Towards a Phenomenology of Values

This book provides a framework for phenomenological axiology. It offers a novel account of the existence and nature of values as they appear in conscious experience.

By building on previous approaches, including those of Edmund Husserl, Max Scheler, and Nicolai Hartmann, the author develops a unique account of what values really are. After explicating and defending this account, he applies it to several of the most difficult questions in axiology: for example, how our experiences of value can differ from those of others without reducing values to subjective judgments or how the values we experience are connected to the volitional acts that they inspire. This provides satisfactory answers to certain fundamental questions concerning the basic structure of value-experiences. Accordingly, this book represents a novel step forward in phenomenological axiology.

Towards a Phenomenology of Values will be of interest to scholars and advanced students working in phenomenology and value theory.

D.J. Hobbs is a Visiting Assistant Professor at Marquette University. His research focuses primarily on systematic phenomenology in the broadly Husserlian tradition, both theoretically and in its application to various regions of what Husserl called the lifeworld.

Routledge Research in Phenomenology
Edited by Søren Overgaard,
University of Copenhagen, Denmark,
Komarine Romdenh-Romluc,
University of Sheffield, UK, and
David Cerbone,
West Virginia University, USA

Imagination and Social Perspectives
Approaches from Phenomenology and Psychopathology
Edited by Michela Summa, Thomas Fuchs, and Luca Vanzago

Wittgenstein and Phenomenology
Edited by Oskari Kuusela, Mihai Ometiță, and Timur Uçan

Husserl's Phenomenology of Intersubjectivity
Historical Interpretations and Contemporary Applications
Edited by Frode Kjosavik, Christian Beyer, and Christel Fricke

Phenomenology of the Broken Body
Edited by Espen Dahl, Cassandra Falke, and Thor Erik Eriksen

Normativity, Meaning, and the Promise of Phenomenology
Edited by Matthew Burch, Jack Marsh, and Irene McMullin

Political Phenomenology
Experience, Ontology, Episteme
Edited by Thomas Bedorf and Steffen Herrmann

Levinas and Analytic Philosophy
Second-Person Normativity and the Moral Life
Edited by Michael Fagenblat and Melis Erdur

Philosophy's Nature
Husserl's Phenomenology, Natural Science, and Metaphysics
Emiliano Trizio

The Bounds of Self
An Essay on Heidegger's *Being and Time*
R. Matthew Shockey

Towards a Phenomenology of Values
Investigations of Worth
D.J. Hobbs

For more information about this series, please visit: https://www.routledge.com/Routledge-Research-in-Phenomenology/book-series/RRP

Towards a Phenomenology of Values

Investigations of Worth

D.J. Hobbs

NEW YORK AND LONDON

First published 2022
by Routledge
605 Third Avenue, New York, NY 10158

and by Routledge
2 Park Square, Milton Park, Abingdon, Oxon, OX14 4RN

Routledge is an imprint of the Taylor & Francis Group, an informa business

© 2022 D.J. Hobbs

The right of D.J. Hobbs to be identified as author of this work has been asserted by him in accordance with sections 77 and 78 of the Copyright, Designs and Patents Act 1988.

All rights reserved. No part of this book may be reprinted or reproduced or utilised in any form or by any electronic, mechanical, or other means, now known or hereafter invented, including photocopying and recording, or in any information storage or retrieval system, without permission in writing from the publishers.

Trademark notice: Product or corporate names may be trademarks or registered trademarks, and are used only for identification and explanation without intent to infringe.

Library of Congress Cataloging-in-Publication Data
Names: Hobbs, Dave (Dave J.), author.
Title: Towards a phenomenology of values : investigations of worth / D.J. Hobbs.
Description: New York, NY : Routledge, 2022. | Series: Routledge research in phenomenology | Includes bibliographical references and index.
Subjects: LCSH: Value. | Values. | Phenomenology.
Classification: LCC BD232 .H63 2022 (print) | LCC BD232 (ebook) | DDC 121/.8--dc23
LC record available at https://lccn.loc.gov/2021018489
LC ebook record available at https://lccn.loc.gov/2021018490

ISBN: 978-1-032-06063-7 (hbk)
ISBN: 978-1-032-06410-9 (pbk)
ISBN: 978-1-003-20218-9 (ebk)

DOI: 10.4324/9781003202189

Typeset in Sabon
by SPi Technologies India Pvt Ltd (Straive)

 Printed in the United Kingdom
by Henry Ling Limited

Contents

Preface vii
Acknowledgements ix

Introduction and Historical Background 1
The Question of Values 1
The Phenomenology of Values: A Long-Unanswered Question 5
The Other Axiologists: Scheler, Hartmann, and Beyond 11
The Dark Age of Values 14
The Axiological Renaissance 16
The Path Ahead 19
Summary of Chapters 20
Conclusion 23

1 **The Necessity of a Phenomenology of Values** 29
  1.1 *Overview of the Phenomenology of Values* 29
  1.2 *Husserl's Three* Vernunftarten 30
  1.3 *Husserl's Limitations: Reason and the* Vernunftarten 36
  1.4 *The Genuine Independence of Values: Scheler and Hartmann* 43
  1.5 *Conclusions: An Independent Phenomenological Investigation of Values* 50

2 **The Identity of Values** 56
  2.1 *What are Values? An Overview of the Question* 56
  2.2 *Examples of Valuation: Three Cases* 58
  2.3 *The Identity of Values: Scheler and Hartmann's Answer* 61
  2.4 *The Impossibility of Values as Objects: A Critique* 69
  2.5 *A Superior Model: Husserl on the Horizonality of Values* 71
  2.6 *The Necessity of Values in Experience: A Controversial Claim* 81
  2.7 *Conclusions: The Essential Nature of Values* 87

3 Pure Values and Valuable Things — 94
   3.1 The True Identity of Values: A More Complete Answer 94
   3.2 Pure Values: The Vanishing Point 95
   3.3 Valuable Things: A More Complex Experience 100
   3.4 Values and Wertnehmen: *Various Examples of Valuation 103*
   3.5 The Modes of Valuation: Four Categories and a Digression 107
   3.6 A Succession of Values: The Good and the Bad 113
   3.7 Conclusions: The Unity of Value-Experience 120

4 Values and Subjectivity — 125
   4.1 The Problem of Subjectivity: An Overview 125
   4.2 The Problem of Subjectivity: A Demonstration 126
   4.3 The Evidence of a Phenomenology of Values: The Apodictic and the Adequate 128
   4.4 Value and Value-For: Values and the Subject 131
   4.5 Valuative Perspectives: The Source of the Difference 134
   4.6 The Acquisition of Taste: A Genetic Account 142
   4.7 The Subjective Structures of Valuation: A Descriptive Phenomenology 149
   4.8 Conclusions: Some Things Change, Some Remain the Same 155

5 Values and Volition — 164
   5.1 Values and the Will: An Overview 164
   5.2 Values on the Horizon: The Motivation of Volition 165
   5.3 Values and Volition: An Essential Connection 169
   5.4 The Value of Living: Values and the Lifeworld 173
   5.5 The Three Modes of Consciousness: A Summation 181
   5.6 Values and Morality: Towards a Phenomenology of Ethics 183
   5.7 Conclusions: The Indispensability of Value-Consciousness 186

Conclusion — 193
   Overview of the Book 193
   Closing Comments 196

Bibliography — 198
Index — 202

Preface

This book is a revised version of my doctoral dissertation, defended at Marquette University in May 2017. Under the direction of Sebastian Luft and with the assistance of my many philosophical mentors – both those whom I know in person and those I have only encountered in books – I was able to put together what I believe is a solid framework for phenomenological investigation into our experiences of value in the world. This is a task in which I remain deeply invested. Naturally, my understanding of this project continues to evolve in many ways, both as a result of my own research and due to my conversations with fellow travelers along these phenomenological roads. Nevertheless, I maintain that the work accomplished in these pages is an important first step towards the goal of understanding values and the ways in which they are experienced while staying as true as possible to the "things themselves." Whether that claim stands up to scrutiny is, of course, to be decided by the reader.

Although I give a more detailed account of the notion of a phenomenology of values in the introduction to this book than would be possible in the space of this preface, allow me to say a few words here about the motivation underlying this project. I first became interested in what I now call the question of values early in my philosophical education. Whether in the context of aesthetics, ethics, or beyond – Nietzsche's notion of the transvaluation of values comes especially to mind – I continued to run into a great deal of fascinating philosophical speculation that relied heavily on value claims. And yet, despite all this speculation, it still seemed to me as if something critical remained missing from the discussion. That is to say, the basic question of *what values themselves are* was often left completely vague in the texts I was reading – and without a solid answer to that question, how are we to make sense of any subsequent claims about what actual values are supposed to obtain?

It was not until I discovered the transcendental phenomenology of Edmund Husserl that I began to see the path ahead towards answering such a question. Husserl's lucid analyses of other regions of experience had, as I began to notice, borne a great deal of fruit over the past century. Why could these very same methods not be turned towards the question of values, I asked myself, and perhaps make similar progress in that sphere? Of course, I was not the first to make such a leap; as I discuss throughout this book, the task of carrying out a phenomenology of values has been taken up by a wide variety of philosophers before me, including Husserl himself as well as the great Max Scheler, who remains, perhaps, its foremost proponent. Indeed, it was in the process of reading through Scheler's famous *Formalism* that the outlines of the task before me finally became clear. I cannot but express my admiration and gratitude once again for the solid phenomenological work carried out by such thinkers, much of which became the foundation for my own project.

Nevertheless, for reasons that I discuss throughout the opening chapters of the book, the purpose of the project at hand is to return to the very beginnings of the task of carrying out such a phenomenology of values in order to explore that problem in as rigorous a manner as possible – though always bearing in mind the remarkable insights of those who have set foot on this path before me. It is my hope that, should my arguments herein be successful, we phenomenologists should have at our fingertips a clearer and more systematic basic framework for our understanding of values than has hitherto been possible. While this book by no means intends to settle all possible questions of value once and for all, it is to be hoped that at least some good will come as a result of such a methodical approach to the topic. In any case, I ask you to take the book in the spirit in which it was intended: as the contribution of one who attempts to add to the edifice of our knowledge of the world of experience by building on the solid work laid down by his forerunners. If my arguments in this book succeed in making such a contribution, of whatever size, then it will have attained its goal.

D.J. Hobbs, Ph.D

Acknowledgements

I would like to express my gratitude to my *Doktorvater*, Sebastian Luft. Not only was he instrumental in helping me to expand my grasp of certain philosophical ideas – phenomenological and otherwise – throughout my doctoral education, his comments during the process of writing this book have been consistently helpful and insightful. This book would not be what it is today without his assistance.

I would also like to express my thanks to the second reader of this work, Michael Monahan. His excellent comments, particularly on Chapter 4, were invaluable in forcing me to attain a greater level of clarity in my ideas and in my writing, and the idea to use a series of running examples throughout the work to illustrate my points came largely from him. I am also grateful to the rest of my dissertation committee – Tom Nenon, Javier Ibáñez-Noé, and Noel Adams – for their assistance with and participation in this project, as well as to the staff at Routledge and the editors of *Routledge Research in Phenomenology* for publishing it.

Finally, allow me to thank en masse all of the colleagues, friends, and teachers who have assisted my philosophical development over the years, whether at Marquette University, at the University of Memphis, or at my alma mater, Christian Brothers University (CBU). I would particularly like to thank Max Maloney at CBU, whose class on the notion of personhood first sparked my interest in philosophy, and who first introduced me to the work of Max Scheler, which has been so influential in my own thought about values. Nonetheless, I am truly grateful to everyone who has had a hand in my evolution as a philosopher.

Introduction and Historical Background

The Question of Values

One of the foremost merits of phenomenological philosophy is the fact that it can be consistently applied to the practical problems that confront us in our everyday lives. In fields as diverse as cognitive science, medicine, and advertising, the theoretical insights unlocked by phenomenological investigations of consciousness have had a tremendous impact, at least within certain circles.[1] Indeed, this emphasis on the practical, on the commonplace, is a central one for phenomenology as such. The very founder of the discipline, Edmund Husserl, was insistent (especially in his later work) on the need for phenomenology to address the real structures of what he called the lifeworld, the world as it is lived and understood through our habitual activities and everyday concerns, rather than focusing only on an impoverished notion of consciousness abstracted from the everyday, and his successors, from Maurice Merleau-Ponty to Dan Zahavi and so on, have, to one degree or another, continued this project. Of course, the theoretical aspects of phenomenology are a strict requirement for any practical results the discipline might yield – we would run far too great a risk of misunderstanding our pragmatic activities if we did not first understand the transcendental structures of consciousness, for instance – but the ultimate aim of phenomenology remains clear: not only to understand reality as such, but to assist us in living it.

Although it is by no means my task in this book to give an overview of phenomenology in general, I should say at least a few words in this introduction about the basic character of the phenomenological project as it is to be pursued herein. Phenomenology, as carried out by Husserl and his successors, is, in one sense, a relatively straightforward task: that of investigating rigorously the genuine content of our experiences in their meaning-structure for us or, as the discipline's famous rallying cry has it, the task of returning to "the things themselves." To some degree, this is a purely descriptive endeavor; the phenomenologist employs certain techniques developed by Husserl and his followers (e.g., the various forms of reduction, the practice of eidetic variation, etc.) as a means

DOI: 10.4324/9781003202189-1

2   Introduction and Historical Background

of isolating certain aspects of those experiences, so that he may subsequently understand their basic character and the relations that they bear towards other elements of our experience. In Husserl's investigations of visual consciousness, for instance, he carefully considers each of the various aspects of a particular visual experience – say, of an ashtray on his desk – in turn, attempting to describe that experience in as much detail as possible, while still remaining entirely faithful to the way in which the ashtray really "gives itself" to his consciousness. And, of course, phenomenological methods can be applied to any of the particular regions of that consciousness as well insofar as they are meaningful for us, from our intersubjective interactions with others to, as will be most important for the present project, our experiences of values and beyond. Any aspect of our experience that has significance for us is part of the lifeworld and is therefore worthy of rigorous phenomenological description. Indeed, according to phenomenologists, it is only through such description that any genuine (or fully developed) understanding of the things around us becomes possible at all. From the phenomenological standpoint, things really are what we experience them to be – or, more precisely, they are that which gives itself in certain ways to our experiencing consciousness, even if such interaction may turn out to be enormously complicated on further examination.

Nonetheless, this descriptive work by no means exhausts the full extent of phenomenological investigation as it is understood within the Husserlian tradition. As I noted above, phenomenology in the full sense must also take into account the fundamental structures underlying our everyday experiences, which are only available in their entirety once phenomenology becomes genuinely *transcendental* in character. While explaining that term in its entirety lies well beyond the scope of this project, it will suffice for the moment to say that it is not enough for the phenomenologist merely to describe his experiences as they occur in fact; rather, he must also give an account of the structures that are *necessarily* operative within experience as such (as well as, in a further move to the level of *eidetic* phenomenology, the structures necessarily operative within experiences of each essential type). That is to say, phenomenology explores not only the particular experiences that the phenomenologist really has, but also, by advancing to the level of the transcendental, the underlying frameworks within the various modes of experience that are imaginable, and which serve as the conditions for the possibility of those modes of experience in the first place.

Returning to the example of visual perception, for instance, Husserl does not merely take note of the fact that his visual encounter with the ashtray happens to occur in such-and-such a way, but also that *any* visual experience that it is possible for him to have must be governed by certain structures. Most notably, these sorts of experiences are always given through what Husserl calls adumbrations. That is, they are not given

Introduction and Historical Background 3

to the perceiver all at once, but rather appear to him only in a series of visual "snapshots" of the object being perceived (for instance, a view of its front side, one of its backside, etc.). Naturally, this characteristic distinguishes visual experiences from, e.g., auditory ones, which are given in quite a different way; these two regions of experience, accordingly, are said to be governed by divergent structures (even if they are also related to one another in myriad ways). Thus, the term "transcendental" may be understood here in an essentially Kantian sense as referring to the "necessary conditions of the possibility," not merely of cognition, but of all experience as such, insofar as it is meaningful. Accordingly, the phenomenological project as a whole must be understood as the task of investigating our experiences (and thus the real givenness of the objects of those experiences), not merely from a descriptive standpoint, but also in light of the difficult-to-discover structures that necessarily regulate all such experiences, whether as a whole or in terms of their differentiation into a variety of experiential types.[2]

In any case, the idea of "reality as such" that phenomenology purports to study, whether it is understood theoretically or practically, is an intensely complicated and multifaceted area of investigation (a claim that is, perhaps, the least controversial of any that will be made in this book!). Despite the fact that phenomenology has made enormous strides in understanding reality and the consciousness that apprehends it, as well as in employing that understanding to yield practical results, a great many regions of consciousness remain largely unexplored – or, at least, unexplored in sufficient detail or with sufficient rigor. Huge swathes of our everyday experience remain concealed to us in their full transcendentality, waiting for the enterprising phenomenologist to uncover the structures that govern them and bring to light what they really mean for our lives. The work of phenomenology is never done; the phenomenologist constantly faces the laborious task of venturing into these hidden crevices of experience in order to catalog with as much systematicity as possible the complex designs he finds within them. With each region that he unveils, new possibilities for the practical application of phenomenology arise. Accordingly, an investigation like the present one, which aims to lay a theoretical foundation for investigation into one such major region of experience, is an indispensable component of the phenomenological enterprise as a whole.

This line of thought leads, to my mind, inexorably towards what I choose to call the question of values. Much of the richness of the everyday experience that phenomenology studies lies in the fact that our world is not simply a realm of dry, dusty facts and analyses, abstracted from our passions, our loves and hates, our desires and drives. Rather, it is a world infused with *value*. When listening to one of Chopin's preludes, we do not merely hear a certain pattern of rhythmic and tonal sounds; we are rather confronted with the *beauty* of the work. An oozing, stinking storm drain clogged with detritus and waste is not merely a particular organization of atoms, but an object of deep revulsion. Many phenomenologists, from the earliest years of the discipline onward, have recognized this notion of value as an essential component of our experience. Many of these historical views, as well as those from the secondary literature, will be discussed – both in terms of their benefits and their limitations – throughout this project, and particularly in this introduction. Nonetheless, despite these previous attempts, the question of values as a whole – What is their nature? In what way do they exist? How can they be understood to function within our everyday lives? – remains elusive. This project will attempt to carry out a rigorous journey into this puzzling region of experience in order to uncover some cogent answers to this question, assisted by the redoubtable methods of phenomenology and by the trails blazed through the wilderness of consciousness by those philosophers who have gone before.

With that portrayal of the focus of this project in mind, allow me to raise one point of clarification regarding the character of this book. Namely, I want to make it clear from the outset that the framework of the project pursued herein is both entirely *systematic* in its aims and nevertheless essentially *Husserlian* in its approach. That is, the project is intended to pursue the basic outlines of a phenomenology of values in its own right, but it does so in a way that is explicitly oriented on phenomenological methods and techniques originally developed by Edmund Husserl himself and refined by his successors in the tradition of transcendental phenomenology. In so doing, it will also take up many of the presuppositions and interpretive frameworks underlying that tradition. As such, this book will not be concerned with defending the utility of the phenomenological method as a whole. That task has already been carried out admirably by men like Husserl and his successors, and, in any case, undertaking such a weighty endeavor would leave no space for the investigation into values that is the primary focus of this project. Nor does this book have the intention of comparing the phenomenology of values that it will develop with alternative approaches to value and valuative consciousness (such as, e.g., theories of value from the analytic tradition). While such a project would indeed be a worthwhile endeavor, it is nevertheless extraneous to the more focused task of this particular book and will therefore have to be entrusted to future projects. In addition, I maintain that it will only be possible to carry out such projects adequately once the task at hand, that of developing a theory of values within the broadly Husserlian tradition, has advanced to a sufficient degree of clarity – a voluminous undertaking in its own right, as subsequent chapters will demonstrate.

Nonetheless, despite its fundamentally Husserlian orientation, this book is by no means intended as a mere exegesis of Husserl's theory of values specifically. In the first place, such exegesis is complicated by the fact that, as will become apparent, Husserl does not have a single theory of values; rather, he developed and refined his understanding of that notion throughout his life. In addition, this project will consult material ranging well beyond the speculations of Husserl himself or those of his interpreters, most predominantly the work of Max Scheler and Nicolai Hartmann, but extending to a variety of other philosophers relevant to the phenomenology of values as well. Although my aim in this book is to take up and carry forward a project inaugurated by the arch-phenomenologist Husserl, I am by no means limiting myself to reiterating his claims on the subject of values. I call on the work of other philosophers wherever doing so is helpful to my project of understanding values as clearly and accurately as possible, and, as will become clear, I do not hesitate to disagree with these thinkers – including Husserl himself – when the task of staying true to "the things themselves" requires it. Accordingly, the book as a whole has genuinely systematic ambitions in that it sets out to explicate its own unique take on the phenomenology of values, albeit one that is oriented on and informed by the work of Husserl, among others. My intention is thus to produce a *Husserlian* work on the phenomenology of values, but not a work *on Husserl* himself. That systematic focus should not be overlooked, since it will structure the entirety of the book, from the (brief) overview of the historical background of the phenomenology of values that I will discuss in the following section to the particular questions that I address in each of the subsequent chapters.

The Phenomenology of Values: A Long-Unanswered Question

The question of values – the question of their real identity – is an immensely broad topic, with tremendous relevance for many different schools and subdisciplines of philosophy. Since the time of Plato's writings about the Good, at the very least, countless philosophers have attempted to deal with the difficult issues surrounding the real existence of such values, as well as the puzzling relationship between them and the objects or situations in the world that we judge to be valuable. Given that fact, the breadth of philosophical speculation surrounding this area of inquiry is far too great to be dealt with as a whole. This project must therefore narrow its focus to one particular strain of thought about values and valuative experiences if it is to be able to say anything of worth on the topic. Since the aim of this project is to deliver a specifically phenomenological account of such values, I will limit my comments on the historical background of this question to its treatment by phenomenologists and certain closely related thinkers. The purpose of this digression, therefore, will be to offer a general (and necessarily abbreviated) survey of the history of phenomenological approaches to the question of values, with a particular focus on the line of tradition established by Husserl, as well as his forerunners and successors. Although this book will not focus on all of these philosophers in any great detail, this historical survey should serve

6 *Introduction and Historical Background*

to establish the context of this project as a whole, and thereby render the task of carrying out a phenomenology of values more comprehensible – though always bearing in mind that it makes no claim to be an exhaustive account of the history of the question of values, even in a specifically phenomenological context.

In general, the historical background of this project really begins in the latter half of the 19th century with the work of Rudolf Hermann Lotze. Although certainly not a phenomenologist himself – Lotze was active well before the rise of phenomenology as a distinct philosophical discipline, and his historical position is rather difficult to pin down exactly in any case – Lotze's work in the realm of values was immensely influential for many of his successors in the German philosophical tradition, including the early phenomenologists. Essentially – and all too briefly – Lotze's fame in this field stems from his rehabilitation and transcendental adaptation of Plato's theory of the Ideas. For Lotze, in addition to the reality of the ordinary objects and situations of the physical world, there are also other genuinely real elements of the world that must be thought of in another way; he accounts for these diverse sorts of reality by making a distinction between the "Being" or "Existence" of the former and the "Validity" of the latter, a claim in line with his transcendental inclinations (Lotze 90). Aspects of reality like the Platonic Ideas are genuine precisely because they are transcendentally valid for all experiences. He thus rejects entirely the psychologistic model that would reduce the realm of truth or validity to the purely empirical laws of consciousness (a stance that he shares with Husserl and the other phenomenologists).

From this standpoint, it is easy to see how Lotze's theories grew to be so influential in the field of value theory during the late 19th and early 20th centuries. Lotze's interpretation of Plato served as the inspiration for the attempts of subsequent philosophers, like the phenomenologists, to inquire into the mode of existence (or phenomenological givenness) of these genuinely existing values.[3] To bring these questions into the realm of phenomenology proper, however, it is necessary to proceed on to their treatment by the "godfather" of that discipline, Franz Brentano. In 1889, Brentano published a text entitled *Vom Ursprung Sittlicher Erkenntnis* (published later in English as *The Origin of the Knowledge of Right and Wrong*) based on a lecture he gave earlier that year in Vienna. In this text, he lays out his own ethical system based on his psychological research and his proto-phenomenological insights about the nature of experience in general. Drawing on the entire history of philosophical speculation about ethics, Brentano lays down his famous ethical dictum, a formulation that he called a "new categorical imperative" and which was later taken up and modified by Husserl: "choose the best among the attainable! That alone will therefore be the appropriate answer" (Brentano 12).[4] In order to explain what he means by this notion of "the best," however, Brentano needed to give an account of something like values, a task which he accomplishes through his investigation of the various "goods" with which we come into contact, as well as into our conception of the good itself. The bulk of his ethical speculation in this text is therefore devoted to his psychological analysis of the multitude of ways in which this notion of goodness is experienced.

Perhaps most importantly for the present investigation, Brentano also develops as part of this investigation the idea of an analogy between different operations of consciousness – specifically, between logical judgments, on the one hand, and acts of (emotive) valuation or of the will, on the other. This analogy, specifically with respect to its later development by Husserl, will be central to this project. Given Brentano's tremendous influence in the development of early 20th-century German philosophy as a whole, an influence felt particularly strongly in the case of early phenomenologists like Husserl and Scheler, the impact of his thought on ethics within that tradition should not be ignored. Brentano can be credited with laying the groundwork for the task of carrying out a rigorous investigation of valuative experience, and so his relevance to the project at hand is difficult to overstate. Granted, this book will not deal directly with Brentano's thought about values in any great detail – except to the extent that this thought has been influential for the phenomenological tradition that succeeded him – but it is imperative that his contributions to this field of study be borne in mind throughout the rest of this project.[5] In particular, Brentano's idea of the analogy among the various modes of possible experience is a crucial component of the framework in which this investigation is to be carried out.

Notwithstanding Brentano's immense influence, then, the background of this investigation lies most clearly in the work of his student and the founder of phenomenology as a distinct philosophical discipline, Edmund Husserl. Despite the fact that Husserl is commonly thought of as a philosopher primarily focused on logic, the analysis of (dispassionate) perception, and so on – an association influenced by the apparent dryness of his early writings, in particular the *Logical Investigations* – his posthumously published work reveals an abiding interest in every aspect of conscious experience, and especially in the experiences of value that are so central to our everyday lives.[6] Husserl was concerned with such issues throughout his academic career. He delivered an influential set of lectures on ethics and value theory from 1908 to 1914 (published as *Hua* XXVIII)[7] and continued (in a modified way) these investigations later in life with his "Introduction to Ethics" lectures in 1920 and 1924 (*Hua* XXXVII) and a series of writings on ethics and other topics composed late in his life and recently published as the *Grenzprobleme der Phänomenologie* (*Hua* XLII).[8] However, all of these texts were published only posthumously; the only explicit work on ethics or values that Husserl published during his own lifetime was a series of articles that appeared in the Japanese magazine *Kaizō* in 1923 and 1924 – though there are, of course, more fragmented references to these issues elsewhere in his corpus. Although many of these texts may have been little known throughout his life and in the decades following his death, at least in comparison with his works on the phenomenology of intellectual or perceptual consciousness, they represent a side of Husserl that was deeply immersed in the study of conscious life in the fullness of its emotive intensity. As such, although this introduction has neither the space nor the inclination to provide an in-depth exegesis of Husserl's developing thought about ethics (after all, my own project, while strongly influenced by Husserl, is predominantly one of *systematic* phenomenology, as well as being focused more explicitly on *axiology* than on ethics), it will be useful to examine briefly at the outset the ways in which these texts can be useful for the task at hand.

Each of these writings opens a window of insight into the nature of values as understood from a phenomenological perspective. In his early lectures on value theory, for instance, Husserl took up and modified Brentano's idea of a parallel among what Husserl now calls the three overarching *Vernunftarten* that govern all conscious acts (i.e., the spheres of the intellect, of valuation, and of the will).[9] For the early Husserl, there is a strong analogy to be made between the rules of logic, which govern all intellectual acts, and the axiological structures that might point the way towards a genuine phenomenological ethics. As he writes, "just as there are laws of consequence, and more precisely of formal consequence in thought, there are laws of formal consequence in valuing, wishing, willing; in one and the other case, these laws are normative expressions of formal laws that are purely grounded in logical and axiological significations, respectively" (*Hua* XXVIII, 237). In this text, Husserl carries this analogy to its farthest limits, proposing to outline a highly structured axiology that could serve as a guideline for a systematic investigation of ethics, just as the laws of formal logic structure rational thought as such. As Ullrich Melle puts it, what Husserl is pursuing in these lectures are the "formal laws pertaining to our acts of feeling and willing analogous to those acts of thinking" (2002, 231). Although this set of axiological laws, being purely formal in character, could never be fully sufficient to its task, Husserl insists here that it is a necessary step along the way.[10] This development of the three *Vernunftarten* as the overarching categories of possible conscious acts is an indispensable insight for the task of separating out acts of valuation as a distinct region of consciousness, worthy of investigation in its own right. As such, although I will not accept Husserl's formal axiology in this text wholesale, I find little to dispute in his division of the acts of consciousness into these three regions – though the precise nature of those regions remains unclear from his early ethics lectures alone.

The "Introduction to Ethics" lectures, delivered later in Husserl's career, outline a somewhat different model of the relationship between valuative acts and other acts of consciousness, albeit with more of an explicit focus on the historical development of ethical theory than on purely axiological concerns. Here, Husserl traces the idea of philosophical ethics from its treatment by Socrates to the formal ethics of Kant (which Husserl, like Scheler, criticizes as *purely* formal, and therefore ultimately unsatisfactory), with a glance at the end of the text towards the then-current state of the field. Throughout these lectures, Husserl continually affirms the centrality of an analysis of genuinely felt values to any attempt to understand ethics; for instance, as part of his chapter on "The Dispute between Moralists of the Understanding and of Feeling in the 17th Century," he identifies the latter as the forerunners of a phenomenological inquiry into the origins of ethics as such. His pursuit of ethics is bound up with his understanding of the entire background of lived experience which could make such an enterprise possible, a background which certainly includes reference to genuinely experienced values. Granted, Husserl's interest in ethics here goes well beyond the borders of any axiology; the late ethics lectures introduce a variety of new and modified positions in the field of ethics as a whole, which carry Husserl's views on the subject a decisive step beyond those expressed in his earlier writings.[11] Nevertheless, these lectures also serve, at least incidentally, as a source of useful speculation on the subject of values that is the focus of the present investigation. Accordingly, while Husserl does not give a fully developed or lengthy account of values or valuative acts here, the text does contain certain important insights and discussions of the subject that will be invaluable to this project – just as they were formative for Husserl's own later research in the field.

There are also key insights into the nature of values within a phenomenological framework contained within some of Husserl's most recently published writings, collected as the *Grenzprobleme der Phänomenologie*.[12] Although much of the *Grenzprobleme* is dedicated to Husserl's thoughts towards a phenomenological account of the unconscious, of instinct, and so on, the sections of this text that are devoted to values and the ethics that are grounded on them bring up tantalizing possibilities for future investigation into the field of value theory – though, given the diversity and the rather tentative character of these writings, as well as Husserl's continuing focus on the notion of the "absolute ought" as a necessary supplement (though, I would argue, not a *replacement*) for his previous ethical speculation, these hints remain mostly undeveloped. In particular, the notion of the horizonality of values that will be central to this project finds its greatest support throughout the corpus of Husserl in this text; Husserl was clearly concerned with developing this notion in the latter years of his life (although it remained mostly obscure even in his latest writings; it will be the task of Chapter 2 of this text to explicate precisely what such a claim would entail). The notion of the horizon makes its appearance again and again throughout these ethical speculations, as befitting its central place in Husserl's later thought. It is here as well that

Husserl delivers his most fully developed revision of Brentano's famous ethical dictum that one should always do the best among the attainable, now taking into account both the variability of the way in which the term "the best" may be understood by different subjects and in different contexts as well as the possibility of absolute obligation in general: "Everyone has his absolute ought, and his choice becomes a reality in the question: 'What should I do?' and, where I should do a number of things, 'Which is now necessary for me?' – not simply 'Which is the better in the comparison of goods?'" (*Hua* XLII, 390).[13] Despite the lack of any great systematicity to these writings and the difficulty which that fact entails for interpretation of the text – after all, Husserl did not intend to publish these speculations on the whole – the *Grenzprobleme* is a rich source of insight into the nature of values in a phenomenological context, quite ready to be incorporated into a more sustained investigation of the question.

There are, of course, other texts in which Husserl discusses values and closely related themes like ethics, virtue, and so on. For instance, the *Kaizō* articles of the 1920s, mentioned previously, focused on the possibility of an ethical renewal of "authentic humanity" in the years following the Great War. This question – though not explicitly one of axiology in particular – certainly has a great deal of relevance for the project at hand. Indeed, the entire motivation for Husserl's inquiry in these articles is a result of the devastation of the entire world of values accomplished in the war, and Husserl's speculation thus stands as an attempt to understand how it might be possible to recapture a truly *worthwhile* human life after that devastation.[14] Although his focus in these articles is chiefly a practical one, therefore, they also contain a great deal of interesting speculation about the nature of values in general that will be worth considering in the current context. Similarly indirect speculation is also found in a number of Husserl's other works, such as his 1917 lectures on Fichte's ideal of humanity, and more focused thoughts in the forthcoming *Verstand, Gemüt und Wille: Studien zur Struktur des Bewusstseins* (to be published in the near future in the *Husserliana*). Nonetheless, despite the fascinating insights to be found in these works, Husserl's most focused writing on questions of axiology that is currently available lies in the three collections mentioned in the preceding paragraphs (i.e., the early and the later ethics lectures, as well as the *Grenzprobleme*). My primary emphasis with respect to Husserl throughout this project will therefore be on those texts, though I will bring in his other speculation on the subject wheresoever it is useful to my overarching project.

Nonetheless, the entirety of Husserl's writings on the subject reveals an ultimate dissatisfaction with the answers he supplies to the question of values. His view on the nature of valuative acts – and especially on the relation of such acts to other acts of consciousness – evolved dramatically throughout his career, and even his late writings demonstrate the incompleteness of his ongoing quest for a rigorous theory of values. Although he first develops his model of the split between acts of the intellect and those of valuation in the early ethics lectures, for instance, he later rejects that model's central claim that the latter are simply *founded* on the former (this claim is certainly incompatible with his later hints about the horizonality of values, for one). Even his later speculation in the *Grenzprobleme*, the product of decades of thought on the subject, is clearly of a provisional character. Many of these texts betray the puzzlement of the author, depicting his search for some way to tie together his various insights into the nature of values and ethical consciousness, but without any truly coherent results.[15] As such, some central elements of the phenomenology of values stand as an unresolved conundrum in Husserl's corpus taken as a whole. Though the necessity of such an endeavor is eminently clear from his writings, and despite the fact that Husserl's investigations illuminate many of the particular characteristics of our experience of values, he was never completely successful in laying the foundation for future inquiries into this region of consciousness. As always, the path of the phenomenologist remained a difficult one, with more work always lying ahead.

The Other Axiologists: Scheler, Hartmann, and Beyond

Given the ultimately unfinished character of these attempts to carry out a phenomenology of values, it is fortunate that Husserl was by no means the only phenomenologist in the early 20th century to take up this difficult work. Alongside other figures working in the early days of phenomenology,[16] perhaps the most famous pioneer in the field of phenomenological axiology is Husserl's contemporary, Max Scheler, who essentially dedicated his (all-too-brief) career to the subject.[17] Indeed, Scheler's idiosyncratic approach to phenomenology is largely rooted in his theory of values, which he sees as a fundamental cornerstone of experience. Throughout his writings, and particularly in his 1913 magnum opus *Der Formalismus in der Ethik und die materiale Wertethik* (translated into English as *Formalism in Ethics and Non-Formal Ethics of Values*), Scheler carefully lays out his argument for a hierarchical system of values that underlies all of conscious experience. This approach posits the existence of an independent phenomenological realm of pure values, which can be the possible objects of our experience and which infuse the objects that we experience as valuable with their particularly affective character. It is this quasi-Platonic set of values, he maintains, that enables us to understand our experience of the world in light of the fact that we constantly feel ourselves inclined to pursue some ends while shunning others.[18] It is therefore the task of Schelerian phenomenology to examine the various modes in which such values can be encountered, as well as to illuminate the necessary relationships among them so that their various ranks can be understood.

It is on this system of values that Scheler attempts to found his entire conception of ethics, the ultimate aim of his appropriately titled masterwork.[19] If he is correct about the existence of a genuine, objective hierarchy among the values that we experience, it is plain to see how a system of morality could be determined by reference to the pursuit of the highest and best of these values (an insight that is intriguingly close to the "new categorical imperative" discussed by Brentano and Husserl). This ethics, Scheler maintains, is finally sufficient to get us past what he sees as the meager formalism of Kantian morality, pushing us towards a view of ethical consciousness that is fuller, richer, and more adequate to our actual lived experience – the material ethics of values, as the title of the text suggests.[20] Scheler's work is therefore, in part, a quite promising defense of the importance of carrying out a phenomenology of values in general. It is not, for him, merely a question of understanding reality – as important as that task may be – but rather of laying the groundwork for any possibility of living a good life. On this level, Scheler's strenuous arguments for a rigorous and dedicated examination of the ways in which we encounter these genuinely existing values (arguments that, in many ways, are even more forceful and well-reasoned than those put forth by Husserl) will be of great relevance to this project. Nonetheless, as I will argue in Chapter 2 of this book, Scheler's conception of values is ultimately just as insufficient to account for the actual content of our valuative experiences as is that of Husserl, albeit for rather different reasons. Despite the tremendous perspicacity of Scheler's thought about values – many of his arguments, especially those defending the independence of valuative experience from other modes of consciousness, will be central to this project – a genuine phenomenology of values cannot rest content solely with Scheler's robust project any more than with the unfinished speculation of Husserl.

Of course, Scheler was by no means the only associate of Husserl to be deeply invested in questions regarding our emotive life. Alongside thinkers like Dietrich von Hildebrand, Edith Stein, a student and assistant of Husserl, was similarly concerned, especially in her 1916 dissertation *Zum Problem der Einfühlung*, with the affective components of consciousness – particularly with their intersubjective aspects. Naturally, such topics have a great deal of bearing for the question of values, particularly as it relates to ethics. Nonetheless, despite Stein's importance in this field, the fact remains that she by no means carried out her investigations in the form of the phenomenology of values that is central to my own project. Rather, Stein's focus – at least in her early work, prior to the conversion to Catholicism that led her deeper into Thomistic philosophy – remains on more specifically ethical and social concerns in phenomenology. While these topics are certainly related to the present project, a fact which necessitates at least a brief mention of Stein in this historical survey, my own focus on the nature of values as such entails that I will not deal with her work in any significant detail (unlike, e.g., that of Husserl and Scheler).

To continue with the historical background of a phenomenology of values in particular, then, we must turn our attention to Nicolai Hartmann. Hartmann, a Baltic German philosopher contemporary with the early phenomenologists and deeply indebted to them in many ways, picks up the investigation into the nature of values where Scheler leaves off: with a detailed investigation into the mode of their existence. While Hartmann is not, strictly speaking, a phenomenologist – it would, perhaps, be better to call him a phenomenologically-influenced ontologist – he was certainly heavily involved with the discipline. Although Hartmann was not personally well-acquainted with Husserl and was often, especially in his later years, critical of his work, he was quite close to Scheler; they were colleagues at the University of Cologne, and Scheler's ethical thought was essentially the point of origin for Hartmann's own work. Accordingly, Hartmann's speculation about the nature of values, particularly as expressed in his voluminous masterwork *Ethik* (published in English as three volumes: *Moral Phenomena*, *Moral Values*, and *Moral Freedom*), provides a crucial window into this difficult question, and is therefore of great relevance for the task of carrying out a phenomenology of values – even if Hartmann would by no means describe his own project in those terms.

Like Scheler, Hartmann envisions values as objects unto themselves, which are then fitted into our experience of ordinary objects and situations in the world in order to give them their valuative character. Hartmann, however, specifically delves deeply into the ontological status of these values, questioning the basic tenor of their existence. Put simply, he lays out a conception of values that identifies them as specifically *ideal objects*, analogous to the mathematical entities that are the common objects of more traditional phenomenological investigation. Just as numbers or pure geometric shapes cannot be said to be instantiated as physical objects in the world, but certainly do make themselves known to us through contemplation and the way in which they affect our day-to-day lives, values too can, on Hartmann's model, be thought of as genuinely existing objects of a similar ontological structure. Of course, values remain distinct from these mathematical objects in important ways and thus deserve their own specialized analysis, which is precisely the task of his *Ethik* (a project that I, though likely not Hartmann himself, would identify as an attempt to carry out the phenomenology of values with which this book is concerned). Hartmann's method for carrying out this investigation runs parallel to his other ontological inquiries, and the rigor with which he executes this task is nothing short of admirable. Nonetheless, as I will argue in more detail in subsequent chapters, Hartmann's ultimate solution to the problem of the identity of values also runs into certain difficulties similar to those that I will discuss in the context of Scheler. As such, Hartmann's *Ethik* will certainly be an important touchstone for this investigation (in many ways, he carries out the task of Scheler's material ethics of value better than does Scheler himself), but it cannot serve as the foundation for a phenomenology of values in general.

Of course, phenomenologists and those influenced by them were by no means the only philosophers at the time – even in the post-Kantian German tradition – to consider these questions of value to be central to a full understanding of reality. Axiology as a general field of study underwent something of a revival at the time (for a variety of reasons, but certainly including the contemporary disruption of many traditional values at least partially inspired by Nietzsche's famous discussion of the death of God). One important example of this turn to axiology is the so-called southwest or Baden school of Neo-Kantianism. Men like Wilhelm Windelband and Heinrich Rickert, with their strong emphasis on the "human sciences" as an essential component of human knowledge and a necessary counterpart to the natural sciences, depicted values as a fundamental cornerstone of such knowledge – and indeed, the conclusions at which the southwest Neo-Kantians arrived mirrored those of the phenomenologists who will be the more direct focus of this book in many ways (which I will not discuss in detail here for the sake of brevity).[21] It is by no means my intention to deny the fact that the same forces which drove phenomenologists like Husserl and Scheler to inquire into this region of experience had tremendous effects beyond that philosophical circle. Nevertheless, since my real point of departure remains strictly within the realm of phenomenology, I will close this section of my historical account with only this brief mention of a few of those wider effects, though always with the realization that there is more to the story of 20th-century continental theory of values than can be told from a phenomenological perspective alone.[22]

The Dark Age of Values

With the stage thus set by these giants of phenomenology (and ontology, to give a nod to Hartmann) in the first half of the 20th century, it would be easy to assume that the field of phenomenological axiology enjoyed a robust development over the ensuing decades. That assumption, however, would be a mistake. Instead, the task of investigating values and valuative experiences as a whole fell out of favor to a certain degree in phenomenological circles in the years following the careers of Husserl, Scheler, and Hartmann. With respect to Husserl, phenomenological scholarship in the latter half of the 20th century focused primarily on his early writings, in particular his work in the region of phenomenological inquiry that he designated intellectual: his studies of perceptual consciousness, time-consciousness, etc. His work on ethics, and on the values which ground ethics, was largely ignored (not least due to the fact that much of this material comes from his literary estate and was only published relatively recently). For Scheler and Hartmann, on the other hand, the story is somewhat grimmer. Despite the fact that both philosophers were deeply influential and admired during their lifetimes, and even seen as the equals of Husserl himself (especially in the case of Scheler, who was more explicitly a phenomenologist), their influence was dramatically reduced after their deaths. Both in Germany and elsewhere, philosophy turned away from these great men towards other pursuits, essentially abandoning the axiological project that they championed in the process.

To some extent, the responsibility for this loss of interest can be laid at the feet of Martin Heidegger, whose writings on *Nietzsche* and especially his *Letter on Humanism* flatly reject the notion that values as such are a fundamental and independent region of philosophical analysis. For Heidegger, any attempt to think of values on their own terms necessarily substitutes an unjustified abstraction for a genuine analysis of valuable things themselves.[23] As he writes in the *Humanism* letter: "Rather, it is important finally to realize that precisely through the characterization of something as 'a value' what is so valued is robbed of its worth ... [Valuing] does not let beings: be. Rather, valuing lets beings: be valid – solely as the objects of its doing" (265). (Heidegger thus, despite the admiration for the work of Scheler that he expresses elsewhere, argues against the very foundations of the latter's approach to phenomenology in general: that values are genuinely independent objects of our experience.) In this case, it would be necessary to engage in an analysis of the valuative character of valuable things only as a *subsidiary* enterprise to a thorough inquiry into the being of those objects themselves; values would be nothing more than abstractions incorrectly derived from our actual experience of objects. A phenomenology of values as such would therefore, according to Heidegger's model, be an entirely misguided enterprise.[24] Given Heidegger's popularity among (certain) phenomenologists, it is, perhaps, unsurprising that this criticism should have borne fruit, and that the pursuit of a phenomenology of values should have been abandoned in favor of Heideggerian explorations into the worldhood of the world, the ethical implications of Heidegger's later thought, and so on.

Nonetheless, perhaps the chief blame for the downfall of phenomenological axiology in the latter half of the 20th century should be attributed simply to the temporary primacy of other regions of inquiry in the field as a whole. Phenomenology has been a tremendously fruitful school of philosophy, bearing useful insights not only for a philosophical understanding of consciousness and reality, but also in more explicitly practical fields, such as cognitive science, medicine, and advertising.[25] These insights are based on careful, time-consuming phenomenological observation of such aspects of experience as time-consciousness or the adumbrations of perception – observations that, notably, lie in that sphere of consciousness that Husserl termed intellectual. Phenomenology can hardly be faulted for focusing on these investigations to a high degree; it is naturally rather difficult to argue with success. Nonetheless, the tremendous dedication that such investigations have required has given relatively short shrift to other possible – and equally important, as I will argue – avenues of investigation. If value-consciousness has received insufficient attention from phenomenologists, therefore, it may only be because they have had their hands full carrying out the necessary inquiries that have established phenomenology as a useful method of philosophical investigation in general. If that is the case, then perhaps it can truly be said that the field is even more ripe for a dedicated phenomenology of values than it was halfway through the 20th century; after all, if phenomenological investigation has been so fruitful already, when it has mostly limited itself to one region of conscious experience, how many more useful insights will become available to us once the rest of consciousness has been opened up to study?

Whatever the reasons for this absence, however, it is certainly the case that relatively little primary or secondary literature on the phenomenology of values was published throughout the latter half of the 20th century. While the field of phenomenology as a whole was booming, those phenomenologists who devoted their careers to specifically axiological investigations (and those close to them, to include Hartmann) were lost in the shuffle. Husserl himself, of course, retained his popularity – perhaps aside from the occasional danger of being overshadowed by Heidegger – but he was mostly known during this period only as a philosopher of logic and of the intellect; his writings on ethics and values went unpublished until late in the 20th century, and any fame he had on the subject during his lifetime quickly dissipated after his death. Scheler and Hartmann, it is sad to say, fell from influence almost immediately after their deaths – a noteworthy fall, given the immensity of this influence during their lifetimes. While Hartmann, for instance, was one of the most common German philosophers of the time to be translated into English while he was alive, this interest tapered away rather quickly after his passing. Of course, there are scattered exceptions to this general lack of interest in phenomenological axiology. Emmanuel Levinas, as perhaps the most notable such example, remained deeply interested in questions of value in his study of phenomenology as a result of his own philosophical interests; his 1986 "Phenomenology and the Non-Theoretical," for instance, takes quite seriously Husserl's early attempts at carrying out a phenomenology of values.[26] Nonetheless, such cases are the exception rather than the rule. Prior to the publication of Husserl's ethics lectures beginning in 1988, the subject remained one of the greatest uninvestigated mysteries of early phenomenology.

The Axiological Renaissance

In recent years, however, the centrality of an investigation of values (not to mention ethics) to a full phenomenological understanding of the world of everyday experience is being rediscovered. In the form of both historical surveys and independent exploration, the field of axiology is, with greater and greater urgency, returning to the forefront of phenomenological research. The cause of this resurgence is primarily attributable to the recent publication of Husserl's ethical writings, which were more or less unknown (except to experts) prior to their appearance in the *Husserliana*. This process began with the publication of Husserl's 1908–1914 lectures on ethics and value theory as *Husserliana* XXVIII in 1988, the first of his major ethical writings to appear publicly. The impact that this publication had on the field of phenomenology as a whole is not to be understated. No longer could phenomenology be thought of only as a tool for purely intellectual introspection, leaving aside the messier and less obviously structured elements of our lives. Instead, phenomenology forced its way into the fullness of conscious life, leaving no stone unturned in its attempt to understand all the structures that could be valid for that consciousness, wherever they might lie. Although this aim had been apparent in the trajectory of Husserlian phenomenology at the least from the much earlier publication of his *Crisis of European Sciences*, the appearance of his rigorously phenomenological discussions of ethics brought this conversation back into the mainstream, making the applicability of the discipline to these broader questions undeniable. After half a century of silence, talk about values once again filled the air throughout the hallowed halls of phenomenology.

In more precise terms, the publication of Husserl's ethics lectures was, at long last, followed by a collective realization of the importance of phenomenology for understanding those aspects of consciousness that go beyond merely intellectual pursuits – especially, for the purposes of this project, the values that we experience. That realization brought along with it a flurry of articles and books eager to make their marks on this newly opened field of phenomenological investigation. This renaissance encompassed both the newly appearing works of Husserl and the tragically overlooked views of Scheler and Hartmann, which also reentered the discussion at this time. The appearance of the *Vorlesungen über Ethik und Wertlehre* in the *Husserliana* was swiftly followed, for example, by James Hart's "Axiology as the Form of Purity of Heart," published in the Fall 1990 edition of *Philosophy Today*, which marks one of the first tentative forays back into the field of phenomenological axiology after the great dismissal of values in the late 20th century. Husserl began once again to be known as a philosopher concerned with affective dimension of conscious experience, while the names of Scheler and Hartmann began to be restored to something of their former fame (though this restoration is a process that remains ongoing).

Nor, by any means, was Hart the sole driving force behind this resurgence. A great number of philosophers took up the banner of a phenomenological axiology during the 1980s and 1990s (and increasingly so in the years thereafter), first and foremost in the secondary literature on Husserl. In addition to the commentators already mentioned, one major name in the field is John Drummond, who has been interested in investigating a (generally Husserlian) phenomenological approach to values at least since his 1995 "Moral Objectivity: Husserl's Sentiments of the Understanding." And certainly, the work of the early phenomenologists on the phenomenology of values has been taken up at times by philosophers whose primary interests lie in related subjects; see, for example, Tom Nenon's 1990 "Willing and acting in Husserl's lectures on ethics and value theory" or Jonathan Sanford's 2003 "Affective Insight: Scheler on Feelings and Values." These works, as well as others mentioned in the bibliography, will be referenced in this book as essential waypoints along the path towards a genuine phenomenology of values.

This tendency only broadened with the publication of Husserl's late ethics lectures in the *Husserliana* in 2004 and continues today due to the appearance of his *Grenzprobleme* in 2014. There is, of course, the already cited text *Husserl on Ethics and Intersubjectivity* by Janet Donohoe from 2004, which pursues, among other things, a historical account of how Husserl's ethical thought evolved over the years as a result of his ongoing research in other regions of phenomenology. In addition, Steven Crowell came out with a 2013 book entitled *Normativity and Phenomenology in Husserl and Heidegger*, which explores the centrality of normative claims to the notion of meaning itself in the work of those two great philosophers – an area of investigation closely related to the question of values under examination in this project (not least because of the dispute between the two on the necessity of an explicit analysis of such values). Susi Ferrarello's 2015 *Husserl's Ethics and Practical Intentionality* and Philippe Merz's 2015 *Werterfahrung und Wahrheit*, among others, represent the same trend.[27] Ferrarello also edited the 2014 collection *Phenomenology of Intersubjectivity and Values in Edmund Husserl*, which contains contributions from a number of noted phenomenologists. Nor, again, is Husserl the only figure in the field whose writings on values are a current topic of discussion; Eugene Kelly's 2011 investigation of the material ethics of value put forth by Scheler and Hartmann brings those two giants of value theory back into the modern conversation admirably. These texts are only a sample of the current renaissance of the phenomenology of values, which shows few signs of slowing – though the fact that this renewal of interest is only in its early stages entails that there may be fewer of these studies than might otherwise be assumed, given the lengthy philosophical pedigree of such a project.

In addition to these historical surveys and analyses in the secondary literature, there have also been recent attempts at a more systematic account of the relationship between phenomenology and value theory. Günter Fröhlich's *Form und Wert*, although certainly rooted in a historical reading of the work of Husserl and Scheler, serves as one such example, as do J. Edward Hackett's rather Schelerian *Persons and Values in Pragmatic Phenomenology* and several recent pieces by Roberta De Monticelli. A number of volumes collecting shorter papers on the subject have also begun to appear in recent years, most notably the 1997 *Phenomenology of Values and Valuing* (ed. James Hart and Lester Embree) and the 2015 *Feeling and Value, Willing and Action* (ed. Marta Ubiali and Maren Wehrle). Related subdisciplines of phenomenology have also been receiving more attention in recent years, as with the 2016 publication of *Phenomenology of Sociality* (ed. Thomas Szanto and Dermot Moran), which investigates the intersubjective dimensions of conscious life (and so is deeply related to questions of value, whose relation to – mere – subjectivity is a point of difficult contention, both in the project at hand and elsewhere).[28] Alongside others (many of which are cited throughout this project), these texts reveal an increasing level of interest, not only in understanding the historical work of Husserl, Scheler, and Hartmann (among others), but in the difficult systematic questions that underlie the necessity of a phenomenology of values.[29]

The Path Ahead

The resurgence of philosophical interest in the phenomenology of values notwithstanding, that task has by no means been carried to completion. As noted previously, and as I will argue in more detail in subsequent chapters, neither any of the models of such a phenomenology explored by Husserl nor those given by Scheler and Hartmann are quite sufficient to answer some of the most fundamental questions about the basic nature of values. The historical analyses of those models carried out in recent literature are, accordingly, not enough to resolve these deep difficulties – even if such analyses do shed a great deal of light on some of the more confusing aspects of those views (particularly with respect to Husserl, whose writing on the subject is often quite vague). As insightful as certain recent interpretations of Scheler's system of values or attempts to carry that system forward may be, for example, those accounts remain likely to go astray in important ways if the basic questions that Scheler's system leaves unaddressed are not given a firm answer. These discussions may well serve as guiding lights on the path towards such a phenomenology, but they have not yet brought us to our ultimate destination.

Even the more systematic investigations of the idea of phenomenological axiology in the recent literature are not, on my view, quite up to the task of carrying out a full-fledged phenomenology of values from the ground up. For the most part, these writings tend to concentrate their arguments on some particularly thorny issue relating to the givenness of values (or some closely related question). They ask, for example, about the way in which our experience of values is related to the essential (inter) subjectivity of our consciousness (as in the *Phenomenology of Sociality* volume) or about the relationship between value-intuitions and the scientific character of phenomenology (as in Eric Mohr's 2015 paper on "Phenomenological Intuition and the Problem of Philosophy as Method and Science"). While untangling these difficulties is by no means a valueless endeavor (in both senses of the word!), that task does not solve the core difficulty associated with the phenomenology of values: it does not speak to the basic nature of values and their fundamental role in experience. These speculations, while useful, are likely to go astray without an accurate and thoroughgoing phenomenology of values as such. What is needed to justify these more specific inquiries is a satisfactory account of the nature and scope of values and their givenness on their own terms – an account that is the explicit purpose of this book.[30]

These recent publications, as well as the historical accounts of Husserl, Scheler, and Hartmann to which they make reference, do, of course, remain invaluable to the present project. They remain essential both as indications of where the phenomenology of values is intended to lead and what benefits it is supposed to provide, as well as for many of the particular insights into the real character of values that they bring up (albeit, in many cases, in a less systematic way than is required for a rigorous phenomenology of values). These texts may get a great deal right about the givenness of values, but it remains necessary to incorporate their insights into an overarching framework of value-consciousness so that they will not be misapplied. Such a general account of values in a phenomenological context is a vital touchstone for any attempt to identify what particular values actually obtain in everyday life or the specific ways in which these values are experienced, and therefore for a full understanding of conscious life as a whole. It is precisely this account that this book is intended to provide. While a difficult task, countless stepping stones have been prepared ahead of time in the work of Husserl and in that of Scheler and Hartmann, as well as by what secondary literature on the subject has already appeared, and so these difficulties are, perhaps, not so insurmountable as they appear to be at first glance.

Summary of Chapters

In Chapter 1 of this book, "The Necessity of a Phenomenology of Values," I discuss in more detail the necessity of carrying out this phenomenology of values, particularly with respect to the genuine independence of this region of phenomenological inquiry from all others. Relying on Husserl's division of consciousness – and, therefore, the reality which that consciousness apprehends – into what he calls the three *Vernunftarten* of thinking, valuation, and volition, I argue that reality as it is experienced cannot be fully understood without paying a great deal of attention to the valuative component of our lives. Further, I go beyond Husserl in claiming that this value-consciousness represents a truly independent and *sui generis* realm of experience, and thus that the phenomenology of values cannot be reduced to any other sort of phenomenological inquiry.

The overarching aim of the chapter is to demonstrate conclusively that a dedicated investigation of values and valuative consciousness is a vital component of a proper phenomenological understanding of the world of lived experience. Without such an endeavor, phenomenology would run the risk of missing important structures intrinsic to valuative consciousness, an error that would only be compounded given the essential relationships between axiology and other regions of philosophical inquiry, e.g., theories of volition or ethics. This chapter thus serves to lay the groundwork for the investigation that lies ahead.

Chapter 2, entitled "The Identity of Values," serves as the beginning of this book's real, positive, and novel contribution to the phenomenology of values. It grapples directly with some of the most difficult questions surrounding our experience of values, especially with the puzzling fact that we never quite seem able to grasp these values directly. Instead, I identify values, not as the direct objects of our valuative experiences, but as entities that lie on the phenomenological horizons of other experiences, influencing and shaping the consciousness that perceives them without ever revealing themselves in any overt manner. Furthermore, I argue that all conscious experience is valuable in some way, whether positively or negatively; there is no such thing as a totally disinterested experience (or experiencing subject). To posit otherwise, I claim, would be to confuse the essentially multi-layered nature of our experiences with a mere abstraction. Under this interpretation of values, their tremendous importance for our everyday lives can be maintained without the need to identify values as something akin to Platonic ideas (as, in certain ways, does Scheler) or to explain how they could be genuinely separated from the objects or situations in the world that we perceive *as* valuable.

Chapter 3, "Pure Values and Valuable Things," furthers this argument by addressing in detail the necessary distinction between values as such, which I have chosen to call "pure values," and values as they are instantiated in valuable things (a technical term that I use to refer to both the objects and states of affairs that we experience as valuable). An understanding of both is necessary for a genuine phenomenology of values, since – as I will argue – each is intelligible only through its connection to the other. I make the claim that pure values function as attractors (or points of repulsion, in the case of disvalues) that can be pursued through the things to which they are attached, but can never themselves be attained. This depiction of values thus permits such concepts as "the good" or "the beautiful" to be made sense of without the excessive metaphysical speculation that would require a Schelerian realm in which they can exist as *objects*. Valuable things, in turn, are valuable only because they "point towards" the pure values with which they are associated, causing the consciousness that grasps them in, e.g., a perceptual experience to apprehend them as favorable (or, for disvalues, as detrimental). This chapter will also explore some of the possible modes of such attraction: our attraction to beauty, for instance, is very different from our attraction to virtue. Laying a firm foundation for future investigations into these particular modes of valuation will be a central task of this project as a whole.

In Chapter 4, under the title "Values and Subjectivity," I apply this view of values and valuative consciousness to one of the most difficult problems of axiology in general: the problem of subjectivity. Values have long been difficult to explain in light of the fact that different evaluating subjects can and do exhibit tremendous variation in the ways that they experience these values. While one person might experience a painting by Salvador Dalí as beautiful, for example, another might be repelled by his modernism and judge the painting to be ugly. One traditional solution to this problem is to declare the valuative judgments expressed by terms like "beautiful" or "good" to be purely subjective, i.e., to be statements about the perceiving subject's own reaction towards a painting, rather than statements about the painting itself. This approach, however, is unsatisfactory. For one, it renders it difficult – if not impossible – to say anything coherent about the structures that underlie such value-experiences, and so gives rise to grave problems with any attempt to carry out a rigorous investigation of, e.g., aesthetics or ethics. My account of values as horizonal, however, offers an alternative. Since values are not, strictly speaking, objects, it is unnecessary to think of them as inhabiting a specific, pre-ordained hierarchy; instead, certain subjective aspects of horizon-consciousness must be taken into account when determining how they are experienced. Pure values themselves do not change, but the mode in which they are grasped may well do so. This account does not imply that values themselves are produced by the subject, any more than the fact that a set of subjects can attain radically different views of a visually perceived object entails that the object itself is not genuinely there. A central task of this chapter will thus be to analyze phenomenologically the various structures that govern value-experiences, in order to explain both how they can vary among different subjects and to examine the commonalities that remain in play throughout all of these experiences.

Chapter 5, "Values and Volition," focuses on the connection between valuative consciousness and that of volition or the will, thereby laying the groundwork for one of the most important potential benefits of this investigation of values as a whole. As horizonal (i.e., as attached to certain experiences in such a way as to call the experiencing consciousness onward towards other possible conscious acts), values are known by their propensity to draw the experiencing subject towards or push her away from the objects that she apprehends as valuable. In that role, they serve to inspire acts of volition on the part of this subject; indeed, such acts cannot be understood at all without some grasp of the way in which they are linked with acts of valuation. For instance, it is only on the basis of the fact that a buyer experiences a painting as beautiful (or valuable in some other way, e.g., as a memento) that her action of handing over money in exchange for the painting makes sense. It is the value with which the painting is connected, and not merely the act of perception that gives the painting to the subject as a visual object, that gives rise to the possibility of the volitional act that leads to the purchase. Further, just as there is no perceptual or intellectual experience without some valuative component, no value-experience can be thought of without some corresponding act of volition (given the horizonality of values, they *essentially* point the way forward to these volitional acts). This connection, at long last, permits the phenomenologist to carry out an investigation into the field of ethics – though only the groundwork for this task will be discussed in this book.

Finally, I will provide a brief conclusion to and overview of the work. In this conclusion, I will recapitulate the main points of each of the preceding chapters, demonstrating also how they work together in order to create an overarching framework for our understanding of values as such. I will then end the book with a few (all-too-brief) closing comments about the path that lies ahead of phenomenology in light of this depiction of values and value-experiences.

Conclusion

Taken as a whole, this text should explain the role and basic functions of values within a phenomenological understanding of consciousness. Certainly, it cannot hope to answer every question that might arise in the context of a phenomenology of values within these all-too-few pages; as mentioned previously, the work of phenomenology is ever ongoing. However, this project will lay the groundwork necessary for that work to be carried out, and thereby point the way towards more specific investigations of particular subregions of valuative consciousness in the future. From this perspective, phenomenology is well positioned to shed light on a difficult area of philosophical investigation in general. Phenomenological investigation into values offers a cogent take on the nature of values as such, allowing us to account for these values as real features of our experience while explaining their potentially troublesome idiosyncrasies (especially in the context of Chapter 4's discussion of subjectivity). Nevertheless, the potential importance of this phenomenology of values for philosophy as a whole should by no means be underestimated. If phenomenology as a discipline is of any value at all (pardon the pun!), such an investigation will be of paramount importance for any attempt to understand the thoroughly valuable world in which we live.

Notes

1 See, for example, the 2001 *Handbook of Phenomenology and Medicine* (ed. S. Kay Toombs), which explicitly announces itself as a practical guide for healthcare professionals interested in better meeting the needs of their patients through phenomenological methods. Another example is the Danish consulting company ReD Associates, which explicitly sets out to apply phenomenological methodology in the field of marketing research.
2 Granted, this account of phenomenology as a transcendental discipline leaves much to be explained about the full extent of that term. Many of the particular points concerning the methodology of transcendental phenomenology as a whole must simply be assumed in the context of the present project, since I am already working here explicitly within the phenomenological tradition as it has been established by Husserl. Nevertheless, these few paragraphs should be sufficient to provide a basic grasp on what transcendental phenomenology entails in this context, even if further explication of that notion remains possible. For further discussion of the transcendental character of Husserlian phenomenology and its necessary conditions (cf., e.g., Hobbs 2018).
3 Not to mention philosophers of other schools, many of whom were also deeply influenced by Lotze's claims. The southwest school of Neo-Kantians, in particular, were greatly indebted to Lotze's interpretation of values. Again, however, my own focus will be limited primarily to the question of values as it appears in the Husserlian phenomenological tradition.
4 All translations from German-language sources are my own, unless otherwise noted.
5 For a more in-depth historical and systematic exploration of Brentano's contributions to this field, see Wilhelm Baumgartner's "Franz Brentano: The Foundation of Value Theory and Ethics."
6 With respect to this criticism of Husserl, see, for example, Theodor Adorno's *Against Epistemology*, which explicitly pits itself against what Adorno calls Husserl's "logical absolutism." Whatever may be said about Adorno's critique, however, it certainly stands in tension with the deeply world-involved aspects of Husserl's later work (not to mention with the traces of this involvement that run throughout Husserl's writings as a whole).
7 As is customary, I will refer throughout this book to texts in the *Husserliana* with the abbreviation *Hua* and volume number.
8 Note that these latter two texts – the "Introduction to Ethics" lectures and the *Grenzprobleme*, as I will refer to it in brief – do not deal with axiology as a distinct discipline of philosophy in as focused a way as do the early ethics lectures (after all, the latter edition of the *Husserliana* gives "value theory" equal billing in its title). Rather, these collections are mostly devoted to Husserl's speculation about *ethics* in particular. They do, however, contain a great many useful insights into the nature of values and valuative acts, which Husserl brings in to support his more focused investigations into the phenomenology of ethical life. It will be important to bear in mind that my purposes in referring to these later texts may be at odds with those of the author, since my intention is to extract from Husserl's writing the insights into valuative consciousness that lie in the background of his arguments, while leaving aside his specifically ethical speculation for a later date.
9 Note that my discussion of Husserl's thought here is merely a brief introduction. I will say more about the three *Vernunftarten*, as well as other points that I will raise in this section, in subsequent chapters.
10 That is, in addition to the formal axiology that Husserl develops in these lectures, he makes it quite clear that any phenomenology of values also requires

an account of the *material a priori* of valuative consciousness (i.e., of the genuine givens which make such consciousness possible at all). Without such an account, Husserl would be totally unable to maintain his critique of Kantian formalism; Husserl is by no means a reductive formalist even in these early lectures, and so he upholds the claim that values themselves must condition, in some way, the real content of our valuative experiences. (Husserl's work here thus prefigures, in some ways and despite their differences, the material value-ethics developed by Scheler, which will be discussed momentarily.) Nonetheless, despite this acknowledgment, Husserl does relatively little to develop this account of the material *a priori* at this time, preferring instead to focus on his analysis of the formal parallels between logic and axiology, etc. Much of the project that this book seeks to undertake can be thought of as an attempt to explicate some of the material *a priori* content of acts of valuation to which Husserl here merely alludes; as always, this project is much indebted to Husserl's insights, even if it also finds it necessary to go beyond him in important ways.

11 For example, Husserl introduces in these lectures the notion of the "absolute ought" as a supplement to the primarily formal obligations discussed in his previous thought on ethics. The question of to what extent this later thought represents a thoroughgoing break with Husserl's earlier conception of ethics can remain open here, once again for the reason that the aim of my own project is systematic rather than exegetical, and that it deals primarily with the conception of values that underlies ethics rather than ethics itself. My own position is that Husserl's thought on ethics throughout his career exhibits more continuities than gaps, with the later ethics refining, building on, and modifying the earlier work without rejecting it entirely, but this historical point is irrelevant to the phenomenology of values that is my own focus, and so I will bracket it throughout the rest of the work. For more detailed discussion of these distinctions in general, see, e.g., the already cited work by Ullrich Melle (2002), Sonja Rinofner-Kreidl's examination of Husserl's critique of Kantian ethics in "Husserl's Categorical Imperative and His Related Critique of Kant," or Janet Donohoe's *Husserl on Ethics and Intersubjectivity*, especially the insightful fourth chapter, which attributes the evolution in Husserl's conception of ethics largely to his increasing focus on genetic phenomenology as a necessary complement to his original focus solely on static phenomenology.

12 Although these writings were composed by Husserl throughout the closing decades of his life, the text itself appeared as a whole only in 2014.

13 This claim, of course, presupposes something like the formal laws of axiology that featured so prominently in Husserl's early ethics lectures. Although the conception of values in the *Grenzprobleme* and the later ethics lectures certainly differs in a number of ways from that found in Husserl's earlier work, there remain common threads that connect them.

14 For the historical background of Husserl's work on ethics and values as a whole, but especially of the *Kaizō* articles, see Michael Gubser's historical survey, *The Far Reaches: Phenomenology, Ethics, and Social Renewal in Central Europe*, which focuses particularly on Husserl in Chapter 2 of Part I. Gubser also addresses the historical context of another great phenomenologist of values whom I will discuss shortly, Max Scheler, in a later chapter, as well as other related figures throughout the rest of the work.

15 Cf. Theodorou (2014a, 70).

16 One important name here, of course, would be Dietrich von Hildebrand, who wrote in great detail on the subject of a phenomenological-psychological ethics and axiology. However, since I have already noted that this project

of exploring the fundamental nature of values as such adopts a specifically Husserlian – that is to say, *transcendental* – approach to phenomenology, von Hildebrand, who inclines much more towards the so-called realist phenomenology of his teacher Adolf Reinach (who was also interested in questions of value), will naturally be a less salient touchstone for my own project – despite the very great utility that many of his insights might have for future, more specific and descriptive investigations in this field.

17 Granted, Scheler too was closely connected with many of the previously mentioned realist phenomenologists (as was, to some degree, his colleague Nicolai Hartmann, who will be discussed momentarily). Nevertheless, it is my position – which I will pursue over the course of this book – that Scheler's work in the field of values stands in closer alignment with the transcendental phenomenological tradition established by Husserl than does that of other such thinkers, and so he (along with Hartmann) will serve as a major point of reference for this project.

18 This quasi-Platonism is also indicative of the fact that Scheler, perhaps even more than Brentano and Husserl, was deeply influenced by Lotze's explicitly Platonic view of values. While Scheler's views do depart from those of Lotze in their specifics, the basic tone of his investigation bears a remarkable resemblance in many ways to Lotze's prior thought.

19 Of course, Scheler's philosophical views range well beyond these insights, particularly in the context of his sociological or cultural discussions. Given the purposes of the present project, however, I will focus primarily on his observations concerning the world of values – which, in any case, form the backdrop for his philosophical endeavors as a whole.

20 Scheler's focus on the material thus mirrors Husserl's insistence that there must be a material *a priori* embedded in any consciousness of values in addition to the formal elements of axiology, though Scheler certainly develops this idea to a far greater degree than does Husserl.

21 Of course, the competing Marburg school of Neo-Kantianism, for example, was also concerned with such issues in the human sciences. Nonetheless, the approaches taken by philosophers like Hermann Cohen or Ernst Cassirer to these questions differ even more sharply from the approach of a phenomenology of values that is being pursued here than do those of the southwest school, and so I will leave them entirely unmentioned apart from this note; for one look at some of these issues in Cassirer, see Arno Schubbach's *Die Genese des Symbolischen*, especially Chapter 3 (the text is forthcoming in English translation by the present author).

22 Admittedly, there may be more of a connection between the phenomenology of values, especially as pursued by Husserl, and this southwest school than is apparent at first glance. Andrea Staiti, for example, has argued that Husserl's later ethics (and thus the conception of values in which it is rooted) must be understood in light of certain developments within that school; cf. his "Husserls Liebesethik im Kontext des südwestdeutschen Neukantianismus." Nonetheless, this historical point will not be pursued here.

23 This criticism thus stands in the context of Heidegger's overall opposition to all forms of supposed Platonism in western metaphysics, or what Heidegger called ontotheology.

24 It is this point that marks my primary disagreement with Heidegger in this context. Although his claim that Scheler's view of values is something of an abstraction will be mirrored, to some extent, in my own arguments, this book maintains that values themselves *are* the proper subject of rigorous phenomenological examination (despite the fact that they can be encountered only

Introduction and Historical Background 27

through the valuable things with which they are associated). This point will be argued primarily in Chapter 1.

25 In addition to the *Handbook of Phenomenology and Medicine* and the business consulting company mentioned in the first footnote, examples of the wide-ranging applicability of phenomenology would include contributions like the work of Shaun Gallagher and Dan Zahavi with respect to cognitive science. There are, of course, many other such cases as well.

26 On a side note, the reader may well be surprised that as central a figure to the intersection between phenomenology and ethics as Levinas receives so little attention in this project. (Levinas will feature in this investigation only in terms of his contributions to a solid understanding of Husserl's early ethics lectures.) The reason for this lack, however, is simple. Despite the fact that Levinas' philosophical work stands as one of the best-known attempts to develop phenomenological insights into a genuine ethics, he does not, for the most part, carry out this ethics on the basis of anything like the phenomenology of values that is the focus of this book. Rather, Levinas' interests – the primordial encounter with the face of the Other, etc. – stem from a different standpoint entirely (perhaps that of the celebrated "ethics as first philosophy," rather than ethics as based on a pre-existing theory of values). Accordingly, while Levinas' contribution to 20th-century continental ethics, like that of Stein, is by no means to be discounted, this project will pursue a very different route of inquiry.

27 From a historical perspective, for example, see also Yvanka Raynova's 2017 *Sein, Sinn und Werte: Phänomenologische und Hermeneutische Perspektiven des Europäischen Denkens*, although that book also ranges far beyond the specifically phenomenological history of the question of values.

28 That is, concerns other than those directly related to axiology as a philosophical discipline, such as the growing interest in the relevance of phenomenology to the study of social ontology, have also been influential in the returning of these issues to prominence. Recent interest in a phenomenological answer to questions of value has been embedded within a vast nexus of overlapping issues that spans many different subfields of the discipline.

29 This brief account of the secondary literature by no means claims to be an exhaustive list of works on the subject. There are, of course, many others, particularly with respect to the application of a phenomenological theory of values to the sphere of ethics: as early as the 1960s, Alois Roth was already discussing the theme in the context of Husserl's manuscripts in his *Edmund Husserls ethische Untersuchungen*, and in more recent years Ullrich Melle, among others, has written extensively on the subject, albeit quite often from a largely historical point of view (see, e.g., his 1988 "Zu Brentanos und Husserls Ethikansatz: Die Analogie zwischen den Vernunftarten" and 1991 "The Development of Husserl's Ethics" in addition to the material already mentioned). Nonetheless, since the focus of this project is exclusively on a systematic, albeit Husserlian approach to the phenomenology of values, rather than on a historical overview of the subject writ large or on the phenomenology of ethics as a whole, it will have to make do with the admittedly partial, but at least representative selection discussed above and with the additional pieces invoked in subsequent chapters. Throughout the book, I will bring in the secondary literature chiefly where it is directly relevant to my own topic, whether as helpful clarification of my primary sources, as support for my own arguments, or as a counterweight to those arguments that might be of use in refining and structuring them.

30 Of course, I by no means claim to be the only one pursuing such an overarching phenomenological theory of values. Although, as noted, the revival of this project after its initial abandonment remains in its early stages, at least some others have seen the same necessity that compelled me to write this book – the work of the aforementioned De Monticelli, for example, inclines in that direction. Nonetheless, I believe that the account that I will deliver in the following chapters offers unique benefits for our understanding of values as they really feature in our experience, and I will defend that claim in more detail as this book unfolds.

1 The Necessity of a Phenomenology of Values

1.1 Overview of the Phenomenology of Values

As demonstrated in the introduction to this book, the question of values has long had a central position both in the field of philosophy generally and in the specific subfield of phenomenology. Quite apart from the historical pedigree of this project, however, any rigorous philosophical investigation must also be capable of being justified on its own terms. Philosophical traditions like phenomenology may be rich sources of insight into the problems that arise in our attempts to understand the world around us, but we should take care to ensure that years of accumulated tradition do not blind us to the real objects of our study. Above all, we want to be certain that our investigations are on track to make genuine progress, and that we are not merely building castles in the air!

These concerns are of particular importance in the context of this attempt to carry out a phenomenology of values. It certainly cannot be denied that the notion of value in general informs a great deal of our ordinary experience; after all, who could go even an entire day without finding some object or event to be beautiful, or tiresome, or impressive? Nonetheless, the goal of giving a fundamental account of *values themselves* as real elements of experience requires further justification.[1] That is, this project does not aim at explaining values as the mere epiphenomena of some more fundamental aspect of reality, as if values could be understood simply as properties of objects or situations, or as subjective judgments about them. Rather, the claim that supports the necessity of a phenomenology of values is that the valuative experiences that we encounter throughout our lives must be understood as stemming from an entirely independent region of consciousness, one that is irreducible to any other (e.g., that of perceptual consciousness or of mere introspection). The task of this chapter will be to examine the outlines of this region, in order to prove that it indeed deserves its own specialized phenomenological inquiry. In particular, I will argue that values themselves must be thought of as really existing elements of consciousness if their

DOI: 10.4324/9781003202189-2

30 The Necessity of a Phenomenology of Values

impact on experience is to be understood at all, and that any worthwhile investigation of values must take this independence into account.

In overview, this chapter will begin its argument by laying out Husserl's view of consciousness (taken from Brentano and most fully expressed in Husserl's early ethics lectures) as divisible into three distinct regions, which he terms *Vernunftarten* ("reason-types"). In addition to the acts of intellectual consciousness that constitute the usual field of phenomenological study and the volitional acts that will be discussed later in this book, Husserl grants the status of *Vernunftart* to acts of valuation (i.e., acts of *Wertnehmen*). Just as perceptual experiences, for instance, are possessed of certain unique conscious structures (e.g., those of adumbration in the case of visual perception), so too are our experiences of value. Employing Husserl's own arguments and supporting them with further phenomenological evidence, this division will serve as an excellent point of departure for the present task of justifying the necessity of a phenomenology of values in general.

Nonetheless, this chapter will also venture beyond Husserl's claims in support of a genuine and thoroughgoing independence for valuative consciousness. The observant reader will notice that Husserl describes all of these regions of consciousness as Vernunft*arten* ("*reason*-types"), thereby allowing for the possibility of their ultimate dissolution into a generalized set of structures that we might term those of pre-theoretical reason. In contrast, this project sides on this point with Husserl's contemporaries, Scheler and Hartmann, who argue for the need to understand valuative experience as a genuinely *sui generis* region of consciousness, completely irreducible to any more general terms. The overarching aim of the chapter is to demonstrate that a dedicated and independent investigation of values and valuative consciousness, one untainted by any assumptions not taken from value-experiences themselves, is a vital component of a proper phenomenological understanding of the world of lived experience.

1.2 Husserl's Three *Vernunftarten*

Far from the opinions of his critics, who often hold the great phenomenologist to be overly concerned with the strictly logical and passionless aspects of human consciousness, Husserl was deeply aware of the great breadth of possible experience. Indeed, he so greatly respected the diversity of experience that one major goal of his phenomenological method was to separate out the various modes of these experiences, in order that each could be studied and evaluated in its own terms. At the time of his early ethics lectures (1908–1914), Husserl formalized the major divisions that he had discovered among conscious acts, leading to his central notion of what he called the three *Vernunftarten*: acts of intellectual understanding, including everything from the (pre-theoretical) perception of visual objects to mathematical thinking, acts of valuation (with which this project is primarily concerned), and acts of volition or the will. Like Brentano, Husserl held there to be an analogy among these three modes of conscious experience. Although different, and so deserving of special attention, each *Vernunftart* would necessarily subject itself to some form of (rational) phenomenological investigation of the essential laws under which it stands, according to Husserl, thereby permitting the enterprising phenomenologist to develop, for instance, a "science of values" parallel to the rigorous study of intellectual consciousness through logic for which Husserl was already well known. This doctrine of the analogy of the *Vernunftarten* will be, in broad terms, taken up by the present project; after all, what would such a science of values be, if not the rigorous phenomenology of values that I propose to carry out?

Nonetheless, given that Husserl's overall view of the task of phenomenology in this context is so influential for this project, it is important to understand precisely what he means by his division of consciousness into its various regions. For Husserl – and for the phenomenologist in general – the study of reality is intrinsically bound up with the study of the way in which that reality is apprehended. If we want to understand fully some object within our experience, the proper focus of our investigation is the experience by which that object is apprehended. But this experience must be taken as a whole, thus with the recognition that it consists of both a subject-pole and an object-pole, noesis and noema, etc. Once this fact is understood, the method for such investigation is clear: we are to examine reality precisely as it is experienced in order to uncover the necessary conditions whereby that reality can exist at all.[2] All of this is no more than the basis of phenomenology as a philosophical discipline. When applied to the study of values in particular, what this method entails is that we must look at the experiences whereby such values are apprehended if we want to understand their real nature – just as we look at the nature of perceptual experiences to understand what the physical objects that we perceive truly are (at least, as *noemata*).

The relevance of Husserl's doctrine of the *Vernunftarten*, in this context, is the insight that these experiences are not interchangeable. This fact was, of course, evident from the very beginnings of phenomenology: the adumbrations of visual perception, to refer to a common Husserlian example, are certainly not a factor when it comes to auditory experiences. Each conscious act that can be imagined is possessed of its own unique experiential structures, which it is the task of phenomenology to discover. Nonetheless, these differences are, in some sense, relatively minor; although an experience of visual perception has its own idiosyncrasies, our understanding of that experience is not so very different from our understanding of experiences belonging to the other senses.[3] The same does not hold true, Husserl rightly maintains, in the case of the differences among the three *Vernunftarten*. To illustrate the point: the acts that he identifies as lying in the region of intellectual consciousness – all forms of perception, for example, or the more abstract, mathematical consciousness that forms the basis for the natural sciences – all have in common a certain essentially dispassionate character. The idea of passion or involvement only arises when valuative consciousness is brought into play, and this element of consciousness stands wholly outside the bounds of anything that could be described in purely intellectual terms. Rather than merely bringing to light another form of perception or intellectual contemplation, it represents a new mode of consciousness entirely. Although valuative consciousness remains, according to Husserl, linked with the other modes – even with the dispassionate mode of intellectual consciousness – this "parallelism" relates primarily to the fact that each mode stands under its own essential laws, which may themselves be investigated in similar (though not identical) ways. As Ullrich Melle puts it, Husserl's chief purpose in making this comparison among the *Vernunftarten* is to emphasize "the parallelism and the analogy among the a priori doctrines of principles: logic, axiology, and practology" (1988, 114).

Indeed, Husserl goes so far as to claim that the various *Vernunftarten* do not merely represent three different possible relations that consciousness could bear towards its objects, but rather must be thought of as grasping different elements of experience entirely (a task which is accomplished through distinct, though parallel, operations of consciousness). He lays out the parallel between acts of the intellect and those of valuative (here, specifically ethical) consciousness clearly in the late ethics lectures:[4]

> With respect to these [i.e., pure things, *pure Sachen*], truths and falsehoods and the logical grounds and logical consequences that belong to them, logical proofs, etc., are not things [*Sachen*], but rather objects of reason, specifically objects of logical reason. And likewise the ethical oughts [*Gesolltheiten*] and the objectivities that are related to them, e.g., appeals, goals of justice, specifically objects of practical reason and not merely things and objective predicates. Theoretical reason, which investigates everything, investigates sometimes the world of things, the empirically real and the ideal, and at other times it investigates reason itself, therefore first of all itself, theoretical reason itself, then, however, other modes of reason, however many there are, e.g., practical reason and the predicates and objectivities that specifically appear in it.
>
> (*Hua* XXXVII, 193)

There are elements to be encountered within the world of experience that answer to a wide variety of different experiential laws, and it would be a grave mistake to fail to recognize that diversity.[5] Thus, passion-inspiring, value-infused aspects of reality like those inhabiting the realm of ethics cannot be grasped by the dispassionate gaze of purely theoretical reason, but only through their own peculiar mode of experience. (Whether or not the laws governing that mode of experience can themselves be understood by theoretical reason, as Husserl posits here, is a separate question – one that will be taken up later in this chapter.)

Why is it, however, that the conscious acts by which values are given must be thought of as radically different from the acts that give the objects of intellectual consciousness? Perhaps, that is, our experiences of value can be thought of simply as a special case of intellectual activity, answerable to the same transcendental laws as any other. If the phenomenology of values is to have validity as a field of phenomenological investigation in its own right, this possibility must be rejected, and valuative consciousness reaffirmed as wholly distinct mode of experience from any intellectual act. Luckily for this project, Husserl answers this concern by appealing to the uniquely vibrant and specifically affective character that our experiences of value possess. He rejects any account of valuative life that does not stem from a subject who genuinely *feels* values. As he asks in the midst of a discussion of how acts of valuation are related to those of the will, "is it conceivable that an act of willing should be free of all valuing, therefore of all feeling? Would not such a willing be as nonsensical as a tone without any intensity or a color without any extension or an imagining without anything imagined? *A priori* in absolute eidetic universality, every willing subject must therefore be a valuing, a feeling subject" (*Hua* XXXVII, 214).[6]

Valuative consciousness thus cannot be disassociated from the act of *feeling* (just as volitional consciousness cannot be disassociated from the act of *willing*, nor intellectual consciousness from the act of *thinking* or *perceiving*), and it is this element that signifies the radical difference between intellection and valuation. While the laws governing visual and auditory perception certainly differ from one another, they can both reasonably be classified as forms of mere (disinterested) presentation; the values of things, however, can only be reached through affect, through value-intuition, i.e., through *Wertnehmen* rather than *Wahrnehmen*. Note that these German terms play a quite useful role in clarifying this distinction. German theorists of value, and in particular Max Scheler, have long made much of the parallel between *Wahrnehmen* ("perception") and *Wertnehmen* (often translated "value-ception," though I will use the somewhat more felicitous, though admittedly cumbersome translation of "value-intuition"). The objects of purely intellectual cognition are given through the former, through the dispassionate presentation of perception, while the latter refers to our encounters with the affective elements of our experience through pure *feeling*.

In any case, this sharp distinction between these two modes of apprehension ensures that the differences among the *Vernunftarten* take precedence over the distinctions that can be drawn among various types of intellectual perception, e.g., between sight and hearing (or, as will be a topic of interest for this book, the differences among the multitude of possible value-intuitions themselves, e.g., between an experience of aesthetic values and an experience of moral ones). Those latter distinctions are not, of course, to be overlooked, but they can be understood within their proper context only after the groundwork for such an investigation has been laid by a basic phenomenological examination of each broader mode of consciousness in turn.

Overall, Husserl's tripartite division of consciousness – and thereby of the reality which that consciousness apprehends – is a good one, adequately capturing the various modes of our experience, at least at the most general level. It accounts for each of the basic ways in which we, as experiencing consciousnesses, encounter the world and the multitude of objects and situations within it. In the intellectual sphere, we encounter these objects and situations through some form of perception, whether through the sensory perceptions by which we are given physical objects or the intellectual intuitions that give us objects like mathematical spheres. But we also encounter objects as beautiful, as pleasant, as detrimental; these valuative impressions are no less important to our daily lives simply because they bring to the table an element of experience that cannot be found in intellectual acts. Finally, on the basis of these other experiences, we *act*, in the ordinary sense of the term: we flee objects that we understand as harmful, we draw nearer to those that attract us, etc. These volitional activities – the term "volitional" here meaning simply "act-generating" by means of the will – differ from either of the other two *Vernunftarten* because they bring to bear the idea of individual enterprise, moving beyond passive observation towards willful activity. Each of these modes of consciousness has its own unique characteristics, and the failure to consider any of them in its turn would result in the failure to understand some essential part of reality as it is experienced. Of course, no definitive claim is made here that these three modes of consciousness represent *all* sorts of consciousness that could ever be imagined. Some creature might well exist who had a fourth such category of conscious acts available to it – though explicating what such a category might look like is no trivial task, and likely beyond any cognition currently possible to any known consciousness. Although Husserl would perhaps formulate this claim more strongly, I maintain merely that these three *Vernunftarten* account well, in broad terms, for the totality of conscious acts available to us as the particular sort of conscious beings that we are, any broader claim being wholly unnecessary to the present project.

Of course, the distinctions among these various *Vernunftarten* are by no means their only salient characteristics. Namely, it is important to note that these modes of consciousness are always inextricably bound up with one another in our everyday experience. Imagine, for example, a situation in which one stands before a beautiful painting at a museum

– say, Salvador Dalí's *Persistence of Memory*. It can hardly be denied that one is having a perceptual (thus, intellectual) experience; one observes – purely dispassionately, mathematically even – the shape of the canvas, the angles of the brushstrokes, and even identifies the objects depicted within the painting as clocks. But there is certainly more to this experience than that! This experience has not only these particular intellectual characteristics, but also certain valuative attributes that have an immense impact on its overall character. Assuming that the perceiver is a fan of surrealism, he perceives the painting not merely as a collection of shapes and colors, but as an object of beauty, an object that attracts him in a way that goes beyond detached observation. To explain the painting merely as a collection of unusually malleable timepieces depicted on a canvas would fail to offer an account of the way in which it gives rise to feelings of admiration in the viewer; both Husserl's intellectual consciousness and his valuative consciousness are simultaneously at play. The same holds true for the final *Vernunftart*, that of volition: depending on the level of beauty with which the painting is given, the perceiver may continue to stand before it in admiration, may walk away, and so on. Perhaps this experience will even lead him to wander over to the museum's gift shop to purchase a print of the piece. In any case, all three modes of consciousness are in play at once; our ordinary experience is quite varied (and therefore notoriously difficult to explain philosophically – although Husserl's attempts to explicate the structures of the *Vernunftarten* are precisely aimed at bringing this variability into some kind of coherent order).

Nonetheless, despite this inseparability in actual experience, the division of the *Vernunftarten* is an indispensable tool for the phenomenologist who is interested in exploring the totality of consciousness. Just as we can, in our phenomenological investigations, abstract from a complete perceptual experience, which naturally (for those whose faculties are not impaired) features objects given by each of the separate senses simultaneously, in order to focus on the purely visual element of that experience, we can analyze each mode of consciousness at play in an experience like that of standing before *Persistence of Memory* on its own terms. Phenomenology has never claimed that experience can be reduced totally to any single substrate, as if there existed some purely independent experience, bound up with no others whatsoever (a claim that would run entirely counter to the spirit of phenomenology in general) – but the various components of any experience-complex can be studied in turn, so long as their essential interrelations to the others are preserved. Indeed, they must be studied in this way if phenomenologists are to be able to make any progress at all; Husserl could not have discovered the adumbrated structure of visual perception had he not isolated this stratum of experience from all others in a *theoretical* abstraction in order to provide a contrast. Accordingly, the independence of valuative consciousness (or volitional consciousness, for that matter) from perceptual or intellectual consciousness does not require their separability in actual experience, but merely that they be governed by separate laws, which admit of distinct phenomenological inquiries.

The upshot of this tripartite division of consciousness with respect to the phenomenological investigation of that consciousness is this: any attempt to carry out an investigation into the eidetic structures underlying a particular act of consciousness (say, for our purposes, the act which gives *Persistence of Memory* as a thing of beauty) must be rooted in a solid phenomenological account of the mode of consciousness governing that act. We are provided with extensive examples of such endeavors throughout the history of phenomenology, most notably in the context of intellectual consciousness. When Husserl lays out his view of visual perception or time-consciousness, he relies on the phenomenological insights that he has gained from regular observation of his own processes of perception, perhaps in the context of contemplation of his famous ashtray (insights that are no longer wholly applicable when, for instance, we introduce volition into the situation).

But these examples also give us a leading thread on our way towards broadening our speculation to other regions of consciousness. Husserl insists that the analogy among the various *Vernunftarten* holds when applied to the *study* of those modes of consciousness. The logic that underlies intellectual acts is parallel to the *logique du coeur*, to use Scheler's term (borrowed from Pascal), that governs acts of valuation.[7] As Ullrich Melle puts it in his lucid essay on Husserl's research into feeling-experience, "there exists an analogy between ethics and logic, which pertains both to the ideal validity of their principles and to the origin and the source of these principles in intentional acts. Just as logical concepts and principles have their origin and their source in acts of the understanding, ethical concepts and principles arise from acts of feeling and acts of the will. Just as logical principles are principles of theoretical reason, ethical principles are principles of valuing-feeling and of willing-acting reason" (2012, 72). Although this analogy is *only* an analogy – the structures of logical judgment are by no means transferable wholesale into the realm of valuation – it nevertheless gives us a route of entry into a difficult area of philosophical speculation: the phenomenology of values itself. The goal of this endeavor will be to uncover the conscious structures that are unique to valuative experiences, insofar as these experiences can be separated from the more complicated manifold in which they are always embedded.

1.3 Husserl's Limitations: Reason and the *Vernunftarten*

Despite laying the necessary groundwork for this investigation with his doctrine of the *Vernunftarten*, however, it is not sufficient for this project to remain content with the stance on the independence of values and valuative consciousness given by Husserl himself. Although Husserl certainly does hold to and argue for the independence of the valuative region of consciousness from all others, my position is that his view of that independence does not go quite far enough. Despite admitting the centrality of values to conscious life, values that are, for the most part, possessed of their own *sui generis* structures, Husserl claims that those structures ultimately remain explicable in terms of certain more primordial structures of reason that govern consciousness generally, and which may be revealed by a phenomenological investigation into conscious life as such. As such, the criticism that Husserl's view of conscious life is mired in an overly reductive form of rationalism – famously made by Heidegger, among others – hits home to some degree, though I will also defend the claim that this criticism is often overblown.

Granted, even such grandiose criticisms are not *entirely* unwarranted. For example, in his early work on ethics (which is also where he develops his conception of the three *Vernunftarten* in its essential details), Husserl takes the notion that values are entirely dependent on reason quite far indeed by claiming that valuative acts, as non-objectifying, are wholly *founded* on the acts of perception that do give objects to consciousness directly – acts which are themselves, of course, governed by the structures of logical judgment. As Günter Fröhlich characterizes this position, "the theoretical level of the understanding, which gives objects [*Gegenstände*], seems therefore to be the primary [level]. Values are added to objects; an object must first be recognized as an object [*Objekt*] (of whatever nature) before feeling can adopt a valuing position towards it" (348). Husserl himself makes this point quite clearly in the early ethics lectures: "According to their essence, acts of feeling [*Gemütsakte*] seem to be founded acts, and indeed founded in intellectual acts" (*Hua* XXVIII, 252).[8] In this case, valuative acts would be entirely subsidiary to intellectual ones, since the latter would be logically prior to and a necessary condition of the former.[9] Naturally, on this interpretation, our valuative acts (and thus the values that inform them) would be completely without their own, genuinely *sui generis* structures in principle; all such structures would necessarily be reliant on the structures of the more primordial intellectual acts that underlie valuation.

Nonetheless, highlighting the strict dependence of values on intellectual acts in the early ethics lectures is by no means necessary to reveal the underlying quasi-rationalism of Husserl's thought about values in general. It is certainly true that Husserl's later views do not necessarily maintain this specific conception of valuative acts as founded on perceptual ones. Although his moves away from this position (like much of his later thought on values) are certainly not unambiguous, there are hints that he ultimately found this view of valuative acts to be unsatisfactory, as we will see in the subsequent chapter. Nevertheless, as will become apparent, the unbroken thread of Husserl's rationalism does remain evident to some degree throughout his writings; even after he retreats from the notion of a strict foundation of valuative acts on intellectual ones, he continues to stress the importance of the more primordial structures of reason that he believes to underlie all types of consciousness whatsoever, including that which governs values. In what follows, I will argue that this view of valuative consciousness must be rejected if we are properly to account for the genuine givenness of values in our ordinary experience – even if many of Husserl's other insights into the subject (e.g., his claims about the horizonality of values that will be the focus of the following chapter) are maintained as a necessary foundation for a phenomenology of values in general.

If we are to pursue this criticism further, however, it is crucial at this juncture to clarify precisely what is meant by the phrase "more primordial structures of reason," if only to avoid mischaracterizing Husserl's position. As demonstrated in Section 1.2, Husserl certainly does not claim that all conscious acts are reducible to those of logical *judgment* or to the acts of merely intellectual or perceptual reason. The three *Vernunftarten* are never able to be collapsed into one another completely; even if they do intermingle with one another in actual experience, they maintain an important separation in terms of the radically different structures that they bring to bear on consciousness. Accordingly, setting aside Husserl's early ideas concerning the foundational structure of the *Vernunftarten*, there is no *direct* connection to be made between the structures of logical reason and those of value-consciousness, at least on the surface, and so Husserl is not a rationalist in the naïve sense that would reduce all experience whatsoever to pure theory. Criticisms of the sort made by certain followers of Heidegger, who claim that Husserlian phenomenology insists on a running thread of explicitly theoretical reason being present throughout consciousness as a whole, miss the mark entirely.[10] As should be obvious from the preceding section, Husserl rejects any account of experience that does not include genuine feeling as a primary component, and this emphasis on feeling is utterly incompatible with a purely reductionist rationalism.

Nonetheless, if Husserl's claim that reason (in its various particular forms) underlies all conscious acts whatsoever does not entail a reduction to mere theory, what sense can be made of it? We must be careful here to distinguish all the levels of meaning in this claim. On one level, it is by no means a grandiose contention. In part, Husserl simply intends to point out the fact that value-consciousness, like any mode of consciousness whatsoever, is governed by *comprehensible* lawful structures that can be unlocked through rigorous phenomenological inquiry. Günter Fröhlich's *Form und Wert* makes this sense of the term clear when discussing Husserl's attempt to lay the groundwork for ethics in his early lectures on the subject: "Apparently there are truths that do not obtain sensory contents, i.e., are grounded on such ... These are, accordingly, also valid for all *rational* beings" (289, emphasis added). In this light, the rationality of value-experiences merely indicates their universal (transcendental) applicability; such experiences are "rational" because they can be made sense of in terms accessible to reason, and therefore to the philosophical speculation which employs that reason to great effect. Valuative consciousness (or volitional consciousness) can be said to be rational here only in the analogous sense discussed above: there is a logic of the heart just as there is a logic of the mind, even if these two supposed "logics" do not resemble one another in any more principled way, and despite the fact that they are certainly not reducible one to the other.[11]

This interpretation notwithstanding, Husserl's use of the term "reason" with respect to all acts of consciousness – he does, after all, identify the various modes of consciousness with the term Vernunft*arten* – goes beyond this uncontroversial (at least, to phenomenologists) meaning. Despite his commendable nuance, Husserl continues to insist on the thoroughgoing rationality of all modes of consciousness, not only insofar as they can be grasped through the employment of reason (through eidetic variation, etc.) in phenomenological investigation, but also in their own right. On his view, there are certain basic rational structures inherent (to some degree) to every experience whatsoever. Granted, these primordial structures are manifest in a way quite different from those of logical judgment – i.e., they are structures of a "pre-theoretical" reason, rather than of the full-fledged reason of logical thought – but that fact by no means obviates Husserl's very real extension of rationality as such into all realms of experience.[12]

This point must be clarified further. After all, these primordial structures cannot be the same as those of perception or of logical judgment in the full sense; on Husserl's model, the structures of pre-theoretical reason are supposed to underlie all three *Vernunftarten* equally. Let us, therefore, turn to an example from Husserl's own writings for the purposes of illustration. In the early ethics lectures, Husserl makes the following claim: "Therefore, when we symbolically describe two durations as t_1 and t_2 and $t_1 > t_2$, then the good G^1_1, which is extended over the duration t_1, is greater than the good G^1_2, which covers the duration t_2" (*Hua* XXVIII, 97). That is, he maintains that value-experiences are susceptible, in some sense, to a sort of mathematical calculus, one part of which is the fact that a value that persists for a longer time in experience is, *ipso facto*, of greater worth than the same value given with a shorter duration.[13] For Husserl, this claim is the expression of one of the formal laws of axiology, and should therefore remain valid in all instances of valuative experience.[14] Just as in the case of intellectual consciousness, Husserl maintains, greater extension is always linked with an increase in that which is extended, and he applies this claim in all regions of consciousness equally. On this model, there are certain laws of consciousness that apply just as much in the case of valuation as they do in that of intellectual thought – even if these regions also possess their own unique and *sui generis* structures as well.

If values were reducible to the structures of logical thought in general, Husserl's claim here might indeed hold true. Nonetheless, although my primary argument against Husserl's position must wait for my discussion of Scheler and Hartmann in the following section of this chapter, I will note here in brief that this particular extension of reason into valuative consciousness contradicts our actual experiences of values in important ways. For instance, it is often the case that a positive value-experience that persists too long can turn into quite the opposite, as when an initially beautiful seaside view becomes tiresome after too many days of vacation (just as a negative value-experience can "lose its edge," so to speak, as one grows more and more accustomed to it).[15] Unlike in the case of intellectual consciousness, values do not necessarily increase continuously as a function of their temporal extension. Any detailed consideration of the world of values or "goods" as a whole thus reveals the inadequacy of Husserl's claim, at least in this one respect; while there may very well be formal laws of axiology parallel to those of logic, this particular law does not hold true in both cases.

The question that now arises, however, is an important one: How could Husserl have come to such an erroneous conclusion? There are two potential answers to this question. On the one hand, Husserl might simply have made the mistake of blurring the lines between two distinct regions of consciousness, i.e., between that of intellectual reason and that of valuation. The law of temporal extension, as one might call it, certainly does apply in the case of the former, and it is not impossible that an insufficiently careful phenomenologist might falsely attribute this law to the latter as well. On the other hand, Husserl was an immensely skilled phenomenologist, deeply concerned with rigor and fully aware of the distinct and *sui generis* characters of the various *Vernunftarten*. As such, I do not attribute to him this amateur error. Rather, a mistake of this sort could also spring from a more substantive claim. Namely, I understand Husserl's position to be that there exist certain *laws of consciousness in general* – a category that, for him, would include the law of temporal extension – that remain applicable throughout all three *Vernunftarten*, and which serve as the basic foundation for all of those various particular regions of consciousness. This reading is consistent with Husserl's actual investigations in the realm of value-experience; although he certainly acknowledges the unique structures that govern this region of consciousness, as demonstrated previously, he also claims that they are governed by further structures that, in a sense, go beyond the notion of valuation as such. It is these more primordial structures that Husserl identifies as the "pre-theoretical reason" that underlies all of consciousness.

This interpretation of the "rational" character of consciousness as such is a momentous claim. If Husserl's assertions here are correct, then while valuative consciousness is distinct from the consciousness of theoretical or perceptive reason and that of volition as a separate mode of consciousness, it is not possessed of its own completely *sui generis* transcendental laws, but merely of laws that are ultimately dependent on the most basic laws of consciousness as such (just as would be the laws of the intellect and of volition). This result has dramatic consequences for the phenomenology of values. Under Husserl's model, that investigation can never be more than a *subsidiary* enterprise to the task of carrying out a *phenomenology of consciousness in general* (a *Phenomenology of Spirit*, perhaps?), which would uncover the most basic principles of consciousness and reality as it is constituted thereby.[16] While the phenomenology of values would remain an important undertaking on this schema, it would not stand as a primordial requirement of phenomenology as such.

In order to demonstrate why this interpretation of the relationship between the various modes of consciousness is incorrect, it is necessary to understand the full extent of how Husserl came to such a conclusion. How might Husserl justify his claim that "the ideal ego of all transcendental capacities," the ego of transcendental apperception that, in principle, is involved in all conscious acts, from those of the intellect to those of valuation and volition, and which is studied by the transcendental phenomenologist from within the phenomenological reduction, is "the ego of a pure reason, and indeed with respect to all possible free formations of logical, of valuative, and of practical reason" (*Hua* XLII, 173)?[17] How can we know, according to him, that all conscious acts are explicable in terms of the structures of this pure, pre-theoretical reason, or even reducible to such structures in principle? In order to get to the root of this issue with respect to the present investigation, we must examine Husserl's arguments for the ultimate rationality of valuative consciousness in particular – although his reasoning here should remain applicable to the other regions of consciousness as well.

Much of Husserl's insistence on the ultimate rationality of values stems from his claim that only intersubjective community is able to root values in any genuine objectivity, i.e., to ground them in their most complete form (as more than *merely* subjective). He writes that "here we necessarily have an agreement of all rational creatures, and the same truth becomes in every subjective realization an identical goal and has an identical ideal value. Here, my value and that of my neighbor are the same ... Every objective value is a moment of possible socialization" (*Hua* XLII, 334). If values are what they truly are only through intersubjective socialization, and if all such socialization is governed (as Husserl believes) by the structures of pre-theoretical reason, then it is certainly true that values must appeal transcendentally to those structures if they are to be meaningful at all. On this model, the very objectivity of values (i.e., the fact that they are not mere creations of the subject, as opposed to their potential objecthood, which would entail their existence *as objects in their own right* – a point that will be argued against in the following chapter) is grounded on their essential relation to the intersubjective community that both shapes and is governed by them, capacities which, for Husserl, are rooted in the shared *reason* of that community, and not merely in the notion of consciousness as such.

As such, Husserl claims, the most important sorts of values that we experience are always, with transcendental necessity, capable of being experienced by all *rational* creatures. As he writes, "on the basis of my love of mankind, which I must have as an ethical human being, every value attains for me a universally human value, value for every rational being that I can re-understand [*nachverstehen*]" (*Hua* XLII, 324). Only on this basis, he maintains, do values attain their true and complete meaning; this explicit unveiling of the unity between felt values and the structures of reason "heightens the value itself and heightens at the same time my joy in thinking on all the joys that it is appointed to realize" (ibid.). On Husserl's model, such values are always already conditioned by rational structures, and so it is not surprising that it is only when they are fully revealed through their (at least possible) application to all reasoning creatures that values can be properly understood.[18] Husserl insists that values must be susceptible to these rules of reason in order to come properly into being as *ethical* values: "There are here rules of ethical behavior and rules of the rational and itself ethically necessary evaluation of happiness and unhappiness, rules of the positive making-fruitful of unhappiness in all [its] forms with an aim towards the 'welfare' of humanity and towards one's own 'welfare'" (*Hua* XLII, 329).[19] The mere *feeling* of values, understood solely in the emotive context that the term "feeling" first calls to mind, is not enough; a phenomenology of values must, for Husserl, reveal the more primordial susceptibility of these values to the structures of reason that govern intersubjective consciousness generally.[20] Values "call forward" to their rational development, and they *must* do so as a necessary part of the mode of consciousness whereby they are experienced.

Husserl's claim is thus that consciousness of value through purely emotive intuition, i.e., what he calls *mere* value-consciousness, is only part of the picture, that the structures of pure feeling are *blind* to their proper objects without an essential connection to reason as such. He claims that:

> every original and <every> acquired instinct is blind. When, however, one introduces value-considerations through reason and pursues the immediate and mediate relationships of values, the instinctive drive, which has a blind absoluteness of the "I must," thus attains the character of a comprehensible [evident] "I should," and which is necessarily directed towards values, just in the evidence of the "I should;" they are entrusted to me, etc. It is therefore said that the

blind drives, the original and the acquired, are not totally meaningless, but rather, as it were, conceal hidden or already known value-opinions in themselves.

(*Hua* XLII, 386)

On Husserl's view, *every* act of feeling conceals an act of (pre-theoretical) reason and can only be fully justified when the latter is made explicit through philosophical examination. Thus, even after all his phenomenological inquiries and attempts to move beyond the formalistic rationalism that he attributes to Kant, Husserl nevertheless maintains the rather rationalist opinion that all acts related to ethics (and to the value-consciousness on which such ethics depends) are characterized by practical *reason*, that value-experiences depend on and can, to some degree, be derived from the same basic set of rational laws that govern all other forms of experience, despite their subregional peculiarities.

While Husserl lays out here a compelling research program for phenomenology, it is predicated on the notion that the same – or, at least, very similar, to the point of being distinguishable only in terms of (non-primordial) regional peculiarities – basic structures apply to all modes of consciousness, from the more obviously *rational* modes of object-perception or abstract, intellectual thought to the *emotive* or *feeling-based* modes more appropriate to value-consciousness. Certainly, when Husserl speaks of reason as the dominant force behind even valuative experience, he does not use the term in any purely theoretical sense (a use that would, of course, run afoul of his own criticisms of such abstract reasoning in works like the *Crisis*); he goes as far as to state in his later writings that such "theoretical reason is itself a particular practical reason," indicating that it is the practical, world-involved functions of reason that take precedence (*Hua* XLII, 474). Theoretical reason is only one branch of consciousness, one *Vernunftart* among others that manifest different sorts of rationality. Nonetheless, practical reason is still *reason*; it is of a type with other employments of reason and cannot grant any genuinely independent structures whatsoever to value-consciousness. Husserl's answer to the question of whether or not values exhibit their own *wholly* independent structures, structures that answer *only* to their own *sui generis* laws and require their own *completely* independent mode of investigation, is, accordingly, negative.[21]

1.4 The Genuine Independence of Values: Scheler and Hartmann

The counter to Husserl's insistence on the extension of rational thought throughout all of consciousness, of course, is the claim that valuative and volitional consciousness are not merely distinct subregions within rational consciousness as such, but rather entirely distinct varieties of consciousness, possessed of their own, wholly *sui generis* transcendental laws. For my purposes, this model entails that an investigation into the phenomenology of values will reveal, at core, only the special laws that apply to valuative consciousness alone, without the ability to trace those laws further back to any more primordial laws governing consciousness in general (though, certainly, the laws of valuative consciousness could make reference to the fact that acts of valuation are always bound up with other sorts of conscious acts; they could *refer* to other modes of consciousness, even essentially, without necessarily being *reducible* to them).[22] This conclusion would render the phenomenology of values even more central to the phenomenological project in general than it is on Husserl's view. Instead of standing as a subsidiary enterprise to phenomenological investigation into the laws of pure reason, the phenomenology of values would be an entirely basic component of any phenomenological understanding of reality whatsoever – just as basic, in fact, as Husserl's own logical investigations. As should be apparent, I will adopt this more fundamental view of the phenomenology of values. Nonetheless, if this project is to go against the arguments given by the master himself, then it is necessary to spell out just where those arguments go awry. This is the task that will occupy us for the remainder of this chapter.

Luckily, the task of going beyond Husserl – at least on this important point, and in no way minimizing his centrality to this project as a whole – is by no means without its own lengthy philosophical pedigree. Even during the early years of phenomenology as a philosophical discipline, there were dissenters in the ranks. Perhaps the most notable of these, at least with respect to the phenomenology of values, was the incomparable Max Scheler. Scheler – along with Nicolai Hartmann, who was heavily influenced by Scheler's account of values – is intensely interested in defending a conception of values that holds them to be totally *sui generis* and completely irreducible to any non-valuative, non-affective terms. As he writes, values can never be derived "from characteristics and properties which do not belong to the sphere of value-phenomena" (Scheler 14). Husserl, as we have seen, insists that a phenomenology of values must be carried out as "a phenomenologically grounded science of axiological and practical reason" (*Hua* XXXVII, 255). For Scheler (and, to a certain degree, for Hartmann – though the latter introduces a uniquely ontological orientation into the investigation), the subject matter of this science might better be characterized as axiological *feeling*, indicating that the modes of givenness which it is to examine are to be sharply distinguished – even at the most primordial level – from those which could legitimately be referred to by the term "reason." Let us, therefore, explore the arguments that these two philosophers give to support the claim that values and valuative acts must be totally *sui generis*, in order that we might be able to avoid some of the errors that led Husserl to so many revisions of his theory of values throughout his lifetime.

Scheler's magnum opus, *Formalism in Ethics and Non-Formal Ethics of Values*, consists, in large part, in a sustained argument for this claim that values are an independent and basic component of experience – albeit one often carried out in the form of an extended criticism of Kantian formalism. For instance, Scheler argues that the possibility of mistaken or disingenuous acts of valuation – situations in which we misapply our valuative judgments due to some error or deception, as in (to give my own example) the famous case of Tom Sawyer and the supposed joys of fence-painting – depends on the real existence of values in general; it is "precisely in the fact that the illusion of the good can be so useful ... that the *independence* of value and virtue from interest [i.e., from pure subjectivity] appears *most clearly*" (Scheler 177).[23] Only by appealing to some genuinely present aspect of conscious experience is it even possible for the moral charlatan to deceive his victims; only because values exist is Tom able to convince his fellow children that painting the fence is a worthwhile activity. But the same argument could just as well have been made by Husserl, who certainly acknowledges the independent *existence* of values in some form. How, then, are Scheler's claims about the *primordiality* of this independence to be justified?

To answer this question, Scheler puts forth a simple argument. If values were only a subsidiary mode of givenness of objects, he notes, rather than possessing their own, wholly unique experiential structures, then it would be possible for objects that are given as valuable *first* to be given in a purely value-free manner. A potentially valuable object like a painting might, in one instance, be given as valuable – as beautiful, as ugly, and so on – but only after the possibility of its being given as a merely perceptual object (i.e., an object with certain colors, shapes, etc., but without any affective significance). But Scheler argues that this is not and cannot be the case. Value, he maintains, is not something added on to that which is experienced as valuable through any *post hoc* process, as if there first existed a value-free experience that could later undergo any number of value-laden interpretations. Rather, as Scheler writes, experiences that demonstrate different values "are basically different *facts*. The nuances of values are *in* the experiences themselves. It is not possible to hold that these experiences are given first as 'value-free' objects – even for a moment – to which one subsequently attributes a value through a new act, or to which one adds a value through a second experience" (195).

This qualification, "even for a moment," is important; while Husserl acknowledges that all value-experiences contain an element of feeling, his assertion that this element is reducible to that of pure reason would entail that value-experiences are not *essentially* or *primordially* given as objects of an entirely valuative intuition, but are rather given first, at least in principle, through the general mode of pre-theoretical rational consciousness.[24] But, in this case, the feeling-aspect of such values (what

Husserl calls *mere* value-consciousness) would not be strictly intrinsic to value-consciousness; the pure feeling by means of which values are apprehended would be a subordinate structure of value-experiences, and an analysis of such experiences at the deepest level could go beyond it.[25] For Scheler, in contrast, value-phenomena are, with transcendental necessity, valuable through and through. No matter how far the phenomenologist delves into such a phenomenon, he will never (without abstracting from the genuine experience itself) reach any substrate that is not characterized by the unique structures of valuation and affective intuition.

On Scheler's account, any attempt to deny the thoroughly *feelable* character of value-consciousness, even to the smallest degree, ignores the genuine evidence of that character in actual experience. Accordingly, Scheler's foremost arguments for the independence of value-consciousness from other forms of conscious life are simple, appealing to the everyday situations in which values are experienced. The richness of human life, he maintains, is unintelligible without acknowledging the independence of value-consciousness from other experiential modes. Any attempt to account for values as mere subsidiaries to other, more primordial modes of experience, or as arising solely from those modes, simply fails to account for the really felt presence of values in everyday life. As Scheler notes, values are "*clearly feelable phenomena* – not obscure X's which have meaning only through other well-known phenomena" (16).[26] Without the real independence of values, they cannot be understood in terms of their genuine content, but only in the purely formal terms that both Scheler and Husserl rightly reject. The central point is that Scheler's conception of human nature – of consciousness itself – is too broad to be described by a single category like that of rationality. As Jonathan Sanford puts it, he holds that "the spirit encompasses more than reason" – even a so-called "pure reason" (Sanford 168). Reason as such would be *blind* to values; the goal of understanding them would remain forever out of reach for the phenomenologist who insists on reducing all experience to the rational structures, even of the pre-theoretical sort, that supposedly underlie it.[27]

Hartmann too agrees with this criticism of Husserl, though he does not prosecute his case quite as confrontationally as does Scheler. Hartmann is insistent that any investigation into values must take seriously the need, valid for any philosophical endeavor, to comply in detail with the specific requirements of its area of study. It is not enough to apply some abstract philosophical method to the problem; the philosopher must pay close attention to what a phenomenologist would call the givenness of value-experiences, listening to what they tell him about the manner in which they are to be investigated. Of course, questions of method are by no means to be disregarded entirely. Comparing the laws of valuation to those of intellectual cognition, Hartmann writes:

> Here, as there, a special philosophical method is needed, which discovers these laws and makes their content and their 'matter' accessible to consciousness and to the conceptual understanding.
>
> (I, 178)

However, he continues:

> Here, as there, such a method is secondary. In ethics it rests upon the primal feeling of value, and can do nothing except draw out from the total emotional phenomenon the aprioristic content which was already within it. The primary seat of the valuational a priori is the valuational feeling itself which pervades our interpretation of reality and our attitude towards life ... The a priori element of worth contained implicitly in living morality belongs therefore in fact – as we have already anticipated – to the given phenomenon, to the situational complex, to the "factum" of ethical reality. And ethics as a science is the logical work of making explicit this implicitly given aprioristic factor and setting upon it the seal of concepts and formulae.
>
> (ibid.)

It is the affective element of value-experiences that comes first, that is the transcendental *a priori* that phenomenology attempts to uncover – and only thereafter can these experiences be subjected to any kind of rational inquiry, setting Husserl's model on its head. At the most basic level, when we look into our acts of valuation, we find only the laws of feeling (even if these laws may in fact be taken up later into the process of rationalization that Husserl emphasizes). We must pay attention to this fact if we are not to substitute a mere abstraction for the genuine content of our experience, i.e., if our phenomenology of values is to have any connection to reality whatsoever.

Thus, in the context of an investigation into values and valuative-experiences, the very goal of phenomenology itself rests on a recognition of their independence as a distinct region of consciousness. Although Husserl himself is well known for the claim that his phenomenology represents the most rigorous realism that it is possible for the philosopher to attain, it remains the case that – if the arguments of Scheler and Hartmann are correct – Husserl has overlooked certain fundamental aspects of the reality that he claims to describe as a result of his over-extension of reason. In the words of Quentin Lauer, Husserl remains "fundamentally a rationalist" despite his phenomenological commitments – though it is important not to take this criticism too far – while

Scheler, "on the other hand, by the recognition of a non-rational element in philosophical thinking itself, is at one and the same time a phenomenologist and a realist" (275). The same description could apply to Hartmann, with the caveat that his connection to phenomenology is rather more tenuous.

Accordingly, the approach taken by Scheler and Hartmann towards the phenomenology of values captures, at least in this respect, the essence of phenomenology as such better than the investigations of Husserl himself. The core mandate of phenomenology as a philosophical discipline is the famous call: back to the things themselves! The insistence of the former two men on the irreducible peculiarity of affect – in contrast to Husserl's attempts to throw value-consciousness in with all other modes of experience under the broad tent of pre-theoretical reason – holds true to the actual content of our valuative experiences. The feeling-aspect of those experiences is wholly intrinsic to them, and not built up from other elements; the affective value of valuable things is part of their essential givenness at every possible level of investigation.[28]

While it is easy to see why Husserl might want to reduce affect to pure reason – such a move would, after all, allow the same structures and methods of investigation that he had long employed in the region of intellectual experiences to apply, *mutatis mutandis*, to valuative and volitional experiences – the work of the phenomenologist is rarely so simple. As Eugene Kelly's exploration of the work of Scheler and Hartmann puts it, a strict insistence on the independence of valuative consciousness is "quite in keeping with the spirit of phenomenology that the givens in any realm of experience be 'cleansed' of all conceptual baggage and existential belief so that the phenomena may stand naked, as it were, in their presence as such to the mind" (61).[29] If Scheler and Hartmann are correct on this point, it is only by avoiding Husserl's conflation of the structures of certain particular regions of consciousness with the fundamental structures of consciousness as such that a phenomenology of values can be done justice – or, indeed, that the great diversity of consciousness in general can truly be understood at all.

This emphasis on a return to the pure content of our experiences, rather than a reliance on a pre-established and purely rational method of analysis, is why Scheler and Hartmann's view of axiology and ethics may justifiably be termed a *material* ethics of value; it is not the formal method that dominates a phenomenology of values, but the content of experience itself. In this sense, Husserl's own view of phenomenology – not to mention his arguments against the ethical formalism that he attributes to Kant – contradicts his conclusions about the primacy of reason in acts of valuation. Husserl himself, as we have seen, argued that it would be impossible to understand the richness of our everyday experiences – of morality, of aesthetics, and so on – without a firm grasp of the uniquely affective content of those experiences, the way in which they are bound up with the act of feeling. Scheler agrees, noting that "[i]t is not only in 'inner perception' or observation (in which only the psychic is given) but also *in* the felt and lived affair with *world* (be it psychic, physical, or whatever), *in* preferring and rejecting, *in* loving and hating, i.e., in the course of *performing* such intentional functions and acts, that values and their order flash before us!" (68).[30] A dedicated phenomenology of values – of one sort or another – is an absolutely necessary condition for understanding our experiential life as a whole, and that point is evident to all of the philosophers currently under discussion.

Nonetheless, Husserl does not carry this conclusion nearly far enough. Although Husserl certainly expands the scope of rationality beyond the level of merely theoretical reason, it is plain to see that his attempt to reduce the structures of value-consciousness to those of *rational thought in general* runs afoul of many of the criticisms that may justifiably be levied against a formalistic conception of ethics and axiology, criticisms with which Husserl's own arguments stand in complete agreement. Husserl might not repeat the formalist mistake of denying the material *a priori* of experience – in the case of valuative experiences, namely, their affective component – but his insistence that all conscious acts whatsoever can be understood, if only at the most basic level, in terms of a *single* set of (rational) structures nevertheless fails to take those aspects of conscious life as seriously as his own arguments demand.[31]

There is no room on Husserl's account for any genuinely independent structures to exist within value-consciousness; such consciousness has its own peculiarities, of course, but these peculiarities can only ever be relatively minor variations on a more universal (and fundamentally *non-affective*) theme. Thus, faced with this dilemma, Husserl must either renounce his own insistence on the importance of feeling to conscious life or he must revise his conception of value along Schelerian lines. Since Scheler and Hartmann demonstrate aptly that any completely rationalistic standpoint is wholly inadequate to the genuine lived experience of values, the latter choice seems to present the best option for the phenomenologist who wants to carry out the phenomenology of values that – as all of these philosophers agree – is central to a full understanding of human existence.

Overall, Husserl's insistence on the reducibility in principle of all conscious acts to the structures of pre-theoretical reason represents the unwarranted extension of a pre-established phenomenological method to every region of experience whatsoever. This extension, made prior to any real consideration of the content of value-experiences, must be thought of as a failure to employ the only phenomenological method that attains the level of rigor that Husserl demands: the method that insists on strict and exclusive attention to the givenness of that which it studies. If we want to be proper phenomenologists at all – a role that I am certainly interested in adopting, since the purpose of this project is precisely to develop a *phenomenology* of values – we must reject Husserl's blanket rationalism with respect to values in favor of adapting our investigative methods to the (affective) peculiarities of its objects. Only by holding the phenomenology of values to be an entirely unique enterprise, one in which the insights that we have drawn from other regions of consciousness do not necessarily carry over, can we be certain that our conclusions will be the correct ones. While some of these insights may, of course, remain applicable in the context of a phenomenology of values, it will take explicit arguments from the givenness of those values to prove that they do; it cannot simply be assumed. Although Husserl himself might not have come to this conclusion in his lifetime, it remains the logical culmination of his own thought about phenomenology as a science. When faced with such a dilemma, it is better to follow the rigor of phenomenology as a philosophical discipline rather than the idiosyncrasies of the man who founded it – the former has less possibility of leading us astray when they part ways.

1.5 Conclusions: An Independent Phenomenological Investigation of Values

At this point, two major questions concerning the nature of a phenomenology of values have been clearly answered. First, following in the footsteps of Husserl, the necessity of carrying out such a phenomenology has been established by reference to its role in uncovering the essential structures underlying one of the major regions of our experience. Consciousness itself, and the reality that is constituted thereby, cannot be understood if the only conscious acts to which we pay attention are those of detached observation or logical judgment. Secondly, the genuine independence of this phenomenological investigation of values from any idea of a "phenomenological method in general," from any attempt to isolate the ground-level structures of "consciousness in general" as the object of a more basic investigation, has been defended, both with the arguments of previous thinkers like Scheler and Hartmann, as well as by claims novel to this book. Although this movement towards the irreducible peculiarity of affect has necessitated a move away from the particular path of investigation followed by the historical Husserl, it is entirely in keeping with the overall theme of phenomenology as a philosophical discipline. Once again, we must go back to the things themselves! If we want to understand values and valuative experiences, we must take them seriously. And taking these uniquely affective elements of reality seriously entails respecting their genuinely *sui generis* character. Any phenomenological investigation of such matters must be willing to take hold of values as they are really given in lived experience. With the foregoing chapter in mind, the path forward for this project should be clear.

Notes

1 Recall that my use of the term "real" here remains within a phenomenological framework. That is, I am not making any claim about the supposed "external reality" of values outside of the conscious acts whereby they are apprehended; rather, the point at this juncture is that values must represent "real components" of experience in that they serve as part of the *noematic content* of certain modes of consciousness. My interpretation is thus "realist" to the extent that that term is *understood from within the phenomenological reduction* (and from a transcendental standpoint).

2 Again, bearing in mind that this claim holds only in the context of a phenomenological understanding of the term "reality," i.e., the world of experience as understood from within the phenomenological reduction. There is no need for this account to posit something like Kantian things-in-themselves (as opposed to the phenomenological notion of things-as-given, which nevertheless have their own noematic structures) to make its case; such a possibility will therefore remain unaddressed here.

3 These smaller-scale distinctions yield what might be termed various *sub-regions* of consciousness, as opposed to the overarching regions described by the various *Vernunftarten*.

4 Although Husserl had moved away from the *Vernunftarten* model to some extent by the time of these lectures – as can be seen from the fact that he refers in this passage to the contrast between theoretical and practical reason, rather than specifically to intellectual or valuative consciousness – it still had a major effect on his thinking. His depiction of the parallel here is particularly clear.

5 Max Scheler agrees with this insight entirely, noting that "it is our whole spiritual life – and not simply objective thinking in the sense of cognition of being – that possesses 'pure' acts and laws of acts which are, according to their nature and contents, independent of the human organization. The emotive elements of spirit, such as feeling, preferring, loving, hating, and willing, also possess original a priori contents which are not borrowed from 'thinking'" (63). Of course, Scheler's take on the separation between acts of the intellect and those of valuation goes far beyond anything Husserl has in mind, a point to be discussed later in this chapter.

6 Of course, this quotation also speaks to the necessity of a strong connection between acts of valuation and those of volition. But this point will be addressed thoroughly in Chapter 5.

7 In the late ethics lectures, Husserl refers to ethics (and thus to the theory of values on which it depends) as a *Kunstlehre*, as a practical or normative doctrine, in contrast to a purely theoretical one. This conception is, for the most part, a correct one – though the precise nature of this practical doctrine requires further clarification.

8 Later in the same text, he applies this conception of foundation to the values themselves: "According to their essence, values are founded objects" (*Hua* XXVIII, 310).

9 Emmanuel Levinas characterizes Husserl's position here succinctly: "'Objectivity,' then, is privileged in the life of consciousness. Husserl says so explicitly. The axiological intentionality – of appreciation, for example, different from representation – would be, according to the terminology of the Third Investigation, non-independent; it requires a substrate. It is based in an independent or concrete objectification which supports it" (112).

10 Hubert Dreyfus, as a famous example, claims in his commentary on Heidegger's *Being and Time* that phenomenologists like Husserl "make our understanding of the world into a belief system entertained by a subject,"

describing Husserlian phenomenologists pejoratively as "cognitivists" (8). Nothing could be further from the truth; valuative experiences (not to mention volitional ones) are of an entirely separate type from the experiences of logical judgment or belief, and not reducible to those terms – even if all of these experiences, for Husserl, ultimately refer back to some even more primordial form of reason that transcends all of them.

11 As Hart puts it, the logic of the heart consists, in this respect, of "bringing to explicit consciousness the eidetics and lawful structures of the heart," a rigorously phenomenological task that is certainly not the work of value-consciousness alone, but which nevertheless depends entirely in terms of its *content* on the unique structures of that form of consciousness (208). "In this sense," he continues, "the heart has reasons which the heart does not know until reason makes them manifest" (ibid.). I agree to a large extent with this formulation, although I would hesitate to call the structures of value-consciousness "reasons," as will become clear in the following paragraphs.

12 This insistence on the underlying rationality of all conscious experience extends beyond axiology into related disciplines like ethics as well. As he puts it in one of his earliest lectures on ethics from the winter semester 1902–1903, Husserl's claim is the ambitious one that rationality lies at the core of any doctrine of values whatsoever. Ethics, he writes, comprises "the total sphere of practical reason ... extended to the total circumference of rational acting. And this discipline again has as its basis a universal doctrine of values, which has to do with reason not in the area of desiring and willing, but rather in the area of feeling. Whoever acts rightly does the right thing, the good; the good is, in this respect, something practically good. Beforehand, however, it must be valid as good, as value, and it does that in 'rational' feeling" (*Hua* XXVIII, 414). He never denies the essential presence of feeling in the sphere of values, but he certainly claims that such feeling must, in order to express values properly, be *rational* feeling, a "correct" feeling parallel to a correct logical judgment. What this idea entails is that such feeling must be subject to other laws than its own, namely, the more primordial laws of rationality itself (the content of which will be explicated momentarily, at least in part).

13 In this sense, Husserl opens the phenomenology of values up to a quasi-utilitarian interpretation, in which the values of things would be subject to calculation in a purely analytical manner. Certainly, this interpretation should not be carried too far, especially in the context of his later work. Husserl does make room for what he calls "absolute" values, values which are not susceptible to this sort of calculation; he uses as his common example the absolute value of the child for its mother, which is unbounded with respect to other values she encounters, her duty to country, etc. – see, e.g., pp. 352f. of the *Grenzprobleme*. Nonetheless, such mathematical calculation does, to some degree, play a role in valuative consciousness according to Husserl, as seen from his claim about temporal extension that was just mentioned, among others.

14 There are, naturally, many other examples of such formal laws that Husserl references throughout his corpus. To give just one more example from his early ethics lectures: "The sum of the existence of two such [equally valuable] goods is twice as valuable as the existence of one of them alone, the collective existence of four equally valuable goods twice as good as that of two, etc." (*Hua* XXVIII, 93). While I do not necessarily dispute all of the laws that Husserl identifies, I emphasize that it is critical for all such formal axiology to be rooted entirely in close observation of the totally *sui generis* structures of valuative consciousness itself, rather than (as I will argue is the case for

Husserl) imported from some supposedly "more primordial" structures of consciousness in general.
15 In addition, certain intriguing valuative claims like Kierkegaard's notion of the "infinite value of the moment" would also be completely inexplicable on Husserl's interpretation – though any further analysis of this sort of claim must be the focus of another project entirely.
16 As Fröhlich puts it: "What is generally valid for cognition should, according to Husserl, also be valid for the specific region of value-cognition" – or to any such region of cognition whatsoever, since this derivative character would also apply to the other *Vernunftarten* (331). The task of uncovering what is "generally valid for cognition," of giving an account of consciousness as such, indeed, a "critique of reason," is one that Husserl takes up in part in the texts currently being collected as his *Studien zur Struktur des Bewusstseins* (although the particulars of this project will not be discussed in detail here).
17 Note that this claim comes from much later in Husserl's career than the preceding quotations from the early ethics lectures. Specifically, it is put forth in the context of Husserl's discussion of the "ego of transcendental apperception" as a necessary ideal for any empirical ego whatsoever, and thus should be valid for any discussion of egos as such. What this fact indicates is that, although the specifics of Husserl's standpoint on values and value-consciousness varied widely throughout his lifetime, the idea that some form of rationality could be extended throughout all regions of consciousness was a common theme from his earliest views on the subject to those he expressed towards the end of his life. While these various standpoints should by no means be conflated with one another, it is important to recognize this common thread.
18 Indeed, it is on this basis of shared, primordial reason that Husserl grounds our ability to make (proper) valuative judgments, not merely intellectual ones. As he writes in the first of the *Kaizō* articles: "To the [intersubjective, communal] acts and their motivations belong differences of reason and unreason, of 'correct' and 'incorrect' thinking, valuing, and willing" (*Hua* XXVII, 8).
19 The close relation between reason and what Husserl sees as the ultimate fulfillment of values in ethics is a major theme of Husserl's later thought on the subject. As Ullrich Melle puts it, primarily in reference to the *Kaizō* articles, Husserl advocates "a radical ethical rationalism in which the Kantian ideas of rational self-rule and of the dualism between irrational impulses and rational self-determination are central ... Ethical life is guided by the ideal of reason" (2002, 242).
20 This focus on intersubjectivity is one of the factors that distinguishes Husserl's late thought on values from that which he expressed earlier in his career. Intersubjectivity itself did not become an explicitly developed region of phenomenology until relatively late in Husserl's writings, and so it is not surprising that his early thought on values might have been somewhat lacking in this regard.
21 Indeed, Melle goes as far as to identify Husserl's entire program for phenomenology as the "comprehensive project of the phenomenological critique of reason" (1988, 109). With the foregoing discussion in mind, it is easy to see how such a claim has its roots in Husserl's own discussions of his project.
22 That is to say, my claim is that, instead of being *founded* on acts of perception, valuative acts are *equiprimordial* with intellectual acts, and thus that each type is governed by its own unique structures – not that these two types are separable from one another entirely in actual experience.

23 To restate this example for those less familiar with the work of Mark Twain, Tom Sawyer is a young boy who, in the story at hand, is being punished for his misbehavior by being given the tedious task of white-washing a fence (an activity that is indeed rife with disvalue for a boy of Tom's age). Dismayed at the loss of his free time, he ingeniously comes up with a plan to trick the other boys in his village into doing his work for him. He pretends to enjoy white-washing very much – i.e., in terms more appropriate to this project, he pretends that the activity holds a great deal of positive value for him – and thereby succeeds in making the other boys jealous of his good fortune and causing them to vie for the chance to paint the fence themselves. As the day passes by, Tom capitalizes on this trickery by generously allowing the other boys to *purchase* (with marbles, a dead rat on a string, etc.) the opportunity of taking his place at the fence, simultaneously enriching himself and getting rid of what really is, as Tom sees it, an onerous chore. This tale serves as an excellent example of Scheler's point that the profitability of the "illusion of the good" is based on the genuine existence of valuative experiences and the values that inform them; it is only because the other boys have previously encountered activities that they found enjoyable that they can recognize Tom's (feigned) pleasure in the activity of white-washing a fence and thereby interpret that activity as bearing a positive value.
24 This consequence is most obvious in Husserl's early writing, where he claims that valuative acts are entirely *founded* on perceptual ones; it is this characterization of values that is the primary target of Scheler's criticism. That criticism remains valid, however, even after Husserl abandoned that early position insofar as he continues to insist on the application of certain "general structures of consciousness" to the region of value-experiences entirely apart from that region's own, wholly *sui generis* structures.
25 Note that this subordination would hold true even if all value-experiences that actually obtain *do in fact* contain the element of feeling once they come to fruition – a point that Husserl certainly acknowledges.
26 Indeed, Scheler goes so far as to claim that values are genuine *objects* of experience in their own right (even if such experiences are always tied to corresponding experiences of valuable objects or "goods" in actual practice). But this point will be discussed further in the following chapter.
27 Scheler compares reason's blindness to certain modes of givenness to the blindness of the faculty of hearing to visual phenomena. As he writes approvingly of Pascal's notion of the *ordre* or *logique du coeur*, "there is a type of experiencing whose 'objects' are completely inaccessible to reason; reason is as blind to them as ears and hearing are blind to colors" (255). Although Husserl speaks of such a logic of the heart as well, he envisions this logic as a subsidiary of a "logic of consciousness as such," a logic of pre-theoretical reason in general, thereby going beyond the merely analogous scope of this term. It is this further move that Scheler rejects.
28 As Sanford puts it, consciousness of such objects must *necessarily* employ "affective faculties such as intuition, feeling, loving, and hating" in addition to the logical and perceptual faculties of Husserl's pure reason: "This is the sphere of our emotional life," which cannot be removed from our experiences without venturing into the realm of mere abstraction (168).
29 Eric Mohr makes a similar claim in his discussion of the rift between Scheler and Husserl: "any use of philosophical methods must presuppose, as well as not distract from, important preconditions of knowledge which pertain more to the philosopher herself than to the method which the philosopher merely applies. Phenomenological method must be based upon the foundation of a 'phenomenological attitude'" (219).

30 With this conception of values as an ineliminable component of genuine lived experience in mind, it is plain to see why Husserl's attempt to argue for their essential rationality from the presupposition of intersubjectivity fails. If all loving and hating, all willing and choosing, and indeed all emotive and ethical life as such necessarily proceeds from feeling in this sense, it is difficult to understand why such feeling could not be a basis for intersubjectivity (i.e. through "fellow-feeling" or empathy) just as much as Husserl's esteemed rationality. Why should reason, even of the most pure and pre-theoretical sort, have an exclusive claim to the realm of shared experience? (Cf. the notion of "social acts" recently in vogue in phenomenology and related disciplines – though the specifics of this notion cannot be discussed in detail here.) Whether or not such a form of intersubjectivity actually obtains is irrelevant. The central point is that, Husserl's claims to the contrary, there are no necessary grounds for presupposing that all conscious acts must be rooted in rationality in order to attain intersubjectivity; Scheler could very well argue (as, indeed, he does) that such intersubjectivity must be rooted in the intuition of certain values that is common to all conscious life. The question of values, accordingly, must be decided on other grounds than those for which Husserl argues so stridently – for instance, by Scheler's appeals to genuine lived experience that are presently under discussion.

31 This insight can be seen most readily in the arguments made by both Husserl and Scheler against Kant, as the supposed representative of formalism in ethics (whether or not that supposition is entirely warranted by Kant's own work). Husserl insists on the genuinely *a priori* character of the affective element of consciousness as a line of argument against Kant, but it takes Scheler to point out that this insistence serves equally well to argue against Husserl's own model. See Wei Zhang's "Rational a priori or Emotional a priori?" for further discussion of this topic.

2 The Identity of Values

2.1 What are Values? An Overview of the Question

At this point, the path that any phenomenological investigation of values and valuative experiences must follow should be clear. The next step is to set foot onto this path by delving deeper into the question of the identity of the values that constantly inform our everyday experience. This step, however, is also one of the most difficult that will confront us throughout this entire project. Values as such are manifestly unlike the ordinary objects we encounter in our day-to-day lives – an understandable point in light of the structural independence of the experiences in which they are given from experiences of ordinary perception. We have many experiences of beautiful objects, for example, but the value of "beauty" itself cannot be seen, heard, or held in the hand. Values seem to be ideal entities, of a sort, and yet they still seem to differ in important ways from other such entities (e.g., numbers or perceptual categories). Countless schemes have been devised throughout the history of philosophy to explain what is meant by the real existence of values themselves, but it will be the task of the present investigation to decide which explanation best accounts for their real givenness to consciousness.

In particular, this chapter will take into consideration two competing accounts of values and their givenness: the view expressed by Scheler and Hartmann, on the one hand, and the position hinted at by the later work of Husserl, on the other. Scheler and Hartmann each envision values as objects of one sort or another, which is to say, in a phenomenological context, that they are the possible intentional objects of a certain mode of consciousness and, accordingly, that they can be *directly intuited* by the valuing subject. Husserl, in contrast, makes certain very interesting points about the ultimately *horizonal* character of values. This interpretation would entail that, like any component of the experiential horizon (a central discovery of Husserl's later phenomenology, which will be discussed in more detail later in this chapter), values would remain ever elusive of any direct experience, although they would continue to have important effects on the experiences to which they are attached. For example, the value of beauty might be horizonal with respect to a perceptual experience of a beautiful painting, associating itself with that experience in certain ways that will be detailed throughout this book, without ever giving itself to direct intuition. Despite the rejection of some important aspects of Husserl's view of values in the preceding chapter, the following discussion will argue that the depiction of the existential status of values that underlies his later work is, in certain respects, superior to the view given by Scheler and Hartmann.

Granted, it is also essential to point out that Husserl never expresses this notion of the horizonality of values fully or embeds this insight within any kind of systematic framework. Husserl's early work on values, such as the early ethics lectures, in which he confronts questions of axiology in the most direct and systematic manner, were composed well before he had developed the notion of the horizon as completely as he does in his later work. In the same vein, Husserl's later writings, although they did have recourse to the notion of the horizon in a general way, are less concerned with pursuing an inquiry into the givenness of values as such than with tangential investigations into specifically ethical values, ethical life as a whole, and so on. I do not intend to claim that what I will call the horizon-model of values can be found in any fully developed form in the work of Husserl himself. Nevertheless, hints towards this way of conceiving of values are present throughout Husserl's body of work, as I will argue, and something very like this model of values can be detected as a background assumption underlying much of his later work on the subject. Accordingly, I will develop in this chapter a fundamental model of values as horizonal that is, I believe, compatible with and, to a large degree, derived from Husserl's investigations into the phenomenology of values – even if a great deal of work with respect to the reconstruction and further development of this model remains to be done beyond what has been explicitly accomplished by Husserl himself.

Once this basic assessment of values as such has been completed – though spelling out the ramifications of this account is a task that will occupy much of the rest of this book, not merely this chapter – it will be possible to explicate certain characteristics of values and value-consciousness that will be of great import for the present investigation. Most notably, an ineradicable link will be established between our experiences of values and our other experiences in the world – a link that, importantly, goes both ways. Given the essentially horizonal character of values, it is impossible (contra Scheler and Hartmann) for any value to be encountered as an object in its own right, i.e., in the absence of some object or state of affairs that is experienced *as valuable*, which must itself be grasped through another sort of experience (e.g., a perceptual one).

However, it is just as much the case that none of these other (non-valuative) experiences can truly be separated from the values with which they are ultimately connected (though by means of an entirely different mode of consciousness, naturally). Although a controversial claim, this chapter will argue that there neither does nor can exist any completely "valueless" (as opposed to *dis*valuable) experience, an experience that is in no way bound up with the structures of valuative consciousness at all. All objects and situations in the world that we encounter have some value for us, whether positive or negative (bearing in mind that this value can be extremely close to neutral). With these claims in mind, it will become apparent just how important a grasp of valuative consciousness is to our understanding of experience in general. It is fortunate, then, that by the end of this chapter we should have a solid basis for understanding what values are on their own terms, and thus a basis on which to continue this investigation in subsequent chapters.

2.2 Examples of Valuation: Three Cases

To begin this investigation, it is necessary to understand just why the question of the identity and characteristics of values has traditionally been such an enigma throughout the history of philosophy, and in particular for phenomenology. As such, it will now be helpful to consider some examples of valuative experiences that might be encountered in day-to-day life, in order to discover whether we can find the value itself lurking within them. Of course, given that there exists a tremendously wide variety of such experiences – axiology deals with all sorts of values, from the moral values that inform ethics to the values of taste that we encounter in aesthetics, etc. – we will have to employ a corresponding diversity in our examples if we want to attain at least some hold on the richness of valuative life. Accordingly, let us now turn our attention to three different situations in which valuative consciousness is clearly in play. Of course, these examples by no means claim to exhaust all the possible structures of valuative acts; that daunting task must be left for future, more particular investigations that can be carried out on the basis of this theoretical account. The workmanlike task of descriptive phenomenology, by which all of these various structures can be examined on their own terms, is certainly necessary to the usefulness of the discipline in general, but this task requires an overarching model of the various modes of experience as such. These three examples, which can certainly be developed further as we go along, are intended merely to help elucidate some of the basic structures of valuation as clearly as possible, and not to address every possible valuative type whatsoever.

> Example I: Two friends, Bert and Ernie, are visiting their local museum. Unbeknownst to them, the museum happens to be hosting an exhibit on surrealism. Partway through their trip, they turn a corner and find themselves face to face with Dalí's famous painting, *The Persistence of Memory*. Bert stands enraptured before the painting, wordlessly appreciating its *beauty*. Ernie, on the other hand, is not a fan of the piece and finds the surrealist work to be *ugly* or *distasteful*, a position he displays with a frown. Afterwards, the two friends discuss their contrasting opinions of the painting.

This example has already been employed in part in the preceding chapter. It will serve as an essential tool for understanding not only the way in which values such as beauty are given through their attachment to objects like works of art, but also (in later chapters) the way in which valuative assessments of such objects can vary among different perceiving subjects (i.e., in a way that does not reduce values themselves to merely subjective judgments).

> Example II: Oscar enjoys an alcoholic beverage every now and again, but – like any drinker – has preferences; for instance, he enjoys beer, but not tequila. He also does not enjoy the taste of scotch, finding its harshness to be *repugnant*. However, he recognizes – having been told of its appeal by others of his acquaintance, whom he trusts – that scotch is a *tasty* and *refined* beverage and that it would be worth his while to acquire a taste for it. He begins to drink scotch despite the fact that he must force himself to tolerate its harsh flavor. Over time, he grows to enjoy the taste and drinks scotch with relish thereafter, finding it to be an even *better* drink than his previous favorites.

This example touches on several issues that will be of great importance for the phenomenology of values. Not only do we have another situation in which certain values, both positive and negative, come to the fore in an individual's experience of an object (as with Example I), but we also find a change in the status of that value with respect to a single experiencing subject. This example will be particularly helpful when we come to the question of how the objects that we perceive as valuable can change over time.

> Example III: Aloysius is a happily married man, as well as a deeply religious man who believes in the sanctity of marriage (i.e., who holds faithfulness in marriage to be both *sacred* and *virtuous*). However, he often finds himself tempted to engage in the act of adultery. Having a weak will, he occasionally submits to these temptations, which he experiences as both *delightful* and *immoral*. Afterwards, he regards himself with loathing, calling himself *wicked*. Nevertheless, he continues to insist on the rightness of remaining faithful, despite his knowledge that he will likely fall into temptation again in the future.

This example takes us, in part, into the realm of moral values, a region that has long been particularly important to axiologists due to its centrality to questions of ethics (though this project will be no more deeply concerned with moral values than with values of any other sort). Further, this example brings in the notion of conflict among values, as when Aloysius' pursuit of faithfulness conflicts with the value he sees in committing an act of carnal pleasure with someone other than his spouse. This example will therefore be particularly useful when the time comes to give an account of the great diversity of values, which may or may not stand in accord with one another, as well as in the context of the connection between values and the will that will be the primary subject of Chapter 5.

With these examples set before us, it is now possible to proceed on to an investigation of why values are so difficult to understand. (Note that the term "values" here refers jointly to what I will call in this book "positive values," i.e., typically values like beauty or virtue, and their opposing "disvalues," such as ugliness or vice; this distinction will be discussed further in Chapter 3.) Let us take as our point of departure the first example, and in particular the moment when Bert rounds the corner to find himself faced with a beautiful painting. At least in a phenomenological context, certain elements of this experience – namely, those that fall under the category that Husserl called intellectual consciousness – are quite easy to explain. As constantly happens in our everyday lives, Bert encounters a visual object, an object that gives itself to his consciousness in certain ways. It gives itself with certain colors, with a certain shape, at a certain distance; it even gives other (represented) objects to his consciousness within the painting itself, e.g., the melting clocks for which Dalí is so famous. Relying on the celebrated work of Husserl and other phenomenologists over the years, we could even go so far as to say that other information is given by the painting in a rather less overt manner, having been sedimented within it for an educated man like Bert: cultural information about the status of surrealism as an art form, aesthetic speculations about what the melting clocks are supposed to "represent," and so forth.

But the question of the painting's beauty – in theoretical terms, since Bert certainly has no trouble appreciating said beauty as a practical matter! – remains unanswered. The painting is a given of experience, with all the baggage mentioned above. But where is *beauty*? Such values cannot be seen like colors, smelled like old paint, or located at a particular distance from ourselves. They are not even given in the same way as the cultural information mentioned above; we can imagine a time when Bert read in a book or heard from a friend about the rise of the surrealist movement, but beauty itself has never appeared on any page or dripped from any tongue. These values are *felt*, not perceived (i.e., they are given through *Wertnehmen* – which, as shown in Chapter 1, always includes this element of feeling – and not through *Wahrnehmen*). But what is meant by this term "feeling" requires further investigation if we are to make any sense of it whatsoever.

2.3 The Identity of Values: Scheler and Hartmann's Answer

Of course, in asking this question about *what values mean*, I am not breaking entirely new ground. Countless answers to this conundrum have been assayed throughout the history of philosophy, from Plato on down the line. But we are here concerned with the task of giving a phenomenological account of this issue. Accordingly, at this point, it behooves us to turn our attention to the work of certain thinkers who have already been employed in this project to great effect: Scheler and Hartmann. In somewhat different ways, both of these philosophers answer the question of the identity of values with a straightforward assertion: values are a particular type of object (ideal objects, as Hartmann terms them) that we encounter through our experiences of value-consciousness.[1] While these experiences are certainly bound up with other experiences that we might have – Bert's visual encounter with *Persistence of Memory* is surely linked with his valuative encounter with beauty in this instance – the values themselves and the perceptual objects that are perceived *as* valuable are not in any way the same, on this model. Rather, the latter is more like a vehicle for the former, which is the real center of valuative experiences. But let us examine this model more closely, in order to determine whether or not it provides a satisfactory answer to the question of a phenomenological account of values as such.

This claim about the ontological status of values arises when we ask ourselves about the mode of givenness that is operative within valuative experiences. Scheler, to begin with, insists that the mode of this givenness is a thoroughly *objective* one. Objectivity, in the strict phenomenological sense, is not the same thing as universality (a term whose relation to values will be addressed later), as it is ordinarily taken to mean. Rather, phenomenologists often use the word in a narrower sense, referring to those aspects of our conscious acts and the reality that is constituted thereby which lie on the object-pole (as opposed to the subject-pole) of our experiences. Of course, the term can also be understood to have a

62 The Identity of Values

broader meaning in phenomenology, one that necessitates the intersubjective availability of that which is objective – but the applicability of this point in the context of values will be dealt with in the discussion of values and subjectivity in Chapter 4. The central point is that values, as objective, would not be mere creations of or judgments by the perceiving subject, as some philosophers have concluded, but rather genuine aspects of experience, in some manner yet to be determined.[2]

But Scheler holds not merely that values lie on the object-pole of valuative experiences, but also that they are themselves the proper *objects* of those experiences. That is, for him, values like beauty (or virtue, deliciousness, etc.) represent possible objects of consciousness just as much as those of perception or rational judgment. Far from merely supervening on the objects of perception, values have an "ultimate independence," Scheler writes, "with regard to things, goods, and states of affairs" (17). Values must, on this model, be the *objects of* certain experiences in their own right; they are, "in their *being, independent* of their bearer" (Scheler 18). For example, just as *Persistence of Memory* can be understood as the direct object of a visual experience, the beauty of the painting would serve as the object of a valuative experience (a *value-intuition* in the most literal sense). These two experiences are, for Scheler, legitimately separate; they are experiences of *two different objects* – even if they remain connected in some manner yet to be examined.

On this model, the conscious act of feeling would always stand in a relationship of intentionality with some value-object (just as the act of perception is intentionally directed towards a physical object). As Scheler puts it, feeling "is not *externally brought together* with an object, whether immediately or through a representation ... On the contrary, feeling *originally* intends its *own* kind of objects, namely, '*values*'" (258). Acts of feeling, understood as the subjective correlates of the values towards which they are intentionally directed, do not have to be mediated through representational thought in order to be meaningful (although certainly the objects represented in such thought can give rise to instances of feeling, as when *Persistence of Memory* gives rise to Bert's encounter with pure beauty); rather, feeling is always directed towards its own objects and governed by its own unique laws.[3] Values themselves, then, are really existent entities on this model, not only in the sense that they structure experience in ways that can be studied through phenomenological observation, as in the present investigation, but even in the much stronger sense that they can be directly intuited by an experiencing subject. Scheler himself makes this point quite clear when he writes:

> The value itself always must be *intuitively given* or must refer back to that kind of givenness ... it follows that there are *authentic* and *true* value-qualities and that they constitute a special domain of objectivities.
>
> (14–15)

Certainly, value-objects and value-experiences can and must be connected with sensible objects and the perceptual experiences in which they are given, a point which makes itself clear in our examples. Bert does not experience the value of beauty out of the blue; he does so precisely in the context of his encounter with *Persistence of Memory*. Scheler by no means denies this point, freely admitting that there exist certain "a priori interconnections *between values* and their *bearers*" (Scheler 85). He notes explicitly, to give just one example, that the values of the morally good and evil are always connected to our experiences of persons, while the value of agreeableness applies only to (impersonal) things or events. And there are many other such cases; it is by no means arbitrary, for Scheler, that Bert's encounter with *Persistence of Memory* should take place alongside an intuition of pure beauty, rather than of some other value – though I will not delve into Scheler's model of these particular structures in any great depth at this time. Nonetheless, these essential interrelations notwithstanding, Scheler maintains that values in general are *genuinely separate objects* from all persons, things, and events – indeed, from all objects of perceptual consciousness whatsoever – and may be intuited alongside these perceptual objects, albeit with a different mode of givenness.

To illustrate the point in more detail: Bert, upon rounding the corner to behold *Persistence of Memory*, has (at the least) two different experiences that are, in principle, distinguishable. On the one hand, he sees the painting, with all of the phenomenological baggage that this act entails. On the other, however, he *feels* the value of beauty via a direct intuition, not mediated by his perceptual experience; as Hackett rightly characterizes Scheler's views here, values themselves "are given in the immediacy of all experience" (18). Granted, it is only in the unity of these two objects, a unity that Scheler terms a "good," that there can be "a *genuine* increase of value in the real world," i.e., that the value in question can be realized in a concrete way (Scheler 21). Nonetheless, Bert's direct experience of the value of beauty is, for Scheler, not strictly dependent on his perceptual experience of a painting, even if the two go hand-in-hand, as it were, in this particular situation. Bert could just as well encounter the *identical* value of beauty alongside an imaginative experience as a perceptual one (even if this imaginative act would lack the further value that pertains to concrete realization), or alongside any number of other such experiences; in none of these cases, Scheler maintains, is his genuine act of feeling directed towards any object other than a value itself.

Of course, it is necessary at this juncture to be precise about what *kind* of objects values are supposed to be on this model. In what manner are such objects supposed to exist? Must we posit some "other realm," even if not a fully Platonic one, to account for them – and, if so, what is the nature of this realm? After all, Scheler remains a phenomenologist; I do not want to oversimplify his standpoint on values in a way that would lead to the wholly unwarranted view that values exist apart from their (at least possible) instantiation within any particular consciousness, a naïvely idealist position that Husserl and his followers have taken great pains to distinguish from phenomenology. Certainly, Scheler's characterization of objective values is not fully Platonic in the pejorative sense; values do not in any way inhabit some "higher" metaphysical reality.[4] As Sanford puts it, Scheler's values neither "inhabit a separate realm of ideal types, like so many Platonic Forms," nor "exist like other things do," but rather "are what might be called neutral with respect to existence. They are, Scheler argues, indifferent with respect to the existential sphere" (171).[5] The "existence" of such values might better be termed their givenness to consciousness; they are correlates of a certain mode of consciousness, not abstract things-in-themselves. Nonetheless, the precise nature of this givenness remains deeply unclear from Scheler's work alone.

The fact that the ontological status of values as such remains obscure in the writings of Scheler himself is something of a curiosity. Although it is not the primary purpose of this project to give an account of the historical circumstances in which the phenomenology of values developed, I will note briefly that I attribute Scheler's puzzling lack of attention to this issue to the fact that he had more pressing concerns in his writing, especially in *Formalism*. That is, Scheler was far more interested in overcoming the arguments of his opponents – the chief of whom was Immanuel Kant, although the question of how closely Scheler's Kant resembles the historical philosopher remains open – and in exploring the intrinsic hierarchy that he saw among values than in answering the theoretical question of *how values exist*, at least beyond a preliminary investigation that he fit into his more polemical arguments.[6] Scheler did note in his opening remarks to *Formalism* that he planned to develop a more extensive account of the phenomenology of values in the future – a supposedly forthcoming work that would carry out "a non-formal ethics of values on the broadest possible basis of phenomenological experience," as he put it – but this work was never published, and possibly never even begun (Scheler 5).[7] Perhaps Scheler intended to clarify the ontological status of values beyond his comments in *Formalism*, but such a clarification remains totally elusive in his available writings.

It is fortunate, then, that Scheler's project was not abandoned after his somewhat premature death. Hartmann, a close associate of Scheler, carried out his own investigations into the nature of values along much the same lines as his colleague. Indeed, Scheler himself wrote in the preface to the third edition of his magnum opus that he considered, for example, Hartmann's views on the ideal and the normative "a valuable refinement of the analyses of 'value' and 'ought' in my *Formalism*," and he noted approvingly that Hartmann's position on the hierarchy of values was "largely in agreement with what I say in *Formalism*" (Scheler XXVIII, n. 10).[8] Hartmann, of course, did not characterize his own work in specifically phenomenological terms, but this shift in focus may actually be particularly fruitful with respect to the task of clearing away the obscurity of the ontological status of values: Hartmann considered himself first and foremost to be an ontologist. For his part, Hartmann spells out the existence of objective values in more specific terms than Scheler ever employs, holding them to exist in the form of *ideal objects*, comparable to – though, importantly, distinct from – mathematical objects like numbers or perfect spheres. Such objects are really existent (and both objectively and universally so; just as the number three can be understood and employed by any thinking subject, so too can values, on this model), but they are orthogonal to reality in a way that entails that they can never be encountered as *real* objects (in Hartmann's technical sense) – thereby eliminating the need to posit some quasi-mystical plane of existence to house them.

Hartmann's arguments for this ideal characterization of values – indeed, for the genuine existence of the ideal as a whole (i.e., its "unreal reality," to borrow terminology from Heinrich Rickert) – betray the heavy influence of Husserlian phenomenology on his thought about ontology. He writes that the only possible objections to the claim that the ideal truly exists stem from certain "prejudices," as he calls them, that are ultimately without any philosophical foundation. Either, he holds, existence as such and so-called "concrete reality," the reality of physical objects, are held to be one and the same thing – a point that simply misses an entire region of our experience, he notes – or ideal existence is (mis)identified with strict subjectivity, as if all ideal objects, from numbers to values, were merely "in our heads" (in the pejorative sense). But both of these prejudices, Hartmann maintains, run afoul of Husserl's famous critique of psychologism in the *Logical Investigations*.

Instead, existence must be thought of in broader terms than these prejudices would allow. As Hartmann writes:

> Logic and mathematics are objective sciences; the same is true of every study of essences, which Phenomenology has opened up. In these sciences the objects are not less genuine than those of the concrete sciences; they are merely not real objects ... There are ideal objects of knowledge which are just as independent of the knowing subject as real objects are – that is to say, there is such a thing as ideal self-existence.
>
> (I, 223)

The fact that such ideal objects are genuine components of our experience is no more susceptible to doubt than the existence of real objects; even if they are given in different modes, both are nevertheless *given*, and thus genuine components of the world in which we live.[9] As this claim is a rather central insight for phenomenology itself (at least in the context of the phenomenological reduction; I will not pursue the question of the robustness of Hartmann's ontological views outside of this context), the

66 The Identity of Values

existence of ideal objects will certainly not be contested in this piece of phenomenological writing! At this stage of the investigation, it could very well be that values stand as ideal objects in the sense that Hartmann so trenchantly defends here.

The gist of Hartmann's characterization of the ontological status of values, thus, depends on the distinction that he lays out between reality and ideality. Values, like mathematical objects, can be known as such because every encounter with them takes place in an ideal mode (thus, lacking physical form, giving themselves through certain "mental" forms of intuition, etc.). But, of course, they must be distinguished from other ideal objects as well; values are certainly not answerable to the same laws of consciousness as numbers, for instance, as demonstrated in Chapter 1 of this book. This task may be accomplished, on Hartmann's model, by reference to the thoroughly *feelable* character of values (i.e., their correlation to acts of feeling) and, more particularly, to the role they play with respect to reality as such. Whereas other ideal objects, e.g., the number three, are set at a great remove from reality and merely observed dispassionately, values thrust themselves upon us with a certain normative force; they call for reality as such to be reshaped according to their dictates. Although values, Hartmann writes, "have no self-existence that is real" – that is to say, they remain ideal objects entirely – they nevertheless serve as "principles of action," and therefore "participate in determining reality, they may even to a great degree be themselves 'actualized' – but for this very reason their existence, their mode of Being, remains merely an ideal mode ... These values as such, in comparison with the actual, always have the character of an 'Idea,' which indeed, when the actual corresponds with it, lends to this the character of a value, but which with its ideal nature still remains on the other side of actualization" (I, 220–221). Hartmann's view of values in general, accordingly, is that they lie in the realm of ideality, but in such a way as to remain apart from other ideal objects by virtue of the mode through which they are intuited and by the effects that they have on the reality from which they are by nature separated.

This explication of the ontological status of these value-objects also allows us to make sense of the claim made by Scheler (and, with important modifications, by Hartmann) that values serve as members of an organic and totally *sui generis* hierarchy, a hierarchy that is, in itself, totally indifferent to the conscious subjects who grasp them. Certain positive values can be known to be superior to other positive values – Scheler puts what he calls the value of "the holy" at the top of the list, above all physiological values, emotional values, etc. – because they *genuinely are* set above those others in a predefined order of ranks. As Scheler writes, "[i]n the *totality* of the realm of values there exists a singular order, an '*order of ranks*' that all values possess among themselves. It is because of this that a value is '*higher*' or '*lower*' than another one. This order lies in the *essence* of values themselves, as does the difference between 'positive' and 'negative' values. It does not belong simply to 'values known' by us" (87). If values truly are ideal objects occupying their own unique realm of experience – a realm which is phenomenologically understood rather than naïvely idealistic, i.e., a realm of *ideal givennesses* – then it is plain to see how such an assertion could be justified. No one who accepts the phenomenological criticism of psychologism could deny that numbers, as ideal objects, are possessed of their own essential hierarchies and inter-relationships (two is less than three, the square root of four is two, and so forth); values, on this model, could be much the same. Of course, the particular rank of these values, and even the particular sorts of ranking to which they submit themselves, would be very different from those of any other kinds of ideal objects, but the possibility for some such order in general is clear.

It is this potential for an essential hierarchy that gives Scheler and Hartmann's view of values its most attractive quality (prior to any questions of the actual validity of that view, of course). Namely, it is this internal ranking of values that permits them to found a robust, value-based ethics. While the further move from axiology to ethics is not, of course, a central topic for this book – due to the limits of space – it is nevertheless obvious just how much of an impact a genuine hierarchy of values could have for this latter field of investigation. If, as Scheler has it, the value of the holy is essentially higher than any other set of values whatsoever, for instance, it does not take much of a leap to understand how a demonstration could be given to establish that an individual agent *should act* in pursuit of such a value. Both Scheler and Hartmann attempt to carry out such demonstrations in their great works on ethics, Scheler in the manner just described and Hartmann in a somewhat more nuanced way, taking into account important differences between the "ought to be" and the "ought to do" of a value, etc.[10] If their conception of axiology is correct, then, philosophy has at long last been able to obtain an answer to the problem of the death of God raised by Nietzsche, the lack of a firm foundation for values or morality that can be appealed to independently of the preferences and drives of any given individual. Both Scheler and Hartmann took up this challenge as the primary motivation for their ethical investigations, and both believe themselves to have been successful in providing a way forward through the objective hierarchies to be found among values themselves.[11]

Let us take a moment, at this point, to spell out the consequences of this view of values in clearer terms by examining how it would account for the examples of valuative experience listed above. Beginning with the case of Bert and Ernie at the museum, we can now attempt to take a closer look at Bert's experience of beauty through his encounter with *Persistence of Memory*. On Scheler and Hartmann's model of valuative acts, when Bert steps around the corner and gets his first glimpse of the painting, there are really *two distinct experiences* occurring at once. In the first place, Bert has a perceptual experience of a painting, including all the various components that have been previously discussed in relation to this example (and which have already been dealt with in detail by the work of Husserl and his followers). Secondly, however, and perhaps even more importantly, Bert has an experience of the *pure value of beauty* itself. He grasps the painting through *Wahrnehmen*, perception, but has an encounter with beauty through an act of *Wertnehmen*, value-intuition. As Scheler would explain it, Bert's experience consists in an intentional feeling of beauty itself, given alongside the painting as its necessary condition, rather than a mere judgment *about* the painting, i.e., that it is beautiful: "we do not feel 'about something'; we immediately feel *something*, i.e., a specific value-quality" (259). There are really, on this model, two events occurring, and these events are in a very strong sense incommensurable.[12]

Now, these two experiences – the visual experience of the painting and the valuative experience of beauty – are certainly not without their own intrinsic and inextricable interconnections. For Scheler and Hartmann, our experiences of values are often bound up, as in the case of Bert and the Dalí painting, with experiences of valuable things. Bert could not have had this *particular* experience of beauty without coming into contact with *Persistence of Memory* as a physical object (even if he could have experienced the same value in other ways).[13] It is only through these unities of value-object and perceptual object, these "goods" (as Scheler and Hartmann term them; "valuable things" will be my preferred appellation, as discussed in the following chapter), that we come to encounter values like beauty *in the concrete world*. However, values, on this model, are a condition of the possibility of encountering such goods in the first place. It is only possible for objects to be understood as good (or as bad) in light of the fact that they ultimately point us towards the positive (or negative) value that grants them their valuative character, and which we immediately intuit *alongside* the object itself. As Hartmann puts it:

> In fact, how could things be accepted by anyone as goods, unless independently of their actuality there were an appreciation of them which told him that they possess a value? Surely value does not inhere indiscriminately in all things; there are bad things as well as good. Now, as there is the same kind of Being in things good and bad, the same reality, wherein could anyone discriminate between them, if his sense of value did not inform him? He must possess beforehand the standard ... Otherwise, as soon as one asked: Why is this good? There would be an eternal circle of back-reference. If one answers "because it is good for that other thing," the question immediately arises: "And what is that good for?" So on to infinity; and so long as it continues to move only in the sphere of goods, it evidently turns in

a circle. It does not come to a rest until one no longer answers with a good but with a value – that is, with what first converts things in general into goods.

(I, 187)

The conscious acts by which values are given are, of course, necessarily connected with those by which we are presented with such goods; to deny this connection would render the investigator unable to make sense of the notion of a "good" at all. And yet, for Scheler and for Hartmann, the acts themselves – and, therefore, the objects that are apprehended by those acts – remain ultimately separate. Bert sees a painting and, simultaneously, intuits the element of beauty within that painting. Indeed, at least in a structural sense, his intuition of beauty *precedes* his visual encounter with the painting, since it is required for that experience to be carried out at all. The entire schema that Scheler and Hartmann construct for values within our experience descends from this one basic claim.[14]

2.4 The Impossibility of Values as Objects: A Critique

Nonetheless, despite the well-thought-out portrayal of values and their internal hierarchies given by these two great philosophers, there remain some important problems with this view, which prevent it from capturing the real nature of values in experience. As shown in the preceding section, the attempt to locate values as the direct objects of a certain form of experience necessarily has as a consequence the division of any encounter with a valuable thing into two distinct (albeit interconnected) experiences, one of a value and one of a perceived object or state of affairs. But this interpretation cannot be valid. Any attempt to separate out two genuinely distinct acts from what is phenomenologically understood as a unitary experience would be nothing more than an abstraction. Certainly, for the purposes of phenomenological analysis, it is possible – and, indeed, necessary – to consider the valuative and descriptive aspects of the acts by which valuable objects are apprehended separately in order to uncover the various structures that govern these experiences (both noetically and noematically). But this separation in abstraction cannot legitimately be extended to a genuine separation in the acts themselves, or in the objects towards which those acts are intentionally directed; to do so would be to mistake the specialized world of phenomenological investigation for the lifeworld that it purports to study, and thereby to run afoul of the very same criticism that Scheler or Hartmann might levy against Husserl's reduction of all experience to the structures of rationality – i.e., that such a separation has allowed unwarranted methodological assumptions to interfere with a direct analysis of the content given in valuative experience.

But, of course, this claim that Scheler and Hartmann have missed an important facet of our real experiences of value cannot merely be asserted. Let us, therefore, engage in a rigorously phenomenological investigation of one such experience – it will be easiest to continue our look at the case of Bert and *Persistence of Memory* – in order to determine at what point the object-model of values begins to break down. To reiterate the point of this model more precisely, its central claim is that values are not only different objects from valuable things, but objects of a separate *type* of experience altogether (even if the acts that accomplish these diverse experiences are inextricably bound up with one another). As Sanford puts it, values are "attached" to our experiences of valuable objects or states of affairs, not as something added on to them, but rather as the ultimate object that they manifest, though naturally on a different level than that of perception or memory (171). So, to return to our example, even if there exists some essential bond between the perceptual act of seeing the painting and the valuative act of grasping its beauty within Bert's experience of *Persistence of Memory* (or in any experience of values), this view entails that there certainly are two *intentions* at stake in this experience: the one an intention of a perceptual object and the other of a value. But this twofold intention is not sufficiently grounded in our actual experiences of value. Value-experiences cannot legitimately be broken down in this way; to deny that it is the *same* object intended in a perceptual act that is also intended as valuable in some way is to make an abstraction of genuine experience. These two modes of apprehension might well represent different *attitudes* towards the intended object, but that fact by no means prevents them from intending the *same* object. The aesthetic value of *Persistence of Memory* is not merely *there* for Bert, as Scheler might claim, to be apprehended alongside the painting understood as a representation, it is *there in the painting itself*, as part of the background that enables the painting to be comprehended at all.

Now, it is certainly true, as both Scheler and Hartmann (not to mention others, including both Husserl and this book itself) have argued, that a genuinely existent value – i.e., in phenomenological terms, a value that is genuinely part of the givenness of the world – is a necessary component for understanding any valuative experience whatsoever. But that fact does not entail, as the proponents of the object-model go on to claim, that this value itself is an object – as long as it is possible to account for it in some other way (which will be the aim of the following section of this chapter). Indeed, the very necessity of values for our experiences of valuable things – best exemplified by Hartmann's contention that values are conditions of the possibility for such experiences – rather supports the contrary thesis to that of the objecthood of values. If beauty is a condition of the possibility for Bert's aesthetic encounter with *Persistence of Memory*, then it will be impossible to isolate his experience of the painting as a physical object from the valuative experience which apprehends that beauty (even if there are multiple structures – even independent structures, in the sense that each is governed by its own *sui generis* laws – that must be accounted for within that experience as a whole). That is, it is a necessary phenomenological presupposition of our ability to recognize the painting as valuable that it be *primordially* given through a *value*-experience. Such an object must be given as something valuable *in-itself*, and does not become valuable by the external influence of a *pure value* that merely becomes instantiated in it (even if that pure value does genuinely exist *within* the painting-experience in some other sense). *Persistence of Memory* must first be understood as a *beautiful thing*, grasped in a unitary perceptual/valuative experience, in which both aspects of the experience are equiprimordial, with neither preceding or supplanting the other – and only afterwards, in the abstraction of phenomenological contemplation, can we begin to understand the various independent structures that go into that experience.[15]

Accordingly, the object-model of values is not tenable, precisely due to its insistence on making values into something which they are not.[16] If axiologists working without recourse to phenomenology had often put too much focus on the physical objects of experience, with values simply written off as their non-essential predicates, Scheler – and Hartmann, to a lesser degree – emphasizes too strongly the existence of pure values themselves, to the point of considering them to be *objectively separate* from the things or situations that are experienced as valuable.[17] Indeed, it is not even clear, on this model of values as ideal objects, just what an encounter with such a pure value is supposed to entail. A perfect sphere can at least be visualized in a rough way – the givenness of its intuition is not inexplicable, even if it never appears in what Hartmann would call the mode of reality – but I, for one, utterly fail when I attempt to conceive of a value itself in the absence of something which is valuable. In phenomenological terms, no instance of eidetic variation of value-experiences ever brings to light a pure value-object "floating in the aether," as it were. These values certainly exist (though in what manner remains to be seen), and they are certainly governed by independent laws of consciousness as has been discussed, but the arguments of Scheler and Hartmann do not prove that they achieve any genuine existence *as objects*, or even that they can be *directly* experienced at all. Another way forward for the phenomenology of values must be found.

2.5 A Superior Model: Husserl on the Horizonality of Values

Instead, Husserl's investigations into a phenomenology of values hint at a different interpretation of their ontological status: namely, the view that values do genuinely exist, but only within the *horizons* of conscious experience, rather than as direct objects of experience in their own right. Primarily in his later work (although certainly hints of it are present

72 The Identity of Values

throughout his corpus), Husserl develops the idea of the horizon as an integral part of conscious experience, but which is never itself directly perceived as the object of any intention. The horizon lies always at the edges of experience, making such experiences possible and revealing itself, as it were, as their hazy background, while nevertheless remaining elusive of direct intuition. Such horizons always, by definition, retain a dynamic, ever-receding character; any attempt to bring that which lies on the horizon into the light of immediate experience only succeeds in giving rise to an endless succession of new horizons.

If I am to make the claim that values lie on the horizons of experience, however, it is necessary at this juncture to give a somewhat more detailed (though still quite brief) account of the notion of horizonality in general as it develops in Husserl's later work. It is unclear precisely when the historical Husserl fully identified this notion as an integral part of consciousness; there are hints towards the horizon already present in *Ideas* I, but that text certainly does not develop the notion fully. Husserl's lectures on transcendental logic, given during the early- to mid-1920s and collected in *Analyses Concerning Passive and Active Synthesis*, are often held to contain the full flourishing of this notion as a distinct element of phenomenological investigation. For the purposes of this project, however, it is sufficient to note that the idea of the horizon had not yet been concretely discovered by Husserl at the time of his early ethics lectures, but had become a central component of his phenomenology by the time of the late ethics lectures and, especially, the *Grenzprobleme*.[18] This is not, of course, to say that Husserl applied the idea of the horizon in any explicit way to the question of *values* in these texts – as I will demonstrate, the link between values and the horizon is only ever hinted at by Husserl himself, and never stated unequivocally – but the notion itself was certainly lurking in the background of his thought, as it were, throughout his later work.

At any rate, Husserl's notion of the horizon refers in all cases to elements pertaining to an experience of a directly given object that, nevertheless, are not themselves *directly* given to the experiencing subject, but which rather lurk in the so-called "background" that enables such objects to appear at all. That is, elements of the horizon are central components of any such experience, but never as its intentional object. The horizon refers to certain elements of these experiences that are not explicitly thematized, but which nevertheless have a tremendous effect on the givenness of the experience as a whole.

To explicate this notion more precisely, Husserl distinguishes between the inner and the outer horizons of intentional objects. Every object, say, of visual perception – let us imagine a ceramic mug – gives certain aspects of itself directly to the experiencing consciousness: for instance, the colors and shapes that appear on the side of the mug that faces the perceiver. At the same time, that experience also contains essential references to other possibilities of experience: the perceiver could turn the object around in order to perceive its as-yet-unseen sides (which must necessarily exist, given Husserl's thought about the adumbrated character of visual perception), she could move towards the mug or pick it up to see it from another perspective or to encounter it in some other way, e.g., through touch, and so on. All of these possibilities of future givenness – possibilities that are not, as yet, directly realized in the experience of the mug, but which are always *available* within that experience – lie on the object's inner horizon, its horizon of self-development with respect to its givenness. As Husserl demonstrates in the *Cartesian Meditations*, "there belongs to every external perception its reference from the 'genuinely perceived' sides of the object of perception to the sides 'also meant' – not yet perceived, but only anticipated . . . Furthermore, the perception has horizons made up of other possibilities of perception, as perceptions that we could have, if we actively directed the course of perception otherwise: if, for example, we turned our eyes that way instead of this, or if we were to step forward or to one side, and so forth" (44 / *Hua* I, 82). These possibilities are genuinely part of the perceiving subject's experience of the object, but are not themselves concretely realized in the same way as her visual experience of the mug's front side.

In contrast, elements of experience that lie on the object's outer horizon do not merely make reference to the givenness of the object itself, but also take into account the relatedness of that object to its surroundings. A visually perceived mug, for instance, is never perceived in abstraction from its immediate environment. Perhaps it sits on a desk, surrounded by all sorts of other objects: papers, pens and pencils, electronics of various sorts. Or perhaps the mug sits underneath a lamp, which provides a certain level of illumination that shapes the manner in which the mug gives itself to visual perception. When the perceiving subject directs her attention at the mug, these other objects (including the desk itself) are certainly part of the givenness of the object in some sense, they are contained within the perceiver's experience thereof, but they are not themselves the direct objects of that experience or the central focus of her attention. These elements of the experience lend themselves to the development of future experiential possibilities in an analogous way to aspects of the inner horizon. The possibility is always open to the perceiving subject to redirect her attention towards any aspect of the outer horizon of the object towards which she is presently directed – but, again, this act would only succeed in giving rise to a new outer horizon of its own (the desk lies on the horizon of mug, the floor lies on the horizon of the desk, etc.). This ever-developing horizon can be extended quite far; the desk is contained within a room, which is located in a building, which stands in a city, and so forth. Every such experience has its outer horizon, in this sense, and so contains within itself countless possibilities of future unfolding – albeit in an indirect way, since these horizonal possibilities are not explicitly given as fully developed in the present experience alone.

Elements of the horizon, thus, in all of these cases, are indeed intended by the experiencing consciousness, but only as that which is "also meant," i.e., in addition to the *directly intended object* of the experience. The horizon refers to all aspects of an experience that are given only indirectly to the experiencing subject, and which can only be brought into the clear light of direct intuition through the further acts towards which they call her. The backside of an object that is given on the inner horizon of any visual experience of that object, to return to Husserl's chief example, can only be brought out of the horizon into direct experience through the act of turning it around or moving oneself around it. Nevertheless, these further conscious acts that the horizon reveals only succeed in giving rise to ever new experiences that themselves contain new horizons in their own right. For example, moving around an object to reveal its backside in direct experience only gives rise to a new adumbration of that object, with its own foreground and background, a new backside, etc. – that is to say, with its own inner and outer horizons. This propensity to call consciousness onward to new experiences and new acts is an integral part of the horizon, on Husserl's model, and it is quite helpful in explicating the nature of the horizon in general.

Of course, it must be acknowledged that the particular examples discussed here in brief by no means exhaust all of the myriad ways in which elements of experience can be horizonally given. There are countless more gradations of the horizon discussed by Husserl and other phenomenologists: the horizon of the lived body, the temporal horizons of experience, the world-horizon as a whole, and so on – not to mention the value-horizon of experience that I will discuss momentarily. It is not at all my intention in this project to give a full account of the horizon as such. Nonetheless, a basic grasp of the way in which this notion functions in phenomenology is necessary to understand how it might be applied in the case of value-experiences, and this elementary account of the horizon is all that I have intended to deliver in the preceding paragraphs.

In some of his later writings, Husserl hints that it is on these ever-developing horizons of experience that we can expect to find values, rather than in an experience of an independent realm of value-objects. Values, that is, might be thought of as elements that have an essential role to play in other experiences we might have, but without themselves being the direct objects that are intended in those experiences; the conscious acts whereby they are apprehended are not direct intuitions of values, but rather acts which bring those values to bear on the edges of, for instance, perceptual experiences.[19] This way of viewing values – not as existing *objects*, but as meaningful components of experience, which imbue value-experiences with a certain unique character (just as the light of a lamp affects the givenness of the visually perceived object on which it shines without itself being the direct object of that experience) – is a running thread throughout Husserl's thought on the subject. Even in his early ethics lectures, which far predate the full development of the idea of the horizon, hints towards this way of thinking were already present: "Value is not a being, value is something relating to being or not-being, but it belongs in another dimension" (*Hua* XXVIII, 340). Of course, it is by no means clear from this early period that this "other dimension" will turn out to be that of the horizon – it would be possible to interpret what Husserl says here along the lines of Hartmann's distinction between the real and the ideal – but this line of thought certainly lays the groundwork for a potentially fruitful characterization of values, and particularly so when the difficulties of the object-model are borne in mind.

As Husserl develops his thought about such value-infused realms of experience as ethics further, particularly in the late, unpublished writings that have recently appeared as the *Grenzprobleme*, it becomes clearer just how this horizonal conception of values could be operative as a background assumption of his phenomenological investigations – though, again, he never explicitly discusses this model in any detail, given his other concerns in this text. Consider the way in which Husserl portrays the relationship between values themselves and the act of feeling that is their subjective correlate in an experience of value-intuition. As he writes:

> In valuing, one "gives oneself up" more or less completely to the values. But is that anything other than enjoying oneself in an ever deeper and richer continuing fulfillment of the same valuation, in which a progressive self-giving of the value ensues, a self-giving in increasing completeness? That concerns values that have wide, indeed unending horizons, in pursuit of which one, insofar as he opens himself to them, pours out from himself ever richer streams of valuing feeling, falls into "enthusiasm" ["*Begeisterung*"].
>
> (*Hua* XLII, 358)

Granted, Husserl here defines values as "having" their horizons, which call the experiencing subject on towards deeper acts of valuation. However, when this process is examined more closely, it becomes apparent that, at least in this formulation, values consist in nothing more than their horizonal effects on the experiencing consciousness. Husserl writes that these values are experienced only through a "progressive self-giving" that always affords the one who values further possibilities of deepening his experience in certain ways (for instance, through Bert's act of aesthetic contemplation, which allows him to encounter the beauty of *Persistence of Memory* in a more nuanced way). Value-experiences, as Husserl portrays them here, consist in nothing but this progressive unfolding and the ever-deepening enjoyment that is its subjective correlate, a fact that distinguishes them, as Husserl notes, from other modes of

76   *The Identity of Values*

experience; he mentions in particular judging and acting consciousness. Although Husserl does not make this connection explicit, it is apparent from the preceding discussion that this notion of progressive unfolding within experience, in which that which unfolds itself is never experienced as such, except in terms of its giving rise to deeper possibilities of future experience, is fundamentally a characteristic of those elements of experience that lie on the horizon. Husserl never thematizes this claim, but it is, nevertheless, a reasonable interpretation of the axiological theory that must underlie his later ethical speculation – even if developing such a theory was not his primary intention in these writings.

This horizon-model of values, further, allows us to account for the close connection between values and the things which we perceive *as* valuable that remained inexplicable on the object-model. Here, values are best understood as *influences* on experience, rather than *objects* of experience at all. They are not themselves experienced as such, except insofar as they represent a unique set of structures that govern any experience which gives some object or situation as valuable (structures that can themselves be intuited in some sense from within the phenomenological attitude). In this sense, they remain absolutely *content-full* (i.e., non-formal) in terms of leading the consciousness that encounters them to particular sorts of valuative acts, while still eluding any direct grasp.[20] Like anything which lies on the horizons of experience, values exhibit the constant tendency to project themselves forward, positing ever-new possibilities of experience as an essential characteristic. As Husserl writes in the *Grenzprobleme*, "Life has its horizon as a horizon of orderly anticipation ... Action is action within a surrounding; personal values, realized, enrich the world and imprint their objective values onto it. Values are built on values, and the ego in its activity heightens itself and inserts into its own life a higher value, not only in an arbitrary aggregate, realizing values in a jumble, but rather building up values systematically" (*Hua* XLII, 421). The appearance of values, for Husserl, always and essentially directs itself towards other possible valuative experiences, a trait that links them inextricably with the idea of the horizon.[21] Granted, the sort of horizonality that values would possess on this model does not directly map onto Husserl's distinction between the outer and inner horizon that is appropriate for, e.g., objects of visual perception. Values, we might say, lie on the *value-horizon* of valuable things, not their perceptual horizon, and this new horizon is possessed of its own unique structures that require their own phenomenological investigation – a task whose basic foundation is precisely the purpose of this book.

Nonetheless, this model may, at this point, seem somewhat abstract. To remedy this problem, let us turn our attention back towards the case of our favorite aficionado of surrealism, Bert, in order to see how the horizon-model of values plays out in actual practice. When Bert rounds the corner and finds himself confronted with *Persistence of Memory*, there are certainly two modes of consciousness simultaneously operative, as we have noted before; on one level, he perceives a physical object and that which this object represents, while on another level entirely he undergoes an aesthetic experience of beauty. But on the horizon-model of values, unlike on the object-model posited by Scheler and Hartmann, there is *only one* experience occurring in this context (albeit an experience that is made up of several mutually independent layers). The only object of Bert's act (at least, the act of looking at the painting that is our present focus) is the painting itself; there is no encounter with the "pure value of beauty" over and above his perception of the painting. And yet, *Persistence* is by no means a *merely visual object* for Bert (or for any perceiver). There is a valuative element to his experience of the painting that cannot be explained simply as one of its attributes, nor through any of the structures of dispassionate perception that serve to account for the painting's shape, its colors, etc. This valuative element is what makes the painting stand out in Bert's experience as an object of sentiment, as that which inspires certain passions within him. That is, a value like beauty is that element of an experience, ungrasped in any direct way but nevertheless given as "also meant," which gives it its uniquely affective significance, and which thereby gives rise to an emotional response by the perceiving subject; as Theodorou puts it, "value-intentionality," i.e., the directedness of consciousness towards an object in a valuative manner, "is 'processed' in what we pre-philosophically know as *emotions*" (2014a, 68).[22]

Furthermore, lurking on the horizons of Bert's painting-experience are a number of further possibilities towards which the painting might call him. Many of these – the possibility of walking behind the velvet rope keeping him from the painting, lifting the frame off the wall, and looking at the backside of the canvas, for instance – lie within the realm of intellectual consciousness, as Husserl describes it. But other possibilities (the most important ones, for our purposes) appeal to different structures altogether. Namely, *Persistence of Memory* calls Bert on to an experience of aesthetic contemplation of its beauty – an experience that is immediately realized in Bert's subsequent actions, e.g., standing in slack-jawed appreciation of the great work. The possibilities that such a horizon opens up are not merely those of dispassionate perception; we could never understand Bert's evaluative stance towards the painting, his subsequently enthusiastic speech about it, etc., if we did not have a firm grasp of the structures of valuation that condition his overall experience of the painting in addition to those of ordinary perception. Ultimately, as I will argue, a connection to acts of volition is required here as well, since the acts towards which a valuing subject is horizonally directed are always acts of the will aimed at bringing the subject and the experienced value closer together (though a full account of this connection must wait until Chapter 5). The horizon-model of values thus explains well the legitimately unique character of valuative consciousness without the further problem of positing the existence of genuine value-objects, which nevertheless always seem to elude our direct experience.

On this horizon-model, it cannot legitimately be said that there are two experiences happening to Bert at one time; what we have, instead, is one experience given in two different modes and, therefore, involving two different conscious acts, one of perception and one of value-intuition – *even though these two acts are part of one experiential structure and cannot genuinely be separated from one another at all*. Bert's experience of the painting is *one* experience, an experience that is intentionally directed towards *one* object, but which is accomplished through two different modes that bring to bear on that experience different conscious structures. Bert perceives the painting as a physical object through the structures of intellectual consciousness and understands it as valuable through the influence of the value of beauty, but he never directly encounters that value itself. The ontological status of that value, accordingly, does not have to be rendered totally independent of the ontological status of the things that are understood to be valuable, even if the structures that govern the apprehension of values differ dramatically from the structures, e.g., of visual perception. Metaphorically speaking, it is as if the value – beauty, in this case – is a source of light shining down upon the perceived object from far above. The source of such light is not directly perceived in the experience (although it is part of the horizon of that experience insofar as it has the potential to call the experiencing consciousness on towards other conscious acts, e.g., to move around the room to see the object illuminated in other ways), but it has dramatic effects on the way in which the perceived object gives itself to consciousness, e.g., whether in fine detail or dimly, with different shades of its colors, etc.[23]

In a like manner, values such as beauty inform the way in which we encounter valuable objects like *Persistence of Memory*, perhaps to an even greater degree than the light shining down on them. It is phenomenologically indisputable that there is something more going on in aesthetic appreciation like that which Bert experiences than can be accounted for through perception or the intellect alone (see Chapter 1), and horizonal values serve well to explain this aspect of such phenomena. Indeed, traces of this interpretation of values run throughout Husserl's work from the very beginning. A quite similar example to this metaphor can be found in the fifth *Logical Investigation*: "Joy, e.g., concerning some happy event, is certainly an act. But this act, which is not merely an intentional character, but a concrete and therefore complex experience, does not merely hold in its unity an idea of the happy event and an act-character of liking which relates to it: a sensation of pleasure attaches to the idea, a sensation at once seen and located as an emotional excitement in the psychophysical feeling-subject, and also as an objective property – the event seems as if bathed in a rosy gleam" (110). While Husserl's formulation here is dependent on the erroneous model of values that informed his early writings – he intimates that values are something like explicit properties of valuable objects – this example certainly hints intriguingly at the horizon-model of values that would, at least in a covert manner, inform his later writings. Values, whenever they are experienced, are encountered through the *effects* that they have on the valuable things to which they are connected.

What the move to the horizon adds to this interpretation is, of course, a greater depth of explanatory power with respect to the manner in which these values are related to the valuable things on which they have such effects. On this model, it becomes clear how values themselves can influence the ways in which we experience the world without the need to define them as *objects* within that world, i.e., the mysterious objects of a direct intuition that would be part of a separate experience from our encounters with valuable things. Such values are essential elements of our experience insofar as they help to explain what distinguishes, say, a beautiful painting from an ugly one; without grasping the way in which values like beauty or ugliness lie on the horizons of the experiences by which these paintings are encountered, we would be at a loss to understand the vast differences in our reactions to each of them. Nevertheless, on this model, we have no need to explain what values are *solely* as abstract objects, as if we could directly intuit "beauty" itself in isolation from a beautiful object, since such values never submit themselves to a direct grasp in the way that the painting as a whole does (although it may still be worthwhile to explain such "values in themselves" or "pure values" in the sense of structures guiding experience, if not as objects – a task that will be taken up in the following chapter).

Indeed, it is only once these insights are incorporated into axiology that Husserl's model of valuation begins to make sense. Although I have rejected Husserl's early thought about values on entirely different grounds (i.e., that it fails to take into account the genuinely *sui generis* character of valuative consciousness), it has also been criticized from other perspectives as well. Most importantly, this model runs into difficulties when the early Husserl, rejecting the object-model of values by holding instances of value-intuition to be *non-objectifying* acts in contrast to those of the intellect, finds himself at a loss to explain what, precisely, such acts accomplish. Henning Peucker writes that the model "runs into trouble if Husserl also claims that feelings or emotions give us a certain access to specific properties which the theoretical acts cannot reveal, namely value-properties. Here the question arises as to how feelings can do this if they are not objectifying acts. How can they open up something from the world when they are not acts that make something objective? How is the givenness of values in feeling consciousness understandable if it is not carried out by objectifying acts?" (2008, 318). Without recourse to the horizon, there are no other options; values are either objects or (static) properties of objects. On the horizon-model, however, this problem too can be neatly avoided, as Peucker acknowledges that Husserl accomplishes in his later work. Here, values can be conceived of as neither objects nor properties; they are horizonal elements of experience, and so have an entirely novel role to play in experience, a role that can only be understood in light of Husserl's later insights.

Ultimately, this horizonal model of values and value-experiences is better justified phenomenologically than the model proposed by Scheler and Hartmann.[24] Most importantly, the former accounts for a central fact of our experiences of value that the latter ignores almost entirely: our encounters with valuable objects, such as the beautiful *Persistence of Memory*, are best understood phenomenologically in a holistic manner. We are immediately given such a work of art as a *beautiful object*; we neither first encounter it as an object of dispassionate perception that only later becomes valuable, as Scheler and Hartmann rightly reject, nor immediately skip past the painting to the pure value that is supposedly the "real object" of our aesthetic appreciation. Paintings do not drop out of our consciousness – becoming latent, as Husserl might put it – when we appreciate the beauty within them. The beauty of an art piece is *in the painting itself*, and is no more alien to it or outside of it than the painting's colors or its shape (even if they are governed by radically different structures).[25]

Here, values do not exist in some quasi-Platonic realm as objects, but rather exist through and are discovered on the horizons of everyday experiences – they are indeed genuinely given to consciousness, but only indirectly, and never given as real via direct intuition. This is not, of course, to deny the independent existence of values, nor their unique phenomenological structures; Scheler and Hartmann's arguments on that count are undeniable. But those arguments do not necessarily prove the further contention that values are *objects* of consciousness, at least when the alternative explanation of their horizonal existence remains possible. The notion of the horizon, then, is necessary to understand how it is that values could exhibit an independence from other modes of experience without being directly intuitable – a point that avoids the grave difficulties associated with the object-model, as demonstrated previously.

Understanding values as part of the horizon of our experiences of value in the world helps us to account for two of the most phenomenologically obvious facts about such experiences: that they are unitary encounters with a genuinely valuable object (or situation, though, admittedly, the valuative structures that apply in this case are rather more complex than those that apply to the encounter with an individual valuable object), and yet that there remains a distinct and independent, purely valuative mode of apprehension operative within that experience alongside its intellectual or perceptual aspects. Both of these claims can be true simultaneously only once the dimension of the horizon is brought into play. Unlike both the object-model, which necessitates an impossible separation between value and object, and the view of values that reduces them to merely intellectual structures, which denies the genuine feeling-aspect of valuative acts, the horizon-model allows the truly multifaceted character of all of our experiences to be maintained, unharmed by any unwarranted assumptions. An *experience of a valuable thing* is one unitary whole, which is valuable through and through, while still allowing us to distinguish between the various modes of consciousness (or conscious acts) that go into that experience, whether these modes are perceptual or valuative (or volitional, as will be discussed later). Only once Husserl's insights about this horizonal character are brought to bear in the context of Scheler and Hartmann's independent value-structures can we truly begin to understand what it means to value something from the phenomenological perspective.

2.6 The Necessity of Values in Experience: A Controversial Claim

One further point must be made in this preliminary exploration of the nature of values before we proceed on to further distinctions and more involved explanations of the role that they play in our experience. Namely, it is my contention that value-consciousness, in the horizonal sense just described, is a fundamental component of all our experiences, a condition of the possibility for any consciousness like ours whatsoever. This is, naturally, a rather weighty and somewhat non-intuitive claim, and so will require strenuous defense. However, that defense cannot be fully carried out at this point in the investigation of values – primarily because a complete account of the valuative character of all experience requires discussion of the essential connection between value-consciousness and volition, a point that will not be taken up until Chapter 5 (at which time I will return to this proof). Nonetheless, a basic understanding of this claim is a vital step along the way towards a phenomenology of values in general; I cannot leave such a discussion entirely for that late point in the investigation. As such, the remainder of this chapter will be devoted to spelling out just what is meant by the claim that values are a basic component of all experience and providing a preliminary justification for that claim, even if some elements of the proof will have to appeal to parts of this investigation that are yet to come.

What, then, does such a claim entail, on the horizon-model of values? Nothing more – though nothing less – than that every perceptual or intellectual experience that we might have is connected in one way or another to some set of values that lie on its horizon. This, of course, implies that *all* experience that is presently conceivable is so connected, given that we have identified the three regions of consciousness available to us as those of the intellect, of valuation, and of volition (whose connection to values will, as mentioned, be explored later). It is not only great or rapturous experiences like Bert's encounter with *Persistence of Memory* that are accompanied by the values, like beauty, that lie on their horizons, but all acts of consciousness whatsoever. There is no such thing as a totally non-valuable (as opposed to disvaluable) experience – or, at least, any such experience would always be a mere abstraction from the real givenness of the object or state of affairs in question, and therefore insufficient to explain reality as such. The value perceived in some objects or situations may be extremely close to neutral, and the values of two different objects may be, on the practical level, nearly indistinguishable, but all things have some unique worth (whether positive or negative). Just as Bert's encounter with the Dalí painting would be misunderstood without reference to its affective character, so too would any other perception that Bert might have – notwithstanding the fact that the affective element within most such perceptions would likely be far less dramatic than that contained in his experience of *Persistence of Memory*.

This claim stands in stark contrast with another doctrine espoused by Husserl: that of the existence of so-called *adiaphora*, objects or situations that are construed as entirely lacking in either positive value or disvalue. Husserl discusses this doctrine most completely in his early ethics lectures, although he continues to make scattered references to it even in his later work. As he writes:

> According to these determinations [i.e., regarding the differences between value-consciousness and perceptual consciousness], it must now be emphasized that we must express a few axioms with respect to the occurrence of adiaphora peculiar to the sphere of valuation. It is to be noted that the existence of adiaphora [*Adiaphorie*] is an occurrence that valuing reason as such has to determine. Whether a pre-given situation has specific value-predicates or whether it is free of values, that is only determined through rational value-considerations.
> (*Hua* XXVIII, 84)

Husserl is insistent on the real existence of these adiaphora within experience, and he formulates his views on the nature of valuative consciousness as a whole in line with this claim. Unlike in the case of intellectual consciousness, where the law of the excluded middle holds sway, he maintains that value-consciousness must appeal to an analogous law of the excluded *fourth*: a valuable object or situation either has a positive value, a negative one, or is an adiaphoron, with no further options.[26] My contention, however, is that this notion of the adiaphoron is, in the end, a term with no real (or even conceivable) application in concrete experience. Consciousness as we know it necessarily involves valuative elements, as I will argue throughout this book, and so no such thing as a genuine adiaphoron can possibly be meaningful for or experienced by us. Any apparently *value-free* experience, I suggest, can ultimately be seen to have some concealed or hidden value lurking on its horizon, which merely fails, for one reason or another, to reach the threshold of explicit awareness or thematization.

But how could such a claim possibly be true? Are there not many experiences that we have that are simply beneath our notice, which hold no value for us whatsoever? Such a counter-claim seems immediately obvious, but further investigation of these supposedly value-less experiences reveals it to be in error. Let us consider a particular example. Let us imagine that, as Bert rounds another corner in the museum, he is confronted not by a work of art like *Persistence of Memory*, but by a bare white wall. (Perhaps the museum has not yet gotten around to filling up this particular nook with artwork due to budget cuts.) In any case, it is easy to see how one might interpret this wall – vis-à-vis Bert's experience of it – as completely lacking in value. The wall certainly does not hold the same kind of attraction for him that a beautiful painting might, nor the repulsion of a hideous one. It is not a particularly majestic wall. Bert's reaction to it might well be described as *apathetic* – literally, without passion or affect. If this is an accurate description of the givenness of such a wall, then it surely cannot be the case that *all* experiences are related to value in one way or another.

And yet, the fact that the bare wall does not strike Bert with anywhere near the dramatic affective significance of an object like *Persistence of Memory* does not entail that he has no feeling towards it whatsoever. It remains possible – and, as I will argue, actually true – that the wall *does* hold some kind of value that Bert can experience, even if that value is nothing particularly noteworthy. (His apathy towards the wall might, therefore, be one of degrees, rather than a total lack of all interest.) There are a vast number of possibilities for the value that Bert could encounter within the wall. One of the most obvious, perhaps, in this case, is that the wall could be an object of aesthetic disvalue. Bert, surrounded by objects of great beauty, suddenly – unexpectedly – finds himself in front of a bare, monotonous wall (a dull and drab object indeed in comparison to a Dalí painting!). Now, the ugliness of the wall is certainly not comparable in scale to the ugliness of a horrific battlefield, an ill-drawn portrait, etc., but that quantitative difference does not entail that such a value does not exist at all.

And there are countless other possibilities as well. Perhaps the wall is, in Bert's experience, not an object of disvalue at all, but rather a welcome respite from the sensory overload of walking through a crowded museum, its calm whiteness a soothing balm to his eyes (or, on the contrary, a glaring, garish brightness that makes him squint and grimace). In this case, the wall would bear the positive value of a refreshing agreeableness (or the negative value of unpleasantness). The wall could be a troublesome obstacle in his path, bearing within it a certain disvalue of discomfort. And so forth and so on, all of which still applies even if these values are so inconsequential that Bert himself is not quite aware of their existence. As phenomenology has rightly pointed out many times, the real existence of something in conscious experience does not require our *active awareness* – see Husserl's distinction between passivity and activity that arose in the context of his late turn towards genetic phenomenology. The point is that, even though these values are quite minor and often easy to overlook, it is phenomenologically vital to include them in our account of everyday experience. Just because we might well ordinarily be inclined to say that Bert sees no value in the wall does not mean that there is nothing of value in that experience, waiting to be uncovered.

There is a useful comparison to be made here between these low-intensity values that constantly surround us and the idea of background noise in auditory perception. In addition to all of the sounds to which we pay active attention throughout our everyday lives – speech, music, alarms, etc. – we are also enveloped at all times by a vast complex of other noises that we, in most cases, simply disregard. Even the quietest country night is filled with the sounds of insects, the rush of the breeze, the swaying of distant trees, and so on. Nonetheless, although these noises are very real and are genuine components of our experiential lives, we say quite often that we are sitting in complete silence despite that fact! That is, our perceptive consciousness is, in the ordinary case, disposed to interpret any noise that falls below a certain threshold (in terms of volume, salience, etc.) as indistinguishable from a *lack* of noise, at least with respect to our thematic awareness. We certainly *experience* these noises – we can even thematize them directly through further conscious acts – but we mostly overlook them in terms of our active attention. My claim is that the low-intensity values discussed in this section are related to us in much the same way; just as background noise is present to us without our thematic awareness, so too are many of the values that we experience concealed to us throughout our daily lives, and for many of the same reasons.

In any case, this same sort of argument could be applied to any other example of a supposedly valueless experience that we might think of, i.e., the claim that such experiences merely *seem* to be valueless as a result of the rather unimpressive quality of the values that really do lie within them, a quality that lies, as we might say, below the threshold of awareness. Such an experience might well be *misinterpreted* as an encounter with a genuine adiaphoron, and for understandable reasons, but that fact by no means entails that this interpretation would be a correct one. The possibility, at least, of my reading of these experiences is unmistakable; counterexamples like that of Bert's encounter with the wall, watching paint dry, etc., are not a knock-down argument against the thoroughly valuable character of all experience. Of course, it remains to be proved that all experiences *are in fact* valuable, at least to some degree, which is quite a different – and more onerous – task than that of establishing the possibility of their being so. As noted previously, this task cannot be carried out in full at this point in this book. A solid case for the thoroughly valuable character of all experience can only be made once the essential connections between values and our acts of volition have been made clear, and so a complete formulation of this argument must appear later in this project, i.e., in Chapter 5.

I can, however, provide at least some further, albeit preliminary evidence for the claim that all experiences are thoroughly valuable. One way of supporting this claim, naturally, is the task of a purely inductive, descriptive phenomenology; we might look at a number of hypothetical experiences that seem, on the surface, to be utterly without value – a theoretical experience like that of Bert and the blank wall, for instance, or a personal experience – in order to determine whether or not some element of value can be located there nevertheless. This is precisely the sort of evidence that I have just been discussing. I could continue enumerating such examples *ad nauseam*, but that would not seem to be a particularly good use of space (exploring further such examples is left as an exercise for the reader!). What my ability to provide such essentially value-based explanations of acts that are seemingly without any pathos implies, however, is that value-consciousness plays a central role in the deeply complex, multi-layered set of experiences that make up consciousness in general. While these considerations are by no means a completely solid argument for this interpretation, they are, nevertheless, evidence in that direction.

Despite what detractors of Husserlian phenomenology might claim about the discipline – Dreyfus' criticisms of Husserl's supposed intellectualism come to mind – phenomenologists (at least, the good ones) do not make the mistake of oversimplifying consciousness. One of the most crucial components of the discipline is its goal of focusing on the real content that is given in experience, and hand-in-hand with that goal is the insight that what is so given is always, first and foremost, the richness that Husserl called the lifeworld, and not any one particular strain of consciousness. The world, as it really is, is not a set of totally discrete experiences, but a unified superstructure containing all of those experiences and much more. Even if such experiences can be analyzed bit by bit, taking each set of structures that govern them (e.g., valuative structures, perceptual structures, etc.) in turn, that separation can never be more than an abstraction away from the real content of experience – a useful abstraction, perhaps, but an abstraction nonetheless. This claim applies just as much to the objects of intellectual perception as it does to those of valuation. As Hartmann notes, any "purely theoretical consciousness of objects is a mere abstraction. Actually, the practical interest is always there, like an undercurrent, and occasionally it breaks powerfully through and disturbs the serenity of contemplation" (I, 35). What is primary in our experience is always the whole, and that whole always includes the passion we feel (to whatever degree, greater or lesser) about every element of our existence.[27] This holistic character of consciousness is good (albeit not yet absolute) evidence that valuative consciousness will always feature as an element within all of our experiences, at least when they are fully understood. *What* value, precisely, a given individual will experience in connection with any particular object, not to mention the relative strength of this value with respect to other values within his experience, cannot be determined ahead of time – a point that will be discussed more fully in Chapter 4 – but the fact *that* some value or other will be tied in with all of his experiences is thus made clear.

Lastly, the vast richness of all of our experiences also entails that the value present within a given object or situation can never be thought of as being entirely independent of all other values. Like any aspect of our experience, valuative consciousness is inextricably intertwined with a wide variety of other experiences – other values, in this case – in a giant nexus that makes up the lifeworld. What this fact means for values on the horizon-model is that (*contra* Hartmann) no two values can ever be entirely the same; the value of an object or situation is always, in this sense, relative (i.e., to the values of other objects or situations for a specific individual, rather than in the thoroughgoing sense of something like *moral* relativism).[28] In the example mentioned above, *Persistence of Memory* is given as beautiful in a particular way; if Bert were to encounter another beautiful painting (say, Dalí's *The Ecumenical Council*), the beauty that this new object held would be potentially comparable to the beauty of *Persistence*, i.e., it would be more or less beautiful. Again, this distinction holds even if the difference is, on the practical level, mostly undetectable; even if the two paintings are roughly equivalent in beauty, one will triumph over the other at least to some degree.[29]

Indeed, much of what accounts for the association between values and the particular objects that they "inhabit" lies in the way that those objects are related to other valuable things in the experience of the conscious subject. If Bert, for instance, finds a blank wall to be disappointingly drab, this is very likely only the case because of the stark contrast between his expectation of rounding the corner to find a beautiful painting and the unremarkable barrier that actually confronts him, a contrast that results in an aesthetic disappointment. Values always appeal to other values for their meaning; this is an integral part of their horizonal character. Again, we could spend a great deal of time spelling out the consequences of such an insight. In the example of Oscar and his scotch, for instance, the beverage has a rather distasteful value in his experience at first, but certainly points towards (in a manner yet to be determined) its development into the positive value of deliciousness that the drink will later attain, e.g., through his associates' praise of its taste. With respect to Aloysius' adultery, the positive value of carnal pleasure and the disvalue of vice are present simultaneously in one action, and therefore absolutely closely related (and, indeed, in horizonal ways; the dominance of the upcoming pleasure over Aloysius' mind when he is first presented with the temptation to engage in the act already has, lurking in the background, the overwhelming guilt that will ultimately come of his doing so, even though that latter value may remain nothing but a vague hint of uneasiness in the heat of the moment). These examples will continue to be discussed throughout this project, but the basically interrelated character of values – both with other values and with all other acts of consciousness – should, at this point, be clear.

2.7 Conclusions: The Essential Nature of Values

The benefit of this chapter is that we now have a template for our phenomenological investigation into the identity of values. After having gone through the arguments of several famous phenomenologists (et al.), we now know where to look to uncover these mysterious entities: not, as Scheler and Hartmann would have it, in some quasi-Platonic realm of ideal value-objects, but always lurking on the edges of other experiences, other conscious acts. With Husserl's notion of the horizon brought into play, we have a way of explaining values and the influence that they bring to bear on our experiences without positing any direct intuition of such values – an intuition that, after all, seems to be missing from our phenomenological worlds. (I have never, for my part, encountered "beauty itself" without the mediation of something beautiful, and I fail to grasp what such an experience would look like at all.) Nonetheless, values are real, and the structures that govern them are independent of those that govern other conscious acts, as established previously. It simply remains the case that, if we want to understand such values, we must always do so in the context of the rich collection of experiences in which they are always embedded – just as any understanding of our experiences in general requires a firm grasp of the values that inform them. With that said, we can now proceed onwards towards a more detailed analysis of the intricate relationships between values themselves and the experiences that they help shape, which will be the task of the following chapter.

Notes

1 Husserl too, in his early thought on values, occasionally made similar assertions (see Ferrarello's "Brentano's and Husserl's Axiology" for an elaboration of these claims). Nonetheless, I will be concerned here primarily with the insights found in Husserl's later thought on the subject, and so I will discuss the object-model of values mostly in the context of Scheler and Hartmann's views.
2 Note that this general objectivity will not be opposed in this book; after all, the entire point of the preceding chapter was to establish that values are an inextricable and independent component of our experiential lives. Husserl

88 The Identity of Values

too defends this basic claim about the objectivity of values in his argument against the reduction of value to subjective desire in ethical hedonism: "*Desire* is a respective condition or act of the feeling subject. Value, however, is suitable to the object. It is known in feeling behavior as a moment in the thing [*Sache*] about which it is said, 'it has a value.' It [i.e., the thing] has, therefore, a value" (*Hua* XXXVII, 68; see also the following chapter of that text). Confusion about this fact, Husserl maintains, only arises when the *act* of feeling is conflated with the *objective validity* of the felt value. Like both Scheler and Husserl, I find this point entirely persuasive – though the *mode* of this objective validity remains to be examined.

3 Of course, while values both can and must be considered on their own terms, for Scheler, to separate them entirely from objects understood as valuable (for instance, by considering them to be purely "mental" objects) would be a failure to recognize the phenomenological character of value itself: "value-phenomena are, in their essence as value-phenomena, thoroughly independent of the distinction between the psychic and the physical" (Scheler 198). His point is simply that values represent possible objects in their own right, not that they can be *wholly* separated from other sorts of experiences in actuality without drifting into abstraction.

4 This claim stands in contrast to that made by Panos Theodorou: "Scheler, a *phenomenological realist*, continues to consider values as species in a Platonic sphere, which get *instantiated* in our intentional emotive acts, as well as on the things that are then experienced as goods" (2014a, 72). While I do hold that Scheler's view of values as objects is mistaken, Theodorou's criticism here fails to give him enough credit for nuance; after all, Scheler is a *phenomenological* realist, and not a naïve (pre-phenomenological) realist at all.

5 Likewise, as Eugene Kelly notes, Scheler's values "do not exist in an inaccessible metaphysical realm, but exist only when they function in human thought and action," i.e. as *intentional* objects rather than objects in any naïve sense (10). Values as objects, properly understood, are *material value-qualities* in their own right, and thus neither merely properties of other objects nor the objects of a naïve (non-phenomenological) realism.

6 Of course, there may be other reasons for this curiosity as well. Hackett, for instance, attributes "Scheler's silence about the ontology of value in the *Formalism*" to his "phenomenological neutrality" and the fact that he works largely from within the phenomenological reduction (21). Nevertheless, the fact remains somewhat puzzling.

7 No such work was found in Scheler's papers after his death. See the editorial note on Scheler 5, n. 1.

8 Granted, Scheler also notes in this preface certain points of disagreement between himself and Hartmann with respect to their conceptions of personhood, Scheler's emphasis on the historical-social character of valuative life, Hartmann's turn towards an explicit ontologism, etc. Nonetheless, none of these disagreements diminish Scheler's appreciation for Hartmann's ability to make "genuine progress in the non-formal ethics of values" (Scheler xxx).

9 Indeed, Hartmann notes that the (objective) presence of such ideal objects to consciousness is exactly the same evidence that we have for the genuine existence of real objects, and the abandonment of either would lead to nothing more than the kind of self-annihilating skepticism that phenomenology as a whole is designed to prevent. As he writes:

> The 'belief' in ideal self-existence stands entirely on the same level as belief in real self-existence ... Whoever, therefore, doubts ideal self-existence

The Identity of Values 89

must also doubt real self-existence. The universal scepticism to which this leads can never indeed be entirely exterminated. But it floats in the air. It is the most precarious of all hypotheses. And as it goes counter to natural comprehension, the burden of proof rests with it.

(I, 224)

10 It is important to note here that Hartmann's view of the hierarchy of values is quite a bit less grandiose than that of Scheler. Hartmann does not, most prominently, hold to a strict and completely worked-out ranking of all values whatsoever. There is room, on Hartmann's model, for genuine conflicts among values to develop; not every value occupies a unique and sacrosanct rung on a static ladder of values. Nevertheless, elements of such hierarchy are certainly present on Hartmann's model, even if to a lesser degree than for Scheler; since values are objects in their own right, they can and do interact with one another in such regimented ways. The peculiarities of Hartmann's system of values in contrast to that of Scheler are not a central topic of this project, given that I intend to reject the object-model of values entirely in favor of a Husserl-inspired horizon-model, however, and so this brief description of their differences must suffice.

11 It is important to note here that what I am calling the "object-model" of values is by no means unique to Scheler and Hartmann, although I do hold that it has its origins (in the particular context of phenomenology) in the work of those two thinkers. Even certain contemporary attempts towards a phenomenology of values take much the same approach. As an example, consider Roberta De Monticelli's attempt to identify "three basic claims or principles that constitute the very foundation of a phenomenologically acceptable theory of feeling": "1. Feeling is essentially a perception of the value-qualities, whether positive or negative, of things. 2. Affective experience in all its parts (including its conative aspects, drives, desires etc.) is founded on emotional sensibility. 3. Sensibility has a structure of layers ('stratification'), corresponding to an objective hierarchy of value-spheres" (2016, 385). For a phenomenology of values rooted in the Schelerian-Hartmannian object-model of values, such a characterization is indeed accurate. However, as I will argue in what follows, a phenomenology of values per se does not need to endorse all of these specific criteria – and indeed has good reasons to be hesitant in accepting at least some of them.

12 My use of the Bert and Ernie example owes much to Quentin Lauer, whose article "The Phenomenological Ethics of Max Scheler" gives a similar demonstration:

> Suppose one strolls through an art gallery and suddenly comes upon a painting one has never seen before, say Rouault's 'Christ among the Fishermen.' Stopping before the picture, it would seem that one would go through two distinct operations (or series of operations) with regard to it. By examining the details one grasps what the painting 'represents,' which is to say its signification. By another process, much more difficult to describe, one arrives at the judgment: 'This painting is beautiful.' By the mere fact of temporal sequence it is clear that the two judgments: 'This painting represents Christ on the seashore among the fishermen of Galilee' and 'This painting is beautiful' are distinct judgments. It would seem, too, that the judgments are materially distinct (in content).
>
> (290)

90 The Identity of Values

It is, of course, the latter point that reveals the major innovation in Scheler's model of values: the representational content of the painting, revealed by logical consciousness, is *totally distinct* from its valuative content, revealed by value-consciousness alone, through a completely separate experience.

13 Nor, in contrast, could Ernie have had his experience of ugliness without coming into contact with *that which is ugly*. The two experiences are mirrors of one another, though this aspect of the example must wait for further discussion until Chapter 4.

14 Note that our other examples may be explained, on this model, in much the same way. When Oscar takes a drink of scotch, for instance, that experience is initially connected for him with an experience of distaste, and later – after his acquisition of the appropriate taste – with an experience of good flavor. Similarly, the act of adultery gives rise, for Aloysius, to experiences both of the positive value of carnal pleasure, on the one hand, and the negative value of immorality, on the other. While there is much more to be said about these examples, naturally, this brief aside should suffice to give a basic account of them in the context of the Schelerian/Hartmannian object-model of values.

15 Panos Theodorou, for one, agrees with this assessment. He gives the example of a perceptual encounter with a bear that is simultaneously a terrifying value-experience of harmfulness. In order, he claims, to become aware that the large creature suddenly appearing in front of me is harmful, "the bear and its harmfulness – or, better, the bear in its harmfulness – must have already been there for me in an analogous pre-predicative experience" if my experience of this value is to have any connection to reality (2014b, 628). Thus, he continues, "we can say that the bear in its harmfulness has to have already been there for me, in a primordial value experience, a value-ception (*Wertnehmung*) of it, as a *Wertlage*, a value-situation" (ibid.). Note that Theodorou uses the term "harmfulness" here to indicate not merely the conclusion of a logical judgment about the bear and its destructive capabilities with respect to the human body, but rather the genuinely valuative feeling that it represents some kind of mortal threat to the individual who finds himself confronted with it.

16 This criticism of the object-model of values mirrors in many ways the famous critique of values as such given by Heidegger, which (as mentioned previously) was instrumental in the move away from axiology in the latter half of the 20th century. Heidegger's criticism is delivered most clearly in his "Letter on Humanism," which I will quote here at length, given its relevance to the project at hand:

> To think against 'values' is not to maintain that everything interpreted as 'a value' … is valueless. Rather, it is important finally to realize that precisely through the characterization of something as 'a value' what is so valued is robbed of its worth. That is to say, by the assessment of something as a value what is valued is admitted only as an object for human estimation. But what a thing is in its being is not exhausted by its being an object, particularly when objectivity takes the form of value. Every valuing, even where it values positively, is a subjectivizing. It does not let beings: be. Rather, valuing lets beings: be valid – solely as the objects of its doing. The bizarre effort to prove the objectivity of values does not know what it is doing. When one proclaims 'God' the altogether 'highest value,' this is a degradation of God's essence. Here as elsewhere thinking in values is the greatest blasphemy imaginable against being. To think against values therefore does not mean to beat the drum for the valuelessness and

nullity of beings. It means rather to bring the clearing of the truth of being before thinking, as against subjectivizing beings into mere objects.

(265)

That is, Heidegger's criticism applies to values thought of as *separate objects*, distinct from valuable things, which grant to those valuable things their affective significance – that is to say, to the object-model of values that I have just rejected. Heidegger, of course, understands this criticism to entail that all talk of values in themselves must be revoked, or at least subordinated to his overarching consideration of Being. I, on the other hand, maintain that we can still carry out a dedicated phenomenology of values if we can come up with a model to account for such values that does not commit this "blasphemy" against the objects in the world that we experience as valuable. It is precisely this task that, with help from Husserl, I will carry out in the following section. (There is, of course, more to be said about Heidegger's criticism of values in general – see Parvis Emad's "Heidegger's Value-Criticism and its Bearing on the Phenomenology of Values" for further discussion, as well as, for a contrasting view, the first chapter of Hackett's *Persons and Values* – but this brief acknowledgement of the validity of his criticism against certain kinds of axiology, while maintaining that other perspectives elude that criticism entirely, should suffice for the purposes of this project.)

17 Further, these early 20th-century philosophers are by no means the only ones to hold to the object-model. Ferrarello's 2014 article on axiology, for one, seems to defend a similar view, as, in some ways, does the work of De Monticelli that has already been mentioned. This stance retains some currency in modern phenomenology, and so the preceding arguments against it are entirely warranted as a necessary counterweight to that position, as well as to clear the way for the horizon-model of values that this book will explore.

18 See Saulius Geniusas' *The Origins of the Horizon in Husserl's Phenomenology* for further discussion of this historical development.

19 This revision entails, of course, that the term *Wertnehmen*, value-intuition, should not be thought of as a form of direct intuition, but rather as an intuition of the valuative element *within* other experiences. Value-intuition is not a conscious act that functions totally by itself, but rather refers to a particular (*sui generis*) set of structures operative within, e.g., perceptual experiences, which also have their own, intellectual structures at work. It remains a distinct mode of consciousness, but one which is inextricably linked with the acts of other such modes, and which never appears completely on its own.

20 In phenomenological terms, they remain the "noematic correlates of evaluative acts," even while they do not permit those acts to be objectifying in their own right (Hart 1997, 193). Husserl's early thought about valuative acts was thus correct insofar as he held them to be non-objectifying, in contrast to acts of perception, but his further claim that the former are founded on the latter must be rejected in favor of this horizonal model in light of the concerns raised in Chapter 1.

21 I am by no means the first commentator to point out this interpretation of Husserl's view of values, as obscure as it may be even in his later writings. Theodorou, for instance, notes that the basic identity of values such as "agreeable" and "disagreeable" lies in their propensity to show us what various experiences could "mean for our overall constitution. They show how what we confront in the world weighs for us, what value it has for the embodied intentional consciousness, for its state and functioning as well as for its

92 The Identity of Values

existentio-praxial possibilities in the lifeworld" (2014b, 639). See also §3 of his "The Aporia of Husserl's Projected Axiology" (2014a). Nonetheless, to my knowledge, this book represents the first time that such an interpretation has been demonstrated to fit in with an overarching phenomenology of values in general, as will be accomplished throughout the rest of this project.

22 Theodorou goes on to clarify the nature of this value-intentionality in the early Husserl: "In Phenomenology, emotions in contradistinction to mere sensory feelings are approached as intentional acts (*Gemütsakte*). Thus, in order to develop the analyses necessary for the founding of a normative axiology, we must delve into the essential structure and function of the emotive acts *as well as* into the texture or identity of their possible – and allegedly intuitable – correlative objects" (2014a, 68). This idea that the *direct object* of a value-intention is a value-object is, of course, abandoned by Husserl's later move towards the horizon-model of values (as well as by this book) – and, indeed, Theodorou dedicates much of this article to the task of illuminating the various aporias of this early position. Nonetheless, the connection between values and emotional responses on the part of the one who encounters them is an important element of this investigation.

23 Of course, this metaphor cannot be taken too literally. A source of light remains itself a physical object, which could be the object of a future direct perception; with values, this not the case – their horizonality gives rise to acts of volition, and not to acts that directly intuit the values themselves. That is to say, sources of light stand on the *outer perceptual horizon* of objects, while values are horizonal in their own way, i.e., they lie instead on an object's *value-horizon*. Nevertheless, this analogy should, in a limited sense, still be useful to shed some light – pardon the pun – on the real givenness of values, which constantly inform our experience of valuable objects, but without submitting themselves to any direct grasp.

24 Indeed, Scheler himself raises a similar point to Husserl's notion of horizonality in the context of what he calls "spiritual feelings," which, on his model, lie at the highest level of the ego's intentional feeling-comportment. As he writes, the "light or darkness of these feelings appears to bathe everything given in the inner world and the outer world in these acts. They 'permeate' all special contents of experience" (343). They are not merely experienced; the fact of their presence to the ego conditions every other experience that this ego either does or can undergo. Just as horizonal awareness is always embedded within a world as a totality, Scheler claims that we become aware of these feelings through their world-conditioning influence. But he does not discuss this connection explicitly, given that the idea of the horizon only comes to the fore in Husserl's later work (i.e., largely after Scheler's death). Even so, while Scheler only applies this notion in the context of certain highly immersive value-experiences, it seems compelling that he at least hints in this direction. Perhaps he would have been amenable to the horizon-model of values had he only grasped this development in phenomenology prior to his passing.

25 And, of course, the same applies (*mutatis mutandis*) to our other examples: Oscar's experience of scotch genuinely contains its harshness (and subsequently its deliciousness, once we have explained the valuative transition that occurs here), while Aloysius' affairs are immediately both pleasurable and immoral. Granted, the specific features of these experiences require further explanation, but their basic structure according to the horizon-model is clear.

26 This parallel is clearer in German, where the law of the excluded middle is expressed as the "*Satz vom ausgeschlossenen Dritten*," i.e., that of the excluded *third*, comparable to the "*Satz vom ausgeschlossenen Vierten*" in value-consciousness.

27 This dependence between the lifeworld and the values that inform it holds both ways. As Theodorou puts it, "[a]n immediate and a mediate world-horizon, or a projected [*cosmos*], are always the prerequisite for every system of values and for every particular value and good" (2014a, 72). Theodorou attributes the origins of this insight to Scheler, although he also claims that Heidegger "added further vital dimensions" to it as well (ibid.). I maintain, as demonstrated throughout this book, that the seeds of such an insight lie in Husserl's writings as well, and especially in his later work.

28 Hartmann does make a similar point about the essentially relational character of values; see pp. 62ff. in Volume II of his *Ethics*. Nonetheless, for him, these relations can include that of total equality, a claim that this model of values denies. This point will be discussed further later in this book.

29 This comparison of beauty can be demonstrated by the fact that, ultimately, Bert will prefer one of these paintings over the other; for instance, if given the chance to take one or the other home with him to display on his own wall, his choice would be informed by the relative values of the two paintings. Further discussion of this topic, however, must naturally wait until Chapter 5 of this book, which deals explicitly with the connection between value and volition.

3 Pure Values and Valuable Things

3.1 The True Identity of Values: A More Complete Answer

The preceding account of values as horizonal with respect to other experiences (e.g., the perceptual experience of Bert looking at *Persistence of Memory*) has gotten us past many difficult problems traditionally associated with a phenomenology of values. Nonetheless, by itself, it is insufficient to stand as a complete phenomenological account of values; the claim that values are a horizonal aspect of all experiences does not tell us much, if anything, about the *content* of that horizon. Without some account of this content, we would be left with nothing more than the purely formal axiology that phenomenologists from Husserl to Scheler and beyond have rightly rejected. The question of the genuine identity of values thus remains unanswered. Values are not objects and cannot be grasped directly; that is understandable, but they still exist in one form or another, and so we still need an account of the mode of that existence. This is a difficult question to answer in light of the fact that we can never directly intuit values; they always remain veiled to us behind other experiences. Accordingly, we must investigate values themselves only through their connections to what we can grasp directly: the valuable things – beautiful paintings, delicious beverages, immoral acts, etc. – that serve as the most obvious content of our experiences of values in the world.

It will therefore be the task of this chapter to draw a sharp distinction between values as such and values as they are instantiated in the world, a contrast between what I will call "pure values" and "valuable things." The term "pure values" can be understood to refer to values as they are in themselves, subject only to the independent laws of value-consciousness and given only on the horizons of experience. "Valuable things," on the other hand, is a composite term for the objects – paintings, etc. – and states of affairs – e.g., the entire complex of actions, beliefs, and emotions that are involved in an illicit affair – that we experience *as* valuable, in experiences that are governed, at the least, by the structures of both perceptual and valuative consciousness. This distinction will form the backdrop for the rest of this investigation. A rigorous phenomenological

DOI: 10.4324/9781003202189-4

inquiry into both of these aspects of valuative consciousness is a necessary task for the purpose of understanding that consciousness fully. As will become apparent, neither pure values nor valuable things can be thought of separately as anything more than an abstraction; both are required for valuative experiences as we know them to exist.

3.2 Pure Values: The Vanishing Point

To begin, the mode of existence of pure values themselves must be analyzed in order to come to an understanding of their role in conscious experience. This task is easier said than done; since values cannot be described as objects, we will be reduced to a rather roundabout means of investigating them. Despite the fact that they can never be grasped directly, values can be meaningfully investigated phenomenologically with an eye towards uncovering the structures whereby the affective quality with which they imbue valuable things comes into effect; that is, they can be studied through the transcendental laws that govern the effects that they have on experience. This investigation, naturally, can only be accomplished in phenomenological reflection; although the ways in which values influence experience are an immediate part of that experience, they can only be explicitly thematized from a reflective standpoint. In this light, pure values can accurately be depicted as attractors (or points of repulsion, in the case of values currently serving as disvalues) that can be pursued (through the valuable things to which they are attached), but never themselves attained or directly intuited – even by the sort of "intellectual intuition" in which, Husserl claims, we can directly encounter idealities like the color blue. This depiction of values thus permits such concepts as "the good" or "the beautiful" to be made sense of without the ontological speculation required by the attempts of Scheler and Hartmann to classify them as objects, already possessed of their own internal hierarchies. Nonetheless, this model of pure values certainly requires additional clarification and justification, so let us turn our attention to what it might mean for a value like "beauty" to serve as an ungraspable point of attraction for the consciousness that encounters it through an aesthetic experience.

To further this investigation, let us return to our primary example: the aesthetic encounter between Bert and *Persistence of Memory*. On the horizon-model of values, as noted previously, Bert's experience of the painting can be described as one, in part, of visual perception, but with a peculiarly valuative twist; built in to his experience is the *beauty* of the painting, which calls Bert onward to acts of aesthetic contemplation. But beauty here is not itself a *thing* and does not feature as a direct part of Bert's experience. In fact, the only way that we can know that the value of beauty is an element of this experience is through its *effects*, i.e., the ways in which it conditions Bert's encounter with the painting, and even shapes the painting itself, understood as the intended object of a certain experience, in terms of its givenness.

What the painting's beauty entails, in this case, is that Bert finds himself to be *attracted* towards *Persistence of Memory* in a number of ways.[1] The painting is not merely an object of Bert's regard – it is not the purely dispassionate object of intellectual perception – but an object of his *desire*, an alluring object. Whenever Bert comes into contact with such an object, he is struck not merely by its physical form, its shape and colors, but by some (at least initially, i.e., pre-reflectively) ineffable aspect it carries with it, which causes him to regard it in a positive light. This component or quality is, of course, not first and foremost in his mind during the experience. He takes as the object of his consciousness only the painting itself, rather than looking past the object to ponder what it is that makes it so attractive. Indeed, while such an investigation is possible – what else are we doing now? – it would seem to be a rather more intellectual experience than the more direct, aesthetic experience that Bert undergoes. Such an investigation of the *value* of the painting would have to take a very different (and explicitly reflective) form from this experience of immediate aesthetic appreciation: perhaps one of aesthetic critique, or of the more philosophical inquiry in which we are now engaged. Nevertheless, such a quality must be present within the painting if we are to make sense of Bert's mode of comportment with respect to the painting (i.e., the fact that his behavior here differs from his reaction to non-beautiful objects). This necessary component of the experienced object is its value (beauty, in the case of positive aesthetic experiences like Bert's).

As such, the value that lurks on the horizons of the painting (the value-component of Bert's overall experience of the painting) is nothing more – and nothing less – than the element of that experience that is capable of accomplishing such an attraction. It is not an object, it exists nowhere other than within the painting, phenomenologically understood as that which lies on the object-pole of Bert's experience, and yet it nevertheless can be known through the dramatic effect that it has on that experience as a whole. The value of beauty is like a force pulling Bert towards a certain mode of experience with respect to *Persistence of Memory*, as if it were an enormous source of gravitational pull urging him closer and closer to itself. This force, of course, only has an effect on Bert through the painting to which it is connected, but the force and the painting understood as a visual object are not the same thing (i.e., they each appeal to different conscious structures, even if they are inextricably bound up with one another in the same *experience*). Beauty itself is the hidden source of Bert's attraction to this painting – just as beauty itself is the cause of his attraction to any beautiful thing (through the fact that it brings a particular set of valuative structures to bear on the objects or situations with which it is connected, as opposed, say, to the structures of moral values). This beauty can be analyzed on its own terms, through

Pure Values and Valuable Things 97

phenomenological reflection on the experiences that it governs, in order to find out what, exactly, structures it entails, even if it can never be experienced in the absence of beautiful things.

It follows from this conception of values that the same sort of analysis applies to values that are understood to be *dis*valuable or unattractive, but in reverse. That is, values like *ugliness*, when they occupy the negative position in contrast to the positive values like beauty that they mirror, can be understood as points of repulsion that condition the things with which they are associated in precisely the opposite way to that just described. To illustrate using our example, let us consider the case of Bert's friend Ernie, for whom *Persistence of Memory* is an object of ugliness rather than beauty (perhaps he just cannot quite wrap his head around surrealism).[2] Ernie's experience of the painting involves the (in this case) disvalue of ugliness in just the same way as Bert's experience involves the positive value of beauty. The ugliness of the painting imbues it with a similarly aesthetic character, but one of a vastly different tone: an aesthetic of discordance, perhaps, rather than of harmony. It repels Ernie, pushing him to grimace, to judge the painting negatively, perhaps to walk away from it in disgust. This process can be quite well understood in the same terms as Bert's experience of beauty, but the peculiarities here have to be taken into account; beautiful and ugly experiences are parallel, perhaps, but not reducible one to the other. Nonetheless, the basic status of the value of ugliness itself here is unmistakable: Ernie never perceives ugliness directly, but it conditions his experience of the painting just as thoroughly as beauty does for Bert.[3]

Perhaps a useful analogy can be made here to a philosophical concept with a long pedigree, in order to elucidate further this characterization of pure values like beauty. Namely, such values resemble – in certain respects, not to be taken too far – Kant's notion of the transcendental idea. Without getting too enmeshed in Kantian distinctions, these ideas – e.g., practical notions like God, freedom, and immortality – are necessary postulates of reason itself and play a tremendous role in shaping the content and activities of rational consciousness. Nevertheless, they are never able to be grasped by that reason *in concreto*, forever eluding any direct intuition or encounter (and even the belief that they might be grasped in such a way leads, for Kant, to nothing more than dialectical illusions). As Kant himself characterizes this idea in the first *Critique*: "I understand by idea a necessary concept of reason to which no corresponding object can be given in sense-experience. Thus the pure concepts of reason, now under consideration, are *transcendental ideas* . . . they are transcendent and overstep the limits of all experience; no object adequate to the transcendental idea can ever be found within experience" (318–319, A327/B383–384).

Such ideas have often been compared (for instance, by Otfried Höffe) to the notion of the vanishing point in the visual arts.[4] The vanishing

98 *Pure Values and Valuable Things*

point is a trick of perspective. It represents a supposed point, far "within" the painting in its illusory third dimension, at which all the lines of perspective converge. Imagine, if you will, a painting of a long railroad tunnel; the vanishing point is the location far down the tunnel at which the tracks, the walls of the tunnel, the ceiling, etc., all meld into one. This point, of course, is not a genuine, physical component of the painting like the various colors, the shapes which one could trace out with a finger, and so on. The point itself – other than the merely representative location on the painting at which it *appears* to occur – is never truly seen. The painting as a physical object (i.e., the canvas and paints themselves, as opposed the *Bild-Objekt* or "image-object," as Husserl would put it, which is experienced *through* that physical substrate, as well as in contrast to that which the painting represents, the *Bild-Sujet*) does not extend into the third dimension in quite the way that the vanishing point indicates; it is only through a clever artist's trick that the painting is able to *represent* such a third dimension at all.[5] And yet, the whole of the painting does not make sense in terms of perspective without the vanishing point. It is this unseen, somewhat illusory point that gives the sense of distance when we look down the train tunnel and makes the painting more than a flat caricature of an image. Transcendental ideas, for Kant, are similar; they are necessary to make sense of our experience, to maintain its unity, but they are never encountered directly – and can never be so encountered, as a result of their peculiar nature.[6]

On the horizon-model, pure values function in much the same way. That is, they are a necessary component of the experiences whereby things are apprehended as valuable, absolutely critical for our ability to explain the meaning that those experiences have for us. It is necessary for the phenomenologist studying Bert's encounter with *Persistence of Memory* to assume the existence of beauty itself in order to explain what it is about the painting that renders Bert's experience of it so uniquely passionate. But this fact does not (and cannot) entail that beauty itself is something that features directly into Bert's consciousness, as if it were a color he could see or a sound he could hear. It is there as a regulative or conditioning factor with respect to his overall experience, and not as an *im*mediate component of that experience at all. Beauty exists, beauty is a *real entity* in the phenomenological sense, we might claim, but it is not the sort of thing that can be understood directly.

Entities of this sort exist throughout our phenomenologically understood experience. Even impossibilities like a square circle feature in our experience in certain ways (e.g., we can use them in thought-experiments), despite the fact that such impossibilities certainly cannot be intuited. Values, of course, have their own unique structures that set them apart from intellectual objects like square circles, as a result of the independence of valuative consciousness discussed in Chapter 1 – they are, for instance, explicitly horizonal in a way that such impossible entities are not – but the fact that such a thing as an *indirectly experienced* element of consciousness can exist is by no means unusual in the phenomenological tradition. Values are simply the essential correlates to a peculiar mode of such indirect givenness, and can only be known through their relationships to the experiences of which they are an essential component. In a very real sense, values are what they do; their ontological structure is defined in terms of the effects that they have on the experiences with which they are connected. They do not exist independently of such experiences – even if the structures that govern them are independent of those which apply to intellectual acts of consciousness – but that fact does not mean that they are not genuinely existent, nor that they can be disregarded by anyone who wishes to make sense of the richness of our valuative experiences. Pure values really are a genuine aspect of the givenness of our experiential world, without ever themselves being given as real through direct intuition.

Of course, as mentioned, this comparison between values and Kant's transcendental ideas must not be taken too far. Most importantly, it is crucial to note that, while values resemble ideas like those of God, freedom, and immortality in the sense that they are held to shape experience without ever being directly experienced themselves, values are a more integral and base-level part of reality than are the ideas of Kant. That is to say, these Kantian ideas are merely *postulated*. They are *necessary* postulates of reason, of course; practical reason, he thinks, can no more get by without making the assumption that the will is free than a human being can exist without a beating heart (or some reasonably good facsimile thereof). Nonetheless, he maintains, since such ideas elude any direct grasp, they must be thought of as stemming solely from reason itself (i.e., as the phenomenologist would put it, they lie on the *subject-pole* of rational activity). This is absolutely not the case for values, phenomenologically understood. Values like beauty are not merely postulated as a necessary condition of acting in the world; rather, they remain *objective* (in the sense that they lie on the object-pole of valuative experiences) without being *objects*.

This difference is subtle, but critically important. What it entails is that values are no more a creation or assumption of the human mind than is reality itself. Phenomenology, unlike Kant's strict separation between the world as it appears to consciousness and the thing-in-itself, allows for there to be really existing, really encounterable entities – entities which consciousness constitutes, but does not create – that are not reducible to the subject-pole of consciousness. This continues to apply even when those entities are never themselves directly confronted by that consciousness. As such, we should not take the comparison between values and the transcendental ideas of Kant too literally. Certainly, this analogy is useful in pointing out how values function with respect to experience. Both Kant's philosophical views and phenomenology in the Husserlian tradition are forms of transcendental idealism, in the sense that each endeavors to be a science of reality *as it is experienced* by a conscious subject. Given that fact, the insights attained by these two traditions often have sufficient overlap to permit such analogies to be quite fruitful. Nevertheless, phenomenology is working from a rather different ontological schema than Kant, and these peculiarities must always be borne in mind.

Overall, pure values can be thought of as horizonal influences on consciousness, rather than as discrete objects in their own right. That is, the consciousness that apprehends an object with which they are associated always finds itself "pointed towards" such pure values, an orientation that shapes the valuative experiences of that consciousness in a number of ways (e.g., by causing those experiences to be regarded as positive or negative, rather than simply as matters of fact, or by directing the experiencing consciousness towards corresponding acts of volition, as will be discussed in Chapter 5). These values are not encountered directly in these experiences, but they play the vital role of making encounters with valuable things possible in the first place. As such, it will be quite a useful task to explicate at least some of the myriad ways in which these values condition our experiences – aesthetically, morally, and so on, each with further subdivisions of its own – in order to apply the phenomenological method of description and classification to this major region of our experiential lives. I will carry out certain prolegomena to this investigation later in this chapter. First, however, it will also be necessary to spell out the essential relationships between these pure values and the objects and situations in which they are instantiated. These relations are, after all, the only way in which pure values can come to be understood, since they remain ever elusive of any more direct grasp.

3.3 Valuable Things: A More Complex Experience

As important as they are to this theoretical account, pure values can neither be the sole focus of our phenomenological investigation into values in general, nor even its real point of departure. While they constitute the most basic, uncomplicated aspect of value-consciousness, that very simplicity renders them nothing more than an abstraction should one ever attempt to separate them concretely from the holistic experiences in the world in which they are always embedded. As such, it is now appropriate for us to turn our attention to values as they are instantiated in *valuable things*, i.e., the objects or situations in the world that we experience as valuable. These valuable things may also be termed "goods," following the convention of Scheler and Hartmann. I will avoid this usage, however, in order that we not lose sight of the fact that valuable things can also include objects or situations that exhibit a *dis*value (e.g., ugly or disturbing things, in the ordinary case) – not to mention to avoid conflating them with mere possessions, as in the phrase "luxury goods." Valuable things run the gamut, from objects of aesthetic worth like *Persistence of Memory* and objects of ugliness to moral or immoral actions or character traits, or even to the world in general, which can be suffused with a generalized sense of well-being (or, on the contrary, unease) – among countless others. Nevertheless, in order to narrow our investigation to a manageable scale, let us, once again, return our focus to the case of Bert's encounter with *Persistence of Memory*. It will always be possible to bring in other aspects of valuable things later (primarily in subsequent chapters) by an appeal to our further examples, once the basics have been covered.

Although, as demonstrated, we can, through phenomenological investigation, discover the pure value of beauty itself lurking within Bert's aesthetic experience at the museum, that pure value is certainly not the primary focus of Bert's encounter. Rather, the genuine object of Bert's experience is, of course, a painting, that unity of image-object, image-subject, and underlying physical substrate discussed so thoroughly in Husserl's works on image-consciousness. Beauty as such does not dominate this experience any more than does one of the painting's colors (say, the blue-white of the sky in the background). What Bert grasps is not a wild conglomeration of different aspects and properties, but a single, unitary object. Granted, this painting and the whole experiential structure that surrounds it can (once that fact has been revealed through phenomenological exploration) be understood to be composed of a vast and interconnected set of structures and elements, but it gives itself primarily in its unity, not its diversity. As a valuable thing or good, therefore, the painting must first be grappled with on its own terms, as the culmination of this interlocking set of acts and modes of experience, and not as a mere "symbol of beauty" or "expression of beauty," as Scheler might have it.

Instead, valuable things must be understood as the primary givens of valuative experience, which nevertheless always point towards some pure value or set of such values that can explain their affective significance. Valuable things are not an abstract component of experience the way that pure values are, but rather are the ordinary objects that we confront every day: paintings, food and drink, the touch of the sun on our skin, our acts of vice or virtue, etc. There is nothing mysterious – at least, on the surface – about these things; they are, in most cases, precisely as they appear to be. Complexities, of course, arise when we attempt to account for the underlying structures that *enable* such objects to be given to consciousness in their particular modes, but their basic ontological structure is not in question. For the past century, phenomenologists in the Husserlian tradition have dealt with the problem of coming up with a rigorous account of the givenness of such perceptual objects to consciousness in general, and, in my opinion, done so quite successfully. The basic givenness of objects like paintings and beverages, therefore, will not be called into question by this project.

What does require more discussion, however, is the second aspect of the preceding definition of valuable things: the fact that they "point towards" the pure value(s) with which they are associated. What does it mean for beautiful objects like *Persistence of Memory* to be related to the pure values with which they are associated? This question can only be answered in the context of our previous definition of a pure value as a point of attraction or repulsion that imbues valuable things with their unique affective characteristics. A valuable thing is valuable not because of any purely internal characteristic (that is, any characteristic that lies within the thing itself, understood solely as an object of *direct* experience). Values are unlike, for instance, colors. The blue-white of the sky in Dalí's painting does not necessarily direct consciousness towards anything other than itself; the whole of the color is there to be seen immediately once the painting is encountered. Values, however, as discussed in Chapter 2, are *horizonal*, which is to say, in this context, that they pull consciousness towards themselves in ways that are not always fully included in the immediate grasping of the objects or situations with which they are associated. Valuable things, understood solely as *things*, i.e., the directly grasped objects of an experience, are never complete in themselves. They always look beyond themselves, through referential implication (*Verweisung*), to the ultimately ineffable values that imbue them with the ability to elicit such passion (whether positive or negative) from their observers.

This claim can be justified by a simple argument. If it were not the case that pure values could be genuinely distinguished from valuable things – if values were simply a property of those things – then it would be impossible to explain how the values that we find in the world can vary over time, or among different people. A full account of this variability will be given in Chapter 4, but the bare existence of the same is indisputable. Consider our examples. Both Bert and Ernie have a similar experience of *Persistence of Memory*, but these experiences diverge in terms of their valuable component; for Bert, the painting is an object of great beauty, while, for Ernie, it holds only ugliness. In the case of Oscar, a sip of scotch begins as an object of distaste – and yet later, the very same scotch becomes the bearer of delicious flavor. These variations occur without any necessary change to the object itself (as would be the case for an object changing color, e.g., a ripening fruit or a blank canvas that is later painted). Rather, the change consists in an alteration of the *relationship* between the valuable things – paintings, beverages – and the pure values to which they are connected. (The structures governing these alterations will, of course, be the object of this investigation in the following chapter.) Such changes are only explicable when this relationship is maintained; only when valuable things are held to direct the attention of their observer towards an ultimately ungraspable pure value is there room for the particular values towards which they are directed to shift without a simultaneous shift occurring in the object itself. The distinction – at least in abstract investigation, if not in actual practice – between valuable things and pure values, therefore, cannot be abandoned.

This is not, of course, to say that pure values are somehow detached from the valuable things that they condition in any thoroughgoing way. This is not and cannot be the case for the horizon of a conscious act; no more could the horizonal backside of an object be detached from that object itself than could the value of a valuable thing be stripped away from it. Values do not exist outside of the conscious acts that are (at least potentially) directed towards them. On the horizon-model, there is never a need to posit some realm or mode of existence for values that can be utterly isolated from the experiences in which those values are embedded; phenomenology in the Husserlian tradition has long maintained that (transcendental) idealism can still attain the status of a rigorous realism, a return to "the things themselves." Pure values are meaningless without the experiences of valuable things by which we come to know them; as De Monticelli rightly puts it, the act of value-intuition "is always accompanied by the exercise of other functions, both sensory and otherwise" (2016, 386). Given that they elude direct grasp, pure values can be understood only through the ways in which they condition our experience of objects and situations in the world (much as a force like gravity can only be understood through the behavior of the objects that it affects). Values and valuable things are, therefore, inseparable in actuality.

Now, it is certainly the case that aspects of any horizon can be *analyzed* separately from the objects for which they serve as the horizon – such an analysis is indeed necessary for phenomenological investigation of the way in which the horizon structures our experience – but the investigating phenomenologist must always return to their primordial union if such an analysis is to bear any relation to reality whatsoever.[7] This fact applies just as much to pure values as it does to any other aspect of a horizon. Accordingly, the necessary next step in understanding valuative consciousness is to investigate in more detail the ways in which pure values can condition our experience of the world of valuable things – bearing in mind throughout this investigation the overarching distinction just made between values themselves and the ways in which we come to encounter them.

3.4 Values and *Wertnehmen*: Various Examples of Valuation

Now that the distinct existences of pure values and valuable things have been discussed in broad terms, we must proceed on to a further analysis of the ways in which they work together to condition our everyday experience of the world. These particularly valuative or affective experiences are accomplished by the act that phenomenologists like Scheler term *Wertnehmen*, value-intuition. As demonstrated, value-intuition cannot be thought of – as Scheler and Hartmann would have it – in terms of a *direct* intuition of values, an act that would require a genuine separation of values from valuable things in actuality, and not merely in analysis. Instead, such an act must be thought of as the intuition of a value through the mediation of the objects and situations that this value conditions by means of its horizonal relationship to them. The basic structure of the act should, at this point, be clear.

Nonetheless, it is the task of this investigation not merely to point out the existence of such acts and claim the glory of a job well done, but rather to peer more deeply into the unique structures that underlie them. Simply knowing that pure values serve as the affective horizon for the acts that apprehend valuable things does not actually tell us very much about the nature of such acts. The wide variety of valuative experiences that we undergo cannot simply be lumped into one major category (or even two categories: the attraction of positive values and the repulsion of disvalues) without further subdivision if we are to make any real progress in understanding such acts. Values come in many different shapes: there are aesthetic values like beauty and ugliness, moral values like vice and virtue, and so forth (and there are certainly gradations of value even within these narrower categories as well). To proceed any further in our investigation, therefore, it will be necessary to explicate some of these particular structures, in order that they might shed more light on the nature of valuation in general.

Let us begin this process of subdivision by returning to our listed examples. In many of these situations, we have rather clear-cut instances of particular types of values being brought into play. In the case of Bert and Ernie standing before *Persistence of Memory* and perceiving it to be (respectively) beautiful and hideous, for example, there can be little doubt that the valuative acts going on are examples of a particularly aesthetic valuation. Beauty and ugliness, the pure values that lurk on the horizon of the painting, certainly serve either to attract the observer towards the painting in various ways or, in the case of the latter, to repel him from it (through grimaces, turning away, loudly proclaiming disapproval, etc.). The basic structures of valuation (attraction and repulsion) are certainly in evidence here, but the special tone or tenor of those structures would be missed without further analysis. Beauty attracts its observer in ways that are demonstrably different from the attraction sparked by other positive values (say, deliciousness). Beauty certainly does not encourage the perceiver of a beautiful object to eat it (at least in the ordinary case!) Rather, it encourages him to gaze upon it, to bask in aesthetic appreciation, and so on. Ugliness, in most cases, functions in a similar (albeit reversed) fashion. And there are certainly subdivisions to be made among each of these values as well; the visual beauty of a painting like *Persistence* is given in a way very different than the beauty of an enchanting song, even if both can reasonably be classified as members of the category of aesthetic values. What this fact tells us is that each value – whether positive or negative; values, like Noah's creatures, come in pairs, as I will discuss later in this chapter – is possessed of its own peculiarities, which play a central role in conditioning the *way in which* those who engage in *Wertnehmen* of that particular value react to it.

To reinforce the essential peculiarities of any set of valuative structures, let us turn our attention to our second example: Oscar and the wonders of scotch. Like Bert and Ernie, we see here exemplified a parallel set of values, one positive and one negative. But in this case, we are dealing with the values involved in a taste for food and drink, and not those of the (visual) aesthetic appreciation dealt with in the previous paragraph. When Oscar drinks scotch at first, unaccustomed to the taste, he finds within his beverage the disvalue of harshness or a bitter distaste; later, through a mechanism that I will discuss in more detail in the following chapter, it acquires for him the positive value of deliciousness or piquancy. (There may well be other values, both positive and negative, involved here as well. Perhaps, as an example, Oscar finds scotch to be a high-class drink, in which case the drink also contains the value of sophistication. But we will focus on the gustatory element of his experience for the moment.) The values of taste, as we shall call them for short, are certainly similar to aesthetic values in certain ways – they are not moral values or spiritual values, etc. – but they nevertheless differ from the latter in the particular way that they draw the perceiving consciousness towards or push it away from the objects with which they are associated.

For lack of a better term, values of taste are more *visceral* than those apprehended through aesthetic appreciation. Tastes, whether pleasurable or vile, present their recipient with a more direct, more assertive instance of value-intuition than many others (which is not necessarily to say that the values they bear are better or worse than those of, e.g., the visual arts; the value of a painting is subtler than that of a strong drink, certainly, but perhaps all the higher for that subtlety). To simply reduce both the value given in a beautiful painting and that given in a delicious beverage to some broad category like that of "positive values in general" would be a grave error; while such a category is a useful tool of analysis, especially when comparing such values to disvalues, it does not capture the richness or depth of valuative experience involved in these various cases. Each particular sort of value possesses its own unique phenomenological structures, which are eminently worthy of their own dedicated investigations (a task that can only be carried out in the broadest of strokes here, i.e., in the form of the brief outline for these future investigations that I will discuss in the following section of this chapter).

There are, of course, countless other examples of the various types of valuative experiences that we could have, and therefore of the various (sub)categories of values. The differences among these experiences range from the relatively minor – such as the difference between the various senses that might be involved in an act of sensual pleasure (e.g., the value of a tasty beverage as opposed to the value of a pleasant odor) – to the major, as when we distinguish broad categories of values from one another. Our third example, the case of the repentantly sinful Aloysius, provides us with a clear instance of very different sorts of values from the aesthetic or sensual ones considered previously. Granted, much of the value involved in the act of adultery as Aloysius experiences it can be described in terms of carnal pleasure similar to that associated with Oscar's newfound love of scotch (though, again, with its own peculiarities; sexual appetites are naturally different from the appetite for a refreshing beverage). Such pleasure, however, is not the only bearer of value for Aloysius in this situation. The act also is infused with the (dis)value of immorality, which explains Aloysius' guilt-wracked state after its completion.

This value has little to do with aesthetics or sensual pleasure, but stems rather from an entirely different realm of value-consciousness: that of *moral* values. While both aesthetics and ethics are strongly tied to the discipline of axiology, their own unique structures must not be ignored. (Indeed, the fact that both sets of values can be in play at the same time, one giving a positive value and the other a negative one as in the case of Aloysius, demonstrates their distinct characters.) Moral values, like any other, direct the experiencing subject towards certain ways of encountering the valuable things that they condition, but the reactions that these modes of experience inspire are wildly different from those of our previous examples. It would be totally inappropriate, for instance, for Ernie to feel guilt in reaction to his distaste for surrealist paintings (barring unorthodox scenarios in which such paintings are connected to some kind of moral code), while such an affective stance is entirely in keeping with Aloysius' experience of adultery. This is not to say that such different categories can never be linked with one another – they often are – but they do represent radically different and independent ways of apprehending values. Each of these modes should be studied on its own terms, though any in-depth investigation of a particular mode of value-consciousness will have to wait for a different project (a project which, I will note, would be entirely dependent on the theoretical work that is being accomplished in this book).

What the great variability of valuative acts indicates for our horizontal model of values is that pure values, in order properly to be understood, must be thought of in terms of the peculiarities inherent to the valuative acts that are the only possible way for them to be comprehended. It is in the differences among valuable things, the differences between an object of taste and an object of visual art, or between the latter and a moral or immoral act, that we can come to know the different shapes of the values that condition our experiences. What a pure value like beauty is, therefore, consists in the effects that it has on these experiences. Beauty – in the ordinary case, setting aside the ever-shifting nature of values vis-à-vis our relationship to them that will be discussed later in this chapter – is a point of attraction that draws the consciousness that perceives a beautiful thing towards itself in the peculiar way that expresses the unique structures of aesthetic experiences. That is, it pulls consciousness towards itself in a way that is subtle and yet refined, a way that sparks acts of aesthetic reflection, and so on. (Even further: since we are concerned here with the beauty of a painting – as opposed to that of a song, for example – we must bring in the eidetic structures appropriate to an encounter with a piece of static visual art: that visual cues must be incorporated in a central way, that the beauty of the piece is given to the observer all at once, etc.) A full account of what beauty is would necessitate a thorough explication of all of these structures – there are certainly more of them than have just been spelled out – but the basic outlines of such a value (as well as how it and other values are to be distinguished from one another) should, at this point, be clear.

In any case, the upshot of this brief and (as yet) unscientific list of examples – and of the countless more that could be added – is that values manifest a vast array of different effects that they can have on the objects and situations with which they are associated. Any investigation into valuative consciousness, then, must take account of this variety. Accordingly, much of what will be required for such an investigation is the long, laborious work involved in laying out the phenomenological structures of each of these various modes of valuative consciousness in turn: a phenomenology of visual art, a phenomenology of taste, a phenomenology of vice and virtue, and so on.[8] While phenomenology has never been averse to taking on board such detailed work, it is certainly a daunting task, given that we already see here the possibility for an apparently endless cavalcade of subdivisions within consciousness. Nevertheless, the future investigations that can be carried out on the basis of this theoretical account remain quite promising with respect to the practical benefits of phenomenology. Once the theoretical issues concerning the givenness of values in general that are being addressed in this book have been resolved, phenomenology will be well positioned to provide accurate and fruitful accounts of all of these various regions of valuative experience – just as it has long done in the realm of perceptual or intellectual consciousness.

3.5 The Modes of Valuation: Four Categories and a Digression

The question thus arises: is there anything concrete that I can say here, in this general investigation into values and valuative consciousness as a whole, that can be of further assistance to these more specific projects? Is there, perhaps, some way in which they can be further organized or categorized, which can help lay out a research program for future inquiries? The answer to this question, happily, is in the affirmative – at least in a preliminary manner. As with any other mode of consciousness, pure values and the valuable things that they condition can be divided into several major regions by reference to the different eidetic structures that govern them within our valuative experiences. All of these regions, however, ultimately lead back to the pure notion of value itself, though that notion must also necessarily be divided into its irreducible components of positive value and disvalue, i.e., the good and the bad.

The fact that there are a nearly endless variety of values, and therefore of different sorts of valuable things, can never be neglected. Nonetheless, this variety does, for the most part and admitting of exceptions, allow itself to be organized in a relatively straightforward way, a way that mimics traditional axiological categories. As I will argue, values can be divided into four major categories, each with its own further subdivisions and gradations: aesthetic values, moral values, sensual values, and spiritual values. There is also a fifth category of "quasi-values" that I will discuss, use-values or values of utility, which resemble values of the other four categories in certain respects, but which remain importantly distinct from values proper. My tentative contention is that this fourfold distinction among values accounts well for the great diversity of our value-experiences, and that it can provide a useful road map for the future investigations that will carry out phenomenological explorations of these value-regions in much greater detail.

Of course, it must be noted here that I am by no means committed to this fourfold categorization of values as an indubitable or completely worked out taxonomy of valuative types. This section of the book is intended to serve merely as prolegomena for more detailed investigations into this question that must be carried out in a future project; the identification and precise specification of every particular region of value-consciousness is far too great a task to be accomplished in full at this time. Accordingly, my remarks in this section will be, to some extent, tentative and open to subsequent revision. I do maintain that this categorization of valuative types is, at least, on the right track towards a genuine taxonomy of values; whether or not it can be maintained as a complete model of valuative types, this fourfold distinction accounts well, in a general way, for at least a large variety of the value-intuitions that are common to experience. Even if this characterization of the various valuative types is subject to possible revision in the future on the basis of a more systematic investigation along these lines, this section of the book will remain useful insofar as it serves to highlight *the manner in which* such an investigation must be carried out. I will certainly use some of the broad distinctions made in this section as a means of inquiring into the essential structures of valuative experience throughout the rest of this text, and that use will in general remain valid even if certain particular elements of this categorization may be amended hereafter. Whatever the specifics of the taxonomy of values, a full-fledged phenomenology of values must include something very like the account that I will deliver here, and so it cannot simply be swept aside entirely.

It is also worth noting at this point that I am building my own sketch of the various categories that values might inhabit to a large extent along the same lines as that given by Max Scheler. In *Formalism*, he similarly divides the realm of values into four groups, although he expresses this categorization in a somewhat different way. Scheler claims that values can be divided into the following categories: values of "sensible feeling," ranging from the agreeable to the disagreeable; values of "vital feeling," such as the noble and the vulgar or weal and woe; "psychic values,"[9] a category which, for Scheler, includes both those of aesthetics and those of morality; and, finally, "spiritual" or "sacred values," especially those of the holy and the unholy (cf. for these distinctions the section of *Formalism* on the "A Priori Relations of Rank among Value-Modalities," pp. 104ff.). Scheler also makes reference to use-values, but distinguishes them (as do I) from values proper. While it is not my intention to give a full account of Scheler's value-categories in this project, it should be apparent that my own formulation of these valuative types owes a great deal to his work.

Of course, I do also depart from Scheler's taxonomy of values in important ways. My fourfold schematization of values breaks with Scheler's most notably in that I do not include his conception of vital values as one of my major categories, and that I divide his notion of psychic values into the two distinct regions of aesthetic values and moral values. In brief, my justification for the former change is that I do not find the category of vital values to be a particularly coherent one; all of the values that Scheler locates in this region, I maintain, can more easily be accounted for among the other valuative categories that I discuss. Similarly, with respect to the latter innovation, I hold that aesthetic and moral values *do* represent quite different and irreconcilable modes of valuation, and so require their own independent categories. Furthermore, unlike Scheler, I deny that these categories represent an objective hierarchy of values, ranging from sensible values at bottom to spiritual values on top. On the horizon-model, such a strict hierarchy of values would make little sense (though I will discuss the notion of valuative ranks in more detail in Chapter 4). Rather, my taxonomy of values merely envisions these four categories as distinct *types* of values, while making no claims about any order of ranks among them. There are naturally other, more minor distinctions between my conception of these valuative types and that given by Scheler as well. Nonetheless, while my depiction of these categories by no means resembles that of Scheler in every detail, I would be remiss if I did not at least acknowledge his influence in this context.

The distinctions among these various valuative types are, in many cases, quite easy to understand. Take, for example, the conventional distinction between aesthetic and moral values. This is a quite obvious distinction even within the small set of examples employed in this book; it informs, e.g., the difference between Bert and Ernie's encounter with *Persistence of Memory* and Aloysius' encounter with the act of adultery. The category of aesthetic values, to begin with, includes all values associated with experiences of art, of passive appreciation of scenes (landscapes, the night sky, etc.), of harmonies and disharmonies, and so on. That is, aesthetics deals primarily with the values of *beauty* or *refinement*, on the one hand, and *ugliness* or *inelegance* on the other (especially in the spheres of visual and auditory perception). Such experiences have their own unique modes of givenness. As mentioned, they often result in acts like aesthetic appreciation (or criticism, conversely), though all the various modes of such acts are deserving of their own independent analyses. The structures governing the visual beauty of a work of art are naturally different from the structures underlying the disvaluable aesthetic experience of a harsh, cacophonous sound. These experiences, nevertheless, all share in common a general valuative "tone" that produces reactions of appreciation or aesthetic disapproval in those who encounter them. Despite their individual peculiarities, all aesthetic values operate in similar ways when compared to other possible sorts of values.

Moral values, on the other hand, present themselves to us with an urgency that aesthetic values lack; the former are possessed, as Hartman might put it, of a stronger, more forceful "ought-to-be" than the latter (with the possibility of a corresponding "ought-to-do").[10] These values – primarily *the morally good* and *the evil* (alternatively: *the virtuous* and *the vicious*) – possess quite different structures than those of aesthetics, often leading the experiencing subject to acts of more direct participation in the instantiation of such values, e.g., by engaging in works of virtue or restraining oneself from sins – an understandable difference given the great relevance that this sort of value has for action in the world. Moral values have a unique salience for our volitional actions, calling us to obey their dictates with a singular gravity – even when we turn against those dictates for other reasons. Values like vice, virtue, and so forth – not to mention their subsidiary values (as just one example, the distinction in Catholicism between venial and mortal sins) – are thus naturally the most suited to ethics, and so play a rather central role in any investigation into values whatsoever. Indeed, as in the case of Hartmann, the propensity of values to contribute to a genuine ethics is often the motivation behind axiology in general.

Certainly, both aesthetic and moral values are absolutely central components of our experience. What, after all, would our lives really be without our experiences of beauty, of refinement, and so on? Without the moral values that serve as the foundation for our ethical lives? Nonetheless, the realm of affect is not reducible to either of these broad categories, or even to both of them together. There are also the even more direct values that are encountered in our various pleasant and unpleasant experiences, such as the deliciousness (or, on the contrary, the nastiness) of scotch. (The directness of these values is a function of the rather immediate character of their givenness – immediate in the sense that they are related to bodily pleasure or pain in a very forthright way, and not, of course, that they are themselves immediately intuited.) These should not be classified as aesthetic values in the same vein as those that inform our experience of a beautiful painting. Rather, they may better be thought of – to adopt Scheler's classification – as sensual values, values of pure bodily sensation or "feeling states."

Essentially, this category includes all values that can be included under the composite values of *the agreeable* and *the disagreeable*, taken in a sense that precludes the subtler call of aesthetic values. Of course, once again, these broad categories are insufficient to express all the detail contained in the wide variety of valuative experiences that they contain. Sensual values include the values imparted by everything from the taste of food – whether savory or vile – to the smoothness or itchiness of an item of clothing, the pleasures of the touch of skin to skin, the pains of illness or injury, and so on. All of these varieties have their own unique characteristics; the awfulness of biting into a morsel of rotten food is quite a bit different from the harmfulness of being bitten oneself, after all![11]

Nonetheless, what they bear in common is their relative immediacy to valuative consciousness, the fact that they present themselves to that consciousness at a very basic, visceral level. This fact is, in particular, what separates sensual values from aesthetic values, their nearest analogue; sensual values do not necessarily direct themselves towards the sort of refined contemplation or judgment as the latter. This is not, of course, to say that such values are always separate *in practice*. Aesthetic and sensual values are often combined in experience; a glass of good wine, for instance, certainly tastes delicious (a purely sensual value), but also can be grasped as something of an art-object – one can admire the color, for example, or savor the feel of the wine's body in a way rather different from a more carnal appreciation of its taste. One can even experience the wine in question as an excellent example of the technical art of winemaking, recognizing its value on the level of professional interest. That fact notwithstanding, however, the structures governing such experiences remain distinct, and therefore susceptible to separate analyses (though both under the banner of axiology in general). Yet again, what we find is that a complex set of structures embedded in ordinary, concrete phenomena submits itself to a more abstract phenomenological investigation through the various independent forms that it takes.

The wide variety of the aforementioned categories notwithstanding, there are values that transcend all of them. Taking another page from Scheler's book (although in a modified sense), we might call this "transcendent" category of valuative acts the realm of "spiritual values." This category is notoriously rather more difficult to pin down than any of those preceding, but it does seem to account for some important aspects of our experience that continually elude those other groups. These values do not correspond to merely bodily sensations like sensual values, but nor are they reducible to the more refined, somewhat detached experiences appropriate to aesthetic values. As Scheler describes it, our apprehension of spiritual values involves the conscious subject being completely "swept away" by the value – e.g., by bliss, catharsis, despair, grief, or awe. There is an element about these values – which I classify under the broad subcategories of *rapture* and *despair*, not in reference to subjective emotional states, but rather to the genuinely existing values that have those emotional states as their subjective counterparts – that goes beyond any particular sensation we might have or judgment we might make, enveloping the subject who encounters them and imbuing his entire experience of the world with a unique character.[12]

But no more are these values equivalent to those we placed earlier under the category of moral values. Bliss, for example, does not speak to us in the commanding tone of a moral imperative; grief is not reducible to any kind of "ought-to-do," as Hartmann puts it. Rather, these spiritual values – and the spiritual feelings that correspond to them – often seem attached to the whole world, rather than to any particular object or set of circumstances.[13] Even in the case of grief, which may be a reaction to some particular event, it is often the case that the entire world seems to be clothed in the black of mourning for the griever; the value washes over more than merely the particular event that was its origin. As such, any account of values would be remiss in ignoring this variety – even if the particularities of the values involved here are rather more difficult to spell out than those of certain other categories that we have examined. As noted above, these four categories – aesthetic values, moral values, sensual values, and spiritual values – should, taken together, serve as a solid foundation for future inquiries into the more specific characteristics of values as they are actually experienced in worldly life.

Nonetheless, I want at this point to introduce one final category of values – though that term must be used loosely, in this case – that must be dealt with by any investigation of the subject. There are certain objects or situations in the world that are experienced as worthwhile pursuits for the experiencing subject (or, on the contrary, as things to avoid) that, nevertheless, do not seem to have the same relationship to their values as do the valuable things that fall into the categories discussed above. I refer, of course, to what Scheler called the values of utility (and placed at the bottom of his hierarchy of values), and which I will term "use-values." The preeminent example of such a use-value is the economic value of money. Aside from caricatures of the rich swimming through piles of gold coins, few men desire money for its own sake, as is the case for all the other positive values mentioned above. Rather, the value of money lies in *what it can do*, i.e., in the fact that it is *useful* for attaining things (experiences, possessions, etc.) that we value more directly. A great many of our actions in the world are done in pursuit of such use-values: not only the jobs by which we earn money, but many political movements, menial tasks, and so on are carried out, not primarily for their own sakes, but for the sake of that to which they lead.

Accordingly, these use-values have quite a different role in our experiential lives to that of all other sorts of values. Beauty, virtue, the sublime – all of these are worthy of pursuit in their own rights, all of them attract the experiencing subject solely to themselves, but *the useful* attracts those who encounter it only in light of some further value towards which it points.[14] (Conversely, *the disadvantageous* is disvaluable only because it presents an obstacle preventing the subject from attaining that which is valuable, or because it drives him closer to something else that is disvaluable in its own right.) Accordingly, use-values lack precisely that characteristic which is most central to values as such: the attraction towards (or repulsion from) *themselves* that they bring to bear on our experiences.[15] And yet, to deny that we genuinely feel *something* towards the things associated with these use-values would be a gross error of phenomenological observation. We do really feel a desire for money, we feel ourselves dedicated to political causes, and so on. But this feeling, which always draws the experiencing subject on to some other value, and not to itself at all, is of a vastly different sort than that which is a feature of values proper. We must, therefore, separate use-values from this group entirely, considering them to be only quasi-values in contrast to the genuine values of aesthetics, morality, sensuality, and spirituality. More precisely, use-values are *second-order values*, entirely contingent on the other values to which they lead. They partake in something of the nature of those genuine values but cannot legitimately be considered their equal. While use-values are certainly a major component of our everyday experiences, however, a deeper investigation of their particular character must wait for another time. The present project is concerned with the theoretical questions underlying values as such; any more in-depth consideration of the quasi-values of utility than that provided in the preceding two paragraphs must be the object of another inquiry; I will not delve any deeper into this subject in this book.[16]

3.6 A Succession of Values: The Good and the Bad

It is obvious, then, that values exhibit a wide variety of modes. These various levels of values and valuative acts – the beauty and ugliness of the aesthetic level, the moral and the immoral of the ethical level, the agreeable and the disagreeable of the sensual level, and the rapturous and despairing of the spiritual level, as well as each level's subsidiary and more specific values (the discordant, the prickly, and so on) – all have unique effects on valuative life in general. Indeed, it is these values that fill in the notion of value itself with meaningful content; there is no sense to the notion of "value" alone, except as it is manifest through its role in describing the way in which all of these particular values are experienced, and therefore only through experiences of the valuable things with which they are associated. (It is this fact, the irreducibility of valuative consciousness to the formal level that would remain abstract from all these particular values, that links the phenomenology of values carried out in this book with Scheler's *material* ethics of values, even if the two differ in important ways.)

Granted, the model that I have explicated here makes no pretension to being an absolutely final list of such valuative types. The categories mentioned above (as well as their sub-categories, many of which remain completely unenumerated here) adequately capture every instance of valuative consciousness that I can think of at the present time, but that is not to say that other regions of value might not be revealed by valuative experiences elsewhere in the world, in the future or in the forgotten past, by other forms of consciousness, etc. This list is included here mainly as a guide to the possibility of such a categorization, and not as the final word on the matter. Nonetheless, this schematization of values as such does open up the path forward for practical investigations into concrete valuative experiences to be carried out. Now that we have attained at least a tentative breakdown of valuative types, the possibility of carrying out a specific investigation into each of these types – a phenomenology of aesthetic values, for instance, or the more specific phenomenology of visual art – is clear. Such a task is a matter for a more dedicated investigation, however, and must be set aside for the present if I am to complete my original mission of examining the underlying structures of values as a whole.

With that task in mind, there are some general, structural comments that I can make about the relationships among the various sorts of values that I have pointed out. Namely, each set of genuine values that has thus far been explicated consists of one overarching pair of values – one positive value and one disvalue – as well as a wide variety of subsidiary values that fall under those banners. In the case of aesthetic values, for example, we see that all of the particular values in this category seem to be comprehended under the blanket terms of beauty and ugliness (or "the beautiful" and "the ugly").[17] These terms capture a tremendous number of other values, all of which have their own subtle gradations; despite the very great differences between them, both an attractive woman and a charming melody can be reasonably described as beautiful, while both a discordant, clashing sound and a grotesque image can be summed up as ugly. The beautiful and the ugly are, therefore, more general values than those other aesthetic values that they comprehend. The same holds true for the other regions of value-consciousness that I have discussed. Sensual values come down to the agreeable and the disagreeable; all pleasures and pains of whatever sort, all instances of smoothness or roughness, pleasing coolness or bitter cold, and so forth, can be positioned under one of these two headings. When it comes to the values of morality, all are either moral or immoral; there may be a wide variety of vices and virtues, even various gradations of moral character, but all fall under this schema. When it comes to spiritual values, the case is more convoluted. It is the (preliminary) position of the author that all such values can be comprehended under the notions of the rapturous and the despairing, but a full account of these values must rely on the more detailed investigation that this book cannot carry out. The parallels here to the other modes of valuation should be obvious; the specifics can wait for a later date.

Nonetheless, the point to bear in mind about these broad categories – the beautiful, the disagreeable, and so on – is that they are meaningless without recourse to the more specific values that they encompass. Let us take as our example the traditional value of beauty, a value that has long had a central pride of place, e.g., in Plato's discussion of the true, the good, and the beautiful. But what can be said about beauty itself, purely on its own terms? Beauty, as we have previously noted, is by no means an object that we can encounter in the world. As with any value, to understand it, we must understand the way it conditions the valuable things that we apprehend *as* beautiful – *Persistence of Memory*, for example, or a beautiful melody like Chopin's "Raindrop" prelude. But these things, as lovely as they are, are not merely beautiful, without further elaboration. Rather, their beauty is always related to some other value that they possess – the specifically visual magnificence of the painting or the auditory charm of the song (terms which, of course, have their own sub-categories). Beauty itself cannot be discovered in the absence of some more specific aesthetic value; beautiful objects are never *merely* beautiful, without further specification, but are always beautiful in some particular way.

In like manner, moral or immoral acts always have some particular moral tone, agreeable or disagreeable sensations have their own specific mode, and so on for the spiritual values of rapture and despair. The overarching categories mean nothing by themselves; their meaning is always bound up in the set of values that they encompass. This lack of purely internal content does not, of course, entail that such values are not a central component of our valuative lives. Again, what would life be without beauty, in all its forms? These category-values are indispensable for illustrating the essential connections between the subsidiary values that they encompass. It is the structures of beauty as such, for example, that permit us to distinguish aesthetic values from all others, grouping them together as their own unique valuative type. Nonetheless, category-values cannot be taken *solely* on their own terms; phenomenologically, their real existence is only spelled out in their subsidiary values, and ultimately in the valuable objects that refer back to them.

This succession of valuative categories – not a succession of abstractions, since beauty and the rest are just as real as their subsidiary values (and just as susceptible to genuine phenomenological investigation), even if they depend for their meaning on the content of the latter – also reveals a set of even more general categories, a set that gets to the core of the notion of valuative consciousness. That is, I have not, until this point, discussed in any detail one of the most important values throughout the history of philosophy: the good itself. Ever since Plato, this notion has been thought of as the absolute cornerstone of axiology (whether or not it was always taken as seriously as by Plato himself, who gave it a rather central ontological position). Clearly, this idea of "the good" as such does not refer to any of the particular values that I have been considering thus far. And yet, each of those values – the positive values, at least – can ultimately be described by this term.

As such, the good can be defined as a really existing value in much the same vein as the broad category-values like the beautiful or the moral – yet at a higher level still in the succession. Each of those category-values (when understood as a positive value) can be thought of as a particular mode through which the good as such makes itself manifest. The good is meaningless without them, just as they are meaningless without their subsidiary values. The real existence of the good – a question that will be examined more closely momentarily – is always bound up in its role as the *summum bonum*, the highest unity underlying all positive values, keeping them all together as being of one type, even while it must refer to values lower down in the succession if we are to make any sense of it.[18] It is never enough, if one wants to be a rigorous phenomenologist, to say that something is simply good; the mode of its goodness must also be specified (though that fact by no means indicates that the idea of the good itself is a useless or abstract notion, any more than that of the beautiful or the virtuous).

Thus, the idea of the good stands at the very top of this axiological system. And yet, it cannot stand there alone. Each of the category-values I have examined has consisted, not of a single (positive) value by itself, but of a pair of values mirroring one another. There is no conception of the beautiful without its counterpart, the ugly; morality cannot be thought of without its negative reflection in immorality; and so on. For every such value, there is always the possibility of a corresponding disvalue. This claim applies to category-values, certainly, but also to the particular values that stand underneath them. For every melodious sound, there is a cacophonous racket; every possibility of a beautiful vista could also reveal some hideous panorama. Values and disvalues, at every level, go hand in hand.

In the present context, the same holds true for the capstone value of the good. If there is a coherent notion of the good, to which all positive values refer, the same must be true for disvalues. The good (contra Plato, et al.) is meaningless without the bad.[19] There must be, then, two ultimate values, to which all others appeal – or, rather, an entwined pair of values that serve as the guiding lights for all others. Like the category-values that are classified directly underneath these two, they mean nothing on their own – but once their content is filled in through those category-values, through the subsidiary values underneath them, and ultimately through the valuable things that we encounter in everyday life, they contain all of the richness of every valuative experience.[20] There is no act of value-consciousness whatsoever that does not appeal to one or the other of this pairing, i.e., which cannot be classified as either good or bad – in whatever particular mode of goodness or badness is appropriate to it. These two notions, despite existing at a relatively high level of phenomenological investigation, are therefore indispensable.

Nonetheless, the question now arises: why should this apparent Manichaeism hold true in the realm of values? Why can we not, for instance, simply reduce all disvalues to the absence of a corresponding positive value, and therefore reduce all thought of "the bad" to an absence of or turning away from the good (as Plato and others – most famously Augustine – would have it)? This solution – while seemingly satisfying the law of parsimony by reducing the number of genuinely distinct values that we need to investigate – cannot, however, be the truth of the matter. Such a reductionist answer fails at precisely the central task of any phenomenological account, which has been a guiding thread throughout this exploration of values: the need to take into consideration the genuine givenness of the things themselves. Despite the ease of simply throwing disvalues in with the positive values to which they are a mirror as their absence, the real, vivid givenness of such disvalues indicates that they must be grappled with on their own terms. Disvalues are just as vibrant a part of our experience as positive values themselves; no more would it be right to eliminate the former from the equation than to remove the latter – a situation that would lead to the utterly comical implication that beauty is nothing more than the absence of ugliness! Such disvalues, while they are certainly correlated with their opposite number, and while the two are analogous to one another in many ways, are distinct enough from those positive values to warrant their own space in the realm of values as such.

Perhaps it would be helpful to demonstrate this point by means of examples. Let us return to the case of Bert and Ernie, and therefore the opposing values of beauty and ugliness. It seems unlikely that anyone could reasonably deny – from the standpoint of the preceding phenomenology of values in general – that Bert genuinely experiences a value, beauty, that must be given its due. The experience that Bert has of *Persistence of Memory* and the reactions that this experience elicits from him all speak to the fact that there is an element to his painting-experience that gives it a uniquely affective character. This value, as we have previously demonstrated, has particular characteristics; the value of beauty is independent with respect to non-aesthetic values like the agreeable or the moral. Without these recognitions, culminating in the identification of a genuinely existing value, we could not make sense of Bert's experience and his subsequent actions at all.

But do not all the same propositions hold true in the case of Ernie's contrary experience? (We will set aside, for the moment, the fact that this experience is an experience of the same *object* as Bert's experience of beauty; that question will be dealt with in the following chapter.) Ernie, it seems, has an experience of the painting that is conditioned by certain unique structures that give it a peculiar affective "tone," that call him on to certain acts, etc. And it does not seem that either the character of his experience or the acts to which that experience gives rise are in any way reducible to a mere inverse of the ones that apply to Bert's encounter with the painting. It is impossible to come to a feeling of disgust with an ugly painting simply by subtracting from ordinary experience the value of beauty – such a subtraction would make no sense, given that these values are defined solely in terms of the effects they have on experience in the first place. And the actions to which these values give rise are by no means always a mirror of one another (except to the extent that reactions to positive values in general stem from attraction, while those to disvalues are a result of repulsion). Ernie's disapproving grimace is not the inverse of Bert's act of staring in aesthetic admiration. There are genuinely two values at play in this situation, even if they run parallel to one another in many respects.[21]

This genuine independence holds true for every pair of values, positive and negative, that we could think about. While it is certainly true that each member of these pairs is linked with its counterpart – it would be difficult to imagine an agreeable feeling without also including the possibility of a *disagreeable* one, for instance – the association between the two is always that of analogy, and never of mere reversal.[22] Beauty is like ugliness in that both are aesthetic values, governing similar sorts of acts, and so on. But they are not the same; just as there is real beauty in this world, so too is there real ugliness. And, since this is the case for all sets of values, the same must hold true for the most general values that it is possible to consider: the good and the bad. It is vital to remember that these highest-level values are wholly derivative in terms of their content from the category-values that lie beneath them, and, in turn, from the subsidiary values on which *those* depend (though this fact, again, by no means entails that they do not meaningfully exist, or that they are not necessary to a phenomenological account of values in general). As such, and given the thoroughgoing distinctiveness of positive values from their corresponding disvalues throughout this framework, it would be inappropriate to reduce all these disparate values to *one* broad category (except insofar as both the good and the bad might be thought of as the opposing representatives of "value itself") – to do so would be to erase the peculiarity of one member of each pair. The fact that such an erasure has often been carried out in the history of philosophy does not obviate our duty to the genuine givenness of values, and so does not stand up as an argument against this division. The real existence of the bad can no more be questioned, once this model is accepted, than the existence of the good itself; the world as a whole is composed of both.[23]

Nonetheless, these speculations tell us little about the nature of the good and the bad as such. What, in general, can we say about the nature of these highest-level values? The answer to this question is subtle. On the one hand, we can say very little about these values at all; as has been emphasized multiple times, no such value can be said to be meaningful apart from its subsidiaries, just as no category at all can be meaningful without an account of that which it categorizes.[24] This is certainly the case for the good and the bad, as the most overarching of all values, even more than for the category-values that they govern. And yet, these top-tier values do genuinely exist; they can no more be dispensed with than the lower-level values that they organize. Their existence in themselves, however, can be described only in the broadest of terms. These values, the good and the bad, must be thought of as exemplifying in the purest possible way the nature of value itself, i.e., they must be thought of in terms of the effects that value itself has on experience.

As such, the only possible definition of the good is that it stands as the point of supreme attraction; what the value of goodness means for us, phenomenologically speaking, is pure attraction. Any value that stands in the light of goodness, as it were, will be a positive value – which is just to say that it will act as an attractor (in some particular way, governed by the specific character of whichever subsidiary values are involved in this case) for the consciousness perceiving the valuable thing with which it is associated. The good is nothing more than this point of pure attraction – though nothing less, either. To describe goodness, one need do no more than explicate the structures by which such an attraction is carried out (a task that, of course, will always involve reference to the particular modes of attraction that stem from more particular values, but one that nevertheless has structures operating at this high level as well). The same applies, in an analogous way, to the bad: badness itself is nothing more than a point of pure repulsion, and to explain it requires only that we explain the structures by which individual consciousnesses are repelled from (dis)valuable things. These two poles govern the whole of valuative experience.[25] We are repelled from the bad and attracted towards the good – albeit in many different ways, accounted for by the successive levels of subsidiary values – and this constant pulling and pushing, to and fro, makes up the richness of our valuative lives. Neither element can be dropped out if we are to make sense of value-experiences, but they always come together in the end to give rise to the endless possibilities of value that confront us every day.

3.7 Conclusions: The Unity of Value-Experience

At this point, the basic nature of pure values – and, importantly, the relationship that these pure values bear to valuable things, which is the only way that they can be known – should be clear. Neither pure values nor valuable things can be thought of without a counterpart. Pure values serve as points of attraction (or repulsion), which lie on the horizons of any experience of a valuable thing; as such, they are subject only (when analyzed separately from the things to which they are connected) to the special and totally *sui generis* laws of value-consciousness. Valuable things, on the other hand, are genuinely "things in the world," meaning that they are subject to all sorts of transcendental laws – the laws of visual perception, for example, in addition to those of valuation. Nonetheless, valuable things always refer to the pure values that they unfold, and which give them their unique character.

The various modes of valuative consciousness have also, to a certain extent, been catalogued. Pure values exist in the form of a succession of valuative types, from the most general (the good and the bad) to the most specific: the particular values that get instantiated in the objects of our experience. All of these values, from the simplest pleasing sensation to the most complex work of art or moral scenario, appeal to one of the two most basic values, goodness or badness itself, depending on whether they are functioning as positive or negative values. These overarching values explain the basic structure that is common to all values as such – pure attraction in the case of the good and the positive values it governs, pure repulsion in the case of the bad and its values. Nonetheless, those most general values are meaningless without further specification of their content. All good things are good in some particular way; the same is true for all bad things. As we explicate these differences, we encounter a number of distinct valuative modes – aesthetic values, moral values, sensual values, spiritual values – each of which can be further broken down to attain greater and greater levels of specificity. Nonetheless, the basic existence and the most general structures of value as such are, at this juncture, quite clear. I thus have a solid basis to pursue this investigation further, into the realm of some of the most challenging questions about values that have long eluded any firm answer: those concerning the relationship between values and subjectivity that I will discuss in Chapter 4, for instance, as well as those regarding the connections between acts of valuation and those of the will that will be the focus of Chapter 5. Given the robust account developed in this book thus far, it is not unreasonable to hope that at least some of these questions can finally be brought to a satisfying conclusion in subsequent chapters.

Notes

1 Ultimately, of course, Bert is attracted to the painting in that it calls him towards acts of volition that bring him closer to it, e.g., approaching it to examine it more closely or purchasing a print of it from the museum gift shop. But this point must look ahead to Chapter 5, where it can be discussed in more detail.
2 This example, of course, raises another important question: namely, how can one and the same object exhibit both a value and a disvalue at the same time (albeit, in this case, for two different perceiving subjects)? Rest assured, reader, that this question has a most satisfactory answer – but that answer will have to wait for the upcoming chapter on values and subjectivity to be discussed in full.
3 This is not, of course, to say that beauty and ugliness always function in these roles, i.e., that of positive value and disvalue, respectively. There are situations in which these roles can be altered, or even completely reversed. But this point will be taken up again later in this chapter.
4 See Höffe's *Immanuel Kant*, 133f.
5 See *Hua* XXIII, *Phäntasie, Bildbewusstsein, Erinnerung*, for this distinction – though I will not address Husserl's view of image-consciousness in detail here, since it is not strictly relevant to the ideas of Kant that are currently under discussion.
6 These ideas are a running theme throughout Kant's work, especially throughout the latter half of the first *Critique*. Perhaps, however, that text sums up this notion best in the opening of the section entitled "The Ideal of Pure Reason," where he writes that such "*ideas* are even further removed from objective reality than are categories, for no appearance can be found in which they can be represented *in concreto*. They contain a certain completeness to which no possible empirical knowledge ever attains. In them reason aims only at a systematic unity, to which it seeks to approximate the unity that is empirically possible, without ever completely reaching it" (485, A568/B596).
7 This conception of the relationship between valuative acts, which appeal to the essential structures of experience that we have termed pure values, and the perceptual or intellectual acts that give valuable things as objects of ordinary perception mirrors, in certain ways, Husserl's *early* account of such a connection. As Ullrich Melle excellently summarizes this view: "All non-objectifying acts are founded in objectifying acts. For Husserl, these objectifying acts are representations and judgments [i.e., those acts of intellectual consciousness that give genuine objects]; non-objectifying acts are emotive and volitional acts as well as intellectual acts like questioning. Accordingly, for Husserl non-objectifying acts are secondary intentions. As valuing, willing, and suggesting, these acts relate to objects and states of affairs that are given to them through the founding acts of representing and judging" (1997, 175). Clearly, the idea that acts of valuation are inextricably related to a larger nexus containing many other acts of consciousness is a running thread throughout Husserl's work. Of course, the precise mechanism of such a relation – one of "founding" as Husserl portrays it here, such that acts like valuation would be entirely *subsidiary* to perceptual acts (rather than bound up with those acts as mutually dependent partners) – must be reconsidered given the inadequacies that made Husserl revise his account of values later in life, a reconsideration that is precisely a major task of this project as a whole, but the basic point that even Husserl's early work was essentially on the right track nevertheless stands.
8 Indeed, such specific investigations have been carried out throughout the history of phenomenology; see, for example, John Brough's article "Image and

Artistic Value." Nonetheless, if these more specialized inquiries want to ensure that their conclusions will remain phenomenologically valid, they must be rooted in an accurate phenomenology of values in general – a requirement that cannot until now have been met in full, if my arguments throughout this project hold true.

9 "*Geistige Werte.*" Frings and Funk render this term in English as "spiritual values," which certainly translates the German accurately, but I will resist this usage. "Spiritual values" does not quite account for the aesthetic and ethical values that this category represents, and I maintain that the term is far better applied to Scheler's fourth category of values, which includes values like that of holiness.

10 Consider the fact that it seems a much simpler task for two persons in the midst of a valuative disagreement to adopt a "live and let live" attitude towards one another when that disagreement concerns aesthetic values rather than moral ones. While Bert and Ernie might well be able to remain fast friends despite their differing opinions on surrealism, the same could surely not be said if they were to disagree on the morality of slaughtering an innocent man in cold blood! Moral values are therefore given with, in some ways, a greater sense of urgency than are aesthetic values. As noted, Hartmann has a great deal to say on the subject of this distinctive characteristic of moral values, as well as the nature of the so-called "ought-to-be" and "ought-to-do" in general. Since the task of distinguishing the different types of values is not the primary focus of this book, however, further exploration of that topic must wait for a later project; for an overview, see Robert Welsh Jordan's "Nicolai Hartmann: Proper Ethics is Atheistic," especially 182ff.

11 Indeed, even values that seem nearly identical to one another can often be distinguished through increasing levels of discrimination. As Scheler writes, for example, "[e]very savory fruit always has its particular *kind* of pleasant taste ... Each of these fruits has a savor that is *qualitatively* distinct from that of the others; and what determines the qualitative difference of the savor consists neither in the complexes of the sensations of taste, touch, and sight, which are in such cases allied with the savor, nor in the diverse properties of these fruits, which are manifested in the perception of them. The value-qualities, which in these cases 'sensory agreeableness' possesses, are *authentic* qualities of a value *itself*" (13).

12 Scheler's characterization of the "spiritual feelings" that are the subjective correlates of these values is illuminating in this respect: "For in true *bliss* and *despair*, and even in cases of serenity (*serenitas animi*) and 'peace of mind,' all ego-states seem to be extinguished. Spiritual feelings seem to stream forth, as it were, from the very source of spiritual acts. The light or darkness of these feelings [i.e., as I would put it, the positivity or negativity of the correlative values themselves] appears to bathe *everything* given in the inner world and the outer world in these acts. They 'permeate' all special contents of experience" (343).

13 There is a fruitful comparison to be made here, not only to Scheler's account of spiritual values, but also to Husserl's thought about "rational spirituality" and the possibility of a "renewal" of "true humanity" in the *Kaizō* articles, as well as to some of his ethical speculation in the *Grenzprobleme* (see, for example, *Hua* XXVII, 42f.). Cf. also the work of Ignacio Ramirez on moods in Husserlian phenomenology. Nonetheless, as interesting as these insights might be, any further development of a phenomenology of spiritual values must await a later project that can be wholly dedicated to such an inquiry.

14 Of course, other sorts of values can lead towards further valuative possibilities as well. The key difference between these cases is that genuine values lead

towards other possibilities *in addition to* their primary function of attracting or repelling the experiencing subject on their own merits, and generally after the fact. In contrast, values of utility have this directedness towards other values as an essential and immediately experienced element of their givenness; the beautiful object can remain beautiful on its own, while the useful object is only useful in relation to some end goal. Scheler's view supports this point: "thus the value of what is '*useful*' is 'founded' in the value of what is '*agreeable*.' For the 'useful' is the value of something that reveals itself as a 'means' to something agreeable, not in terms of a conclusion, but in terms of immediate intuition. This is the case with regard to 'tools.' Without the 'agreeable,' there would not be the 'useful'" (94).

15 Cf. Hartmann's discussion of utility in Volume II of his *Ethics*, 28f. He too agrees in essence with my claims here – stating, e.g., that "utility is not a value on its own account" and that it "can only be the value of a means to something valuable in itself" – even if his particular formulation of the point differs to some extent from mine as a result of his contrasting views on the nature of values in general.

16 As a possible wellspring for future investigation into this question, Husserl carries out in the late ethics lectures a very interesting discussion of what we might call "chains of motivation" leading from genuine values to motivated action by way of intervening values and judgments; see *Hua* XXXVII, 77ff.

17 The precise words used for these values matter little. Beauty is traditional, of course, and so that is the term I have chosen to use, but titles like "the fitting" and "the ill-fitting" or "the elegant" and "the inelegant" would work just as well; it is the eidetic structures referred to by these terms that matter, and not the terms themselves.

18 This fact, of course, distinguishes the good, as the highest or most general of all positive values, from the beautiful, which represents merely one broad *category* of positive values. Plato's close relation between the true, the good, and the beautiful cannot be maintained under this conception of values.

19 Note that this notion of "the bad" is not equivalent to "the evil." The latter is a specifically moral value, and must be dealt with by a phenomenological investigation into ethics. All disvalues whatsoever can be categorized as "bad," but it would be the height of nonsense to consider, e.g., an unpleasant prickling sensation to be evil.

20 Hartmann makes a similar point in his discussion of the "emptiness" or "irrationality" of the notion of the good itself: "Such is the Platonic 'Idea of the Good,' the peculiarity of which is that it lacks all distinctive marks, that in content it remains simply indefinite. What man cannot discern may for all that exist in itself. In this sense one cannot deny that Plato's thought is justifiable. The disadvantage in it is simply that the idea of the supreme value remains empty for our sense of values. With such a principle nothing but a postulate is set up; no valuational insight is gained" (II, 66). This is not to say that the notion of the good (or the bad) is *essentially* empty, but merely that it is devoid of content *when taken in abstraction* from its subsidiary values.

21 Perhaps an example from personal experience will help as well. As an arachnophobe, spiders – particularly those in close proximity to me – are given with a tremendously negative value, say, the disvalue of vileness. This value is by no means equivalent to the inverse of a positive value, as if my distaste for spiders were merely a reaction to the *absence* of some positive value that I associate with a "vicinity without spiders." The feeling of revulsion that spiders inspire cannot be traced merely to the lack of a positive value, but must be thought of as possessing its own unique – and uniquely negative – valuative structures.

124 *Pure Values and Valuable Things*

22 This claim stands in tension with a point made by Husserl in the *Kaizō* articles. He writes that "all negative striving, namely the striving away from disvalues (e.g., 'sensual' pain), is only a transition to positive values. The painlessness in which the striving away relaxes itself – just like desirelessness in the case of the final relaxation of striving for pleasure through the enjoyment of the savored value to the fullest – immediately motivates new, positive strivings aimed at filling up the developing emptiness with positive values" (*Hua* XXVII, 25). For example, an individual who flees the sensual disvalue of a disgusting aftertaste might attempt to fill the ensuing void with the positive value of sweetness through the act of eating something that tastes much better. I do not necessarily disagree with this claim on its own terms; our lives certainly consist (in part) of a long series of value-experiences and our reactions to them, and it is by no means a stretch to imagine that an individual who has just experienced a disvalue of one sort or another might choose to "cleanse his palate" by pursuing a related positive value. I will discuss the connection between values and volition that would underlie such a claim further in Chapter 5. Nonetheless, this fact should not be taken to entail that positive values enjoy some intrinsic privilege over disvalues or that disvalues are somehow simply the absence of positive values, for the reasons I have given above. If that is the claim that Husserl intends to make in this passage, it is sorely misguided – even if his point is insightful in other respects.
23 The relationship between these highest-level values and that world, of course, must be subjected to rigorous examination. But this is a task for later in this book (see Chapter 5).
24 The reverse, of course, is also true; particular values make no sense without the structures of the categories on which they depend, nor without the notions of the good and the bad that stand at the highest level of categorization. Hegel would be proud of this thoroughgoing structure of mutual implication.
25 On this level, the values that I call the "good" and the "bad" are comparable to what Husserl terms the values corresponding to "pure love" and "pure hate," i.e., that which is of the greatest attraction or repulsion for the individual who encounters such values – see the section of the *Grenzprobleme* on the "Absolute Ought and Absolute Love" (*Hua* XLII, 343ff.). Of course, Husserl's insights here venture beyond pure axiology into the realm of ethics, and so require further attention in that more specific context.

4 Values and Subjectivity

4.1 The Problem of Subjectivity: An Overview

Now that this project has come to a foundational understanding of what values are and how they relate to valuable things, it is in a better position to answer some of the most troublesome questions of axiology. Perhaps the most notable of these questions, and certainly one of the most vexatious among them, is what I choose to call the problem of subjectivity. Since at least the time of Nietzsche's proclamation of the death of God (not to mention long before), it has been a matter of grave concern whether or not the values that inform our experience of the world are reducible to merely subjective variations among experiencing subjects, i.e., whether or not anything truly universal can be said about values at all. This problem can be illustrated by a simple observation: despite the fact that many experiences of value are, for the most part, quite similar – there is a reason why Chopin, for instance, is held up as a great composer by almost everyone – it remains the case that our judgments about the values of particular things can nevertheless differ quite markedly. An object or situation might be the source of great positive value for one individual, while another individual finds it to be immensely *dis*valuable. Such cases of valuative disagreement are not only possible, but frequently encountered in everyday life – in the realm of aesthetics, in well-worn phrases like "*de gustibus non est disputandum,*" for example, and perhaps especially in the case of judgments about ethical values, about the morally good and bad, which have certainly been put into (often-violent) dispute. Any genuine account of values and valuative consciousness must give some interpretation of this fact, given its centrality to the way in which we live our ordinary lives.

This insight continues to present a problem in the context of a specifically phenomenological investigation into values. Namely, how are we to account for the apparent variability of values, given the fact that we have identified them as part of the horizons of conscious acts? By placing values on the horizon, we have located them on what phenomenologists call the *object*-pole of a conscious act, and not the *subject*-pole; by definition, such horizontal elements cannot themselves be entirely subjective. But if values are not simply subjective, then how is it possible for a valuable thing to hold two distinct, even contrary values at once (admittedly, for two different conscious subjects)? This difficulty is not as irresolvable as it first appears, but demonstrating that fact will require a careful analysis of the relationship between valuative acts and the conscious subjects who perform them. It is precisely this investigation that I will take up as my major task for this chapter.

4.2 The Problem of Subjectivity: A Demonstration

Luckily, it will not be necessary for me to discuss this problem solely at the level of abstract theory. My previous examples will be quite helpful in elucidating both how subjectivity plays an important role in value-consciousness and how values themselves can nevertheless remain objective. Let us begin with the first example: that of Bert and Ernie and Salvador Dalí. Hitherto, I have been primarily concerned with what this example has to say about the values – beauty, ugliness, and their subsidiary values – involved in the experiences of the two men. But the fact cannot be overlooked that, although Bert and Ernie are each having an experience of the same painting, in very nearly the exact same circumstances, the valuative components of those experiences could not be more different from one another. For Bert, *Persistence of Memory* is an object of great beauty; the painting is conditioned by the structures of the value of beauty and everything that entails. For Ernie, on the other hand, the *very same painting* is an object of ugliness – and, indeed, for many of the same reasons for which Bert finds it to be beautiful: its surrealism, its playful stance towards the objects it represents, etc.

The view of values developed in this book seems, on the surface, to stand in tension with this twofold valuation. Is the painting both beautiful and ugly at the same time? But beauty and ugliness are supposed to be valuative opposites, two paired values, one positive, the other negative. And regardless, if the painting were both beautiful and ugly simultaneously, how would one be able to tell which value any given subject would be able to ascertain in it? Is it simply the case that both Bert and Ernie are missing a valuative element essential to the painting-experience as such? Is it possible for these two values to coexist? These quandaries must be explained if this model of valuation is to be accurate; after all, the central task of the phenomenologist is always to stay true to the things themselves, to explain all the various structures that shape our experiences of the world.

We also see a similar case with the example of Oscar and his newfound love for scotch. This example involves, both before and after Oscar's acculturation to the drink, a single sort of object: a glass of good scotch. (The fact that it is not precisely the *same* glass of scotch in both cases matters little; the important thing is that the two glasses have essentially the same chemical makeup, the same taste, etc.) And yet, as with Bert and Ernie's disagreement on *Persistence of Memory*, we find two distinct and opposing values at play within this single object – in this case, the negative value of harsh disagreeableness followed by the positive value of deliciousness. Here we find, perhaps, an even more troubling level of variability in value-experience. Not only are there two conflicting values operative within the same object (over time, in this example), but these values are even, in this case, opposing values *for* the same perceiving subject.

Just as in the case of Bert and Ernie, this possibility – not an uncommon one in everyday experience, from the purposeful acquisition of tastes to the natural shift in values that happens to human beings over time – demands explanation from anyone who would seek to engage in axiology. How are we to account for the fact that the value of a glass of scotch changes so dramatically in Oscar's case? Does the scotch itself undergo some alteration? This possibility seems unlikely; as stipulated, it is the same variety of scotch in both instances, and there seem to be no major discernible differences from one drink to the next that would account for such a massive reorientation. And yet, on the horizon-model (or any genuine phenomenological model), we cannot attribute these values – harshness and deliciousness – to Oscar himself, as if he were the one imbuing the scotch with its special valuative character. The values are "in" the scotch itself (understood as the object-pole of a particular experience-complex), serving as part of its endless object-horizon. But how can this claim be reconciled with the facts before us?

To answer all of these questions, it will be necessary to delve more deeply into certain matters that I have hitherto left unobserved, both concerning some technical issues in phenomenology and about the genuinely subjective aspects of value-consciousness. First, I will make a few prefatory remarks about the central distinction made in phenomenology between apodictic and adequate evidence, which will serve to address some concerns that might arise throughout this chapter. Secondly, I will discuss the real and essential connection between values themselves and the subjects who encounter them in value-experiences. Despite the fact that values are objective (in that they lie on the object-pole of experiences, as part of their horizon), every such experience continues to have its subject-pole as well, and this element cannot be ignored if we are to understand values to the fullest. Remember: values are not objects, and cannot be thought of solely as detached from the perceiving consciousness or the conscious act whereby they are apprehended.[1] As such, when we want to investigate values, we cannot do so without looking at the *whole act* in which they appear, the valuative experience as such. This act always includes several components: most notably, for our purposes, an object (whether an actual, independent object or a situation, such as a musical performance or a fireworks show), the value that conditions that object, and the subject for whom the object is a thing of value. It is in the complex interrelationships among these various components that values themselves come to life; it is by means of these interrelationships that values and valuable things come to have meaning. Accordingly, after a brief discussion of some technical matters in the following section, it is to these relationships that this project must now turn its attention.

4.3 The Evidence of a Phenomenology of Values: The Apodictic and the Adequate

At this point in the phenomenology of values, it is necessary to address a crucial distinction made in the broadly Husserlian phenomenological tradition between two different sorts of evidence that can be offered in support of a philosophical claim. For the most part, this project has hitherto been concerned only with the various structures underlying values and valuative consciousness in general, whether in the context of the distinction between positive values and disvalues, in a broad taxonomy of valuative types, etc. However, these structural comments leave unaddressed some of the most important questions that we might want a full phenomenology of values to answer, most particularly questions concerning the actual everyday experiences in which we encounter particular values in a concrete way. Not all of these questions can be answered in precisely the same way that has permitted us to understand the basic structures of values as such. Accordingly, we must now turn our attention to some of the various levels at which phenomenological investigation can take place, a topic that has a tremendous role to play in determining both the extent of our inquiries into the subject of value-consciousness and the degree of certainty to which those inquiries can reasonably aspire. It may not be immediately obvious how these technical concerns might be relevant to our ongoing investigations in the field of values and value-experiences, but the rest of this book will, I guarantee, bear out the importance of the present discussion.

Predominantly in his *First Philosophy* lectures, Husserl attempted to give a solid answer to a question that has troubled phenomenologists from the earliest days of the discipline. Namely, should phenomenology be thought of as a transcendental science or a merely descriptive one?[2] Husserl himself constantly stressed the need to establish phenomenology as a "system of universal and absolutely justified truth," i.e., a discipline founded on absolutely justified evidence – the evidence of direct, indubitable experience (*Hua* VII, 24).[3] It is to this sort of evidence, which Husserl terms apodictic, that the phenomenologist, in a rather Cartesian move, makes his primary appeal. Apodicticity is what Husserl refers to as the absolute "self-givenness" of an insight to consciousness, in the sense that such evidence cannot be revoked by any other act of that consciousness; no possible counter-evidence is conceivable.[4] And indeed, many of phenomenology's most famous conclusions appear to be justified by evidence of this sort. The fact that, in visual perception for instance, only one side of an object is given at a time, with other sides present only on the object's horizon, cannot be abandoned; without this characteristic, it would not be justified to term any given intentional act an instance of perception (though it could well be another sort of intentional act, such as a memory). This characteristic of perception is a universal structure of consciousness that is revealed as such because it cannot be revoked by any possible act of consciousness; apodictic evidence is thus that which Husserl finds most proper to the pursuit of phenomenology as universal science.[5]

In terms of the present inquiry, it is obvious that many conclusions about the nature of values and valuative consciousness in general attain this level of apodicticity. If my arguments are correct – and the assumptions it makes about the general validity of a phenomenological view of reality hold true – then it is indubitable that values lie on the horizons of other experiences, that positive values act as attractors and negative values as points of repulsion, etc. These claims cannot be doubted because they are grounded on the conditions that are necessary for valuative experience to occur at all; for example, the claim that values are horizonal rests on the grounds that values like beauty are a genuine and irreducible component of consciousness (i.e., we do in fact have genuine aesthetic experiences that differ from other sorts of experiences we undergo), but also that values can in no way be accounted for as the direct objects of that consciousness – as has been discussed at length. For these sorts of claims, we have the best of all possible phenomenological evidence: the absolute self-givenness of the structures that govern valuative consciousness.

This apodicticity even applies to certain conclusions that can be made from more particular investigations into the phenomenology of specific values. When a phenomenologist analyzes the unique structures that apply, for example, to consciousness of the melodiousness of a beautiful sonata, many of the structures that he identifies there will be absolutely certain insofar as any given experience must possess these structures if it is to be an experience of that particular value at all. (This apodicticity is parallel to that of the adumbrations of visual perception; certainly, there are many experiences that do not involve such adumbrations, but those experiences would *ipso facto* not be instances of visual perception.) Accordingly, much of the phenomenology of values does satisfy Husserl's requirements for phenomenology to be a rigorous science, capable of attaining such absolutely certain conclusions.

Many of the claims we might make about values, however – perhaps including those that might be most relevant to our everyday lives – are by no means equal in apodicticity to these broader structural claims about valuative consciousness in general. In particular, any claims we might make about the ways in which values are actually experienced – not their merely structural features, but their instantiation in particular acts of consciousness through the apprehension of valuable things – can never be completely certain. This lack of precision is a result of the fact that such experiences can be dramatically shaped by any number of factors (characteristics of the experiencing subject, as I shall discuss momentarily, as well as contingent facts about the valuable things themselves, etc.) that can never be predicted ahead of time. We can never, for instance, be absolutely certain what particular objects will be experienced as the bearers of any given value. As such, while it is not wholly useless to make specific claims about the way in which values are experienced in the world (especially given the fact that conclusions of this sort are one of the greatest motivating factors behind an investigation such as this one), such claims will always have a tentative character, subject to constant revision in light of changing or newly discovered circumstances.[6]

Nevertheless, if phenomenological claims about these matters of genuine lived experience must always be conditional, then what sort of value (pardon the pun, once again) do they have for the scrupulous phenomenologist, who wants to ensure that his investigations remain as rigorous as possible? Certainly, these conclusions cannot be apodictic, but – luckily – that gold standard is by no means the only level of justification to which phenomenologists can appeal. Throughout his corpus, and especially in his later work, Husserl was careful to make room for the validity of less elevated forms of evidence. In lieu of apodictic evidence, he maintained, the phenomenologist always has the option of appealing to evidence that is merely *adequate* to its object in his arguments.

Adequate evidence – while it remains a genuinely useful source of appeal for Husserl – is characterized precisely by its lack of the distinguishing characteristic of apodictic evidence: indubitability.[7] Namely, evidence which is merely adequate always remains susceptible to change, since it is always possible that it might be, or might have been, otherwise. Adequate evidence, as opposed to the apodictic, is that which can be conceived of otherwise than it is. Husserl uses as his example for this sort of evidence the actual content of perceptual experiences, as opposed to the essential structures that govern perception in general: while it is impossible for objects of visual perception to be given otherwise than through adumbrations, it can reasonably be wondered whether the silhouette in a window that is given as a fellow human being is really a mannequin instead. We might certainly *believe* that it is a real human being, even experience it *as* another person, but that claim is always subject to later disproof. The same, clearly, holds for many of the claims we might make about values as they are instantiated in the world: the claim that *Persistence of Memory* is beautiful, for instance, or that scotch is delicious.

It is quite evident, in light of phenomenology's attempts to establish itself as a thoroughly rigorous science, that this adequate evidence is, in terms of its (lack of) certainty, inferior to the apodictic evidence of the discipline's more transcendental conclusions. Nonetheless, adequate evidence remains a central tool for the phenomenologist despite this lack; Husserl does call it "adequate" evidence, and not "inadequate," after all. It is important to note that the susceptibility of adequate evidence to doubt by no means entails that such doubt must inevitably occur. Quite the opposite; adequate evidence is adequate precisely because we have no *reason* to doubt it, because it gives itself to us directly (just as does apodictic evidence, though with an absoluteness that adequate evidence cannot attain). In general, we have no need to revise our interpretation of such evidence, though that possibility always remains open to us.[8]

The fact that adequate evidence is never given with the indubitability of apodicticity does not mean that it provides no evidence at all or leaves us with no conclusions about the objects and situations in the world that it addresses; rather, any change in the evidence available to us always gives rise to new sorts of adequacy, a possibility always present in the horizon of such evidence. (Returning to Husserl's example: a shift in my perception of a lady in the window does not leave me with no evidence whatsoever, but gives rise to the newer and more complete – though still merely adequate – evidence of a mannequin.) Accordingly, while adequacy is a less lofty standard than apodicticity, it does remain a useful and necessary ground for our claims about reality. Indeed, it is fortunate for the phenomenological project that this is the case, since the sphere of the apodictically given is itself rather small, limited to purely undeniable structures of consciousness like the adumbrations of perception or, in this case, the general structures of pure values. Without admitting adequate evidence to the scope of phenomenology, little enough can be learned (though it remains vital to consider purely apodictic evidence as its own sphere of investigation, since it is only this sort of evidence that unlocks the truly transcendental truths that ultimately serve as the ground for any other claims that phenomenology could make). In any case, this distinction will be quite useful as the phenomenology of values continues to be developed throughout the rest of this book.

4.4 Value and Value-For: Values and the Subject

Now that the distinction between apodictic and adequate evidence has been addressed, at least to some degree, we may return to the topic of the subjective elements of value-consciousness. Just as no value can be imagined without the simultaneous positing of some *thing* which is valuable, it is also impossible to separate values and valuable things from the subjects who experience them. Let us illustrate this fact by our examples. When I first described the Bert–Ernie–Dalí scenario, it is noteworthy that

132 *Values and Subjectivity*

I did not start off by detailing the painting itself – its textures and colors, or even the value lurking "inside." Instead, the focus of the example lay in the value-*experiences* of the painting undergone by the two friends, the subjects of such experiences. The value (beauty or ugliness, in this case) lies within the painting-experience, certainly, but that experience must be understood as a whole. It is critical to remember just what sort of meaning an aspect of the horizon like these values possesses: values *are* what they *do*, they are known by the ways in which they structure consciousness and call it onwards towards further conscious acts. What this fact means in practice, in an actual example, is that values do not condition "consciousness in general" (even if that is a useful notion for phenomenological investigation), but rather the consciousness of particular subjects – Bert, Ernie, etc. Accordingly, if we want to know what a value "means," we must always explicate that meaning in terms of its relationship to these particular subjects.[9] Values as such are never a direct part of our experience, unlike the valuable things that they condition.[10] When we encounter values in ordinary experience, what we always find prior to any *epoché* is value-for, i.e., value as it is given to a particular consciousness, rather than the pure values discussed in Chapter 3.[11] Granted, values certainly possess structures that are not unique to any one consciousness in particular, but these structures only – ultimately – make sense in their application to the concrete experiences of value-for that we encounter in everyday life.

As a consequence of this fact, it is always an essential part of any horizon that the precise details it conveys can change depending on the perspective of the conscious subject *to whom* it presents itself. Again, a useful demonstration of this point is that of the backsides of visually perceived objects that are Husserl's most common example of the horizon. These backsides certainly exist; they are real components of the object-experience in question. And yet, no one would quarrel over the fact that the specific content of this horizonal experience can vary tremendously depending on the perspective that the perceiver takes up with respect to the perceived object. Imagine, if you will, a photograph standing on a table in the center of a room. One subject, standing directly in front of the photograph, is given one view of the object, with the actual backside of the frame serving as the horizonally-given backside within his experience. Another subject, however, standing to the right of the first, will have entirely different parts of the frame concealed from him as its backside, as will yet a third subject standing behind the frame. It is clear that all of these subjects are having a visual experience of the *same* object, and even that their experiences are parallel to one another in many ways. Yet, in each of these experiences, we have different particular content appearing as a result of the different perceptual stances that they adopt, i.e., as a result of the *subjective elements of horizon-consciousness*.[12] (Indeed, this difference can be so great as to render their experiences entirely the

Values and Subjectivity 133

opposite of one another; what serves as the backside of the photograph for the first observer is the front side for the third, and vice versa.) These differences do not imply that there is no objectivity to what stands on the horizon of their experiences; it merely entails that the particular content of that horizon is malleable with respect to perspective.

How, though, does this analogy apply to the case of values, which are certainly not given in the same (visual) way as the backside of a physical object? The answer to this conundrum hinges on a thorough understanding of the distinction made in the previous chapter between pure values and valuable things. Centrally, it is important to remember that pure values are not identical with the things to which they are attached; beauty as such, for instance, is not limited to its instantiation in one particular beautiful object (even if it can only be known through such objects). Instead, values stand apart from valuable things to some extent, connected to them only through the conscious acts of value-intuition that give meaning to both. What this fact entails is that the subjective aspects of those conscious acts can affect the *relationships* between values and valuable things (though not the values themselves) in many important ways. Just as changes in what we might call physical perspective produce tremendous variations in the horizons of a visually perceived object, other sorts of perspectival changes can have enormous ramifications on the way that a given subject will perceive the world of valuable things. These alterations do not change the values themselves, but do condition the ways in which those values are grasped, and therefore produce very different, or even opposing, valuative experiences.

Let us illustrate this possibility with a metaphor (though, again, constantly remaining aware that the metaphor cannot be taken literally). Imagine that a valuable object of some sort – let us use as our example a ruby, as a potential object of aesthetic value – lies on a table in a sparse room, just like the photograph in the preceding discussion. As any phenomenologist could attest, when one observes this stone, a vast array of content is built into that experience – and, as we know from the axiological investigations up to this point, part of that content is the values (e.g., beauty) that inform it. These values are not strictly properties of the object, but are essential components of any *experience* thereof. They can therefore be imagined as floating points of light hovering around the room, forming the backdrop to different possible perspectives of the ruby on the table. And, of course, these values come in pairs – beauty, for one, might be hovering at one end of the table, while its opposite, ugliness, takes up its position on the opposite side.

Given this imaginative scenario, it is easy to see how different perspectives in the room would be informed by drastically different values, purely depending on the subject's own position with respect to the ruby. A man standing at one end of the room would have as part of his experience of the ruby the value that floated in the background of his observation, say, beauty. A man standing opposite him, however, would have an entirely different value bound up in his experience, perhaps even one that is entirely incompatible with the value given to the first man. Both of these experiences are genuine, and both are genuinely experiences of the same object; they simply are given in two different valuative modes. This difference is not the result of any change in the values themselves, which continue to float in the same locations and which continue to condition the objects they govern in the same ways. Nor is it due to a change in the ruby; the object remains exactly the same as it ever was, despite the two men's differing views of it. No, this change can be attributed solely to an alteration in the *perceiver*'s phenomenological position, an alteration that, combined with the horizonal givenness of values, necessitates a change in the value-experiences that these perceivers undergo. One man might experience the ruby as beautiful in one way while another man experiences it as beautiful in an entirely different way, or even as ugly, all without changing anything about the ruby itself or the values to which it appeals. (Of course, a question could now arise as to whether any of these valuative perspectives is "better" or "more accurate" that the others; this concern will be dealt with in the following section of this chapter.)

Now, as mentioned, this metaphor is only included for illustrative purposes. It is useful to imagine values as lying "in the background" of the valuable objects to which they are connected, because that makes it easier to visualize the complex relationships between the two. However, this image is by no means sufficient when taken literally; the real meaning of the relationship between values and valuable things lies in the complex structures that govern it, and not in the simple fact that they are connected. It is necessary, then, at this point to examine the precise ways in which values stand in the background of valuable objects, in order that we might understand more fully the reasons for evaluative differences among various perceiving subjects. In the metaphor above, these differences could easily be explained: one subject perceived a different value than another because the values were *physically located* in different positions, in such a way as to appear in the background of the object when perceived from one standpoint in the room and to fail to appear in that space when seen from another. But these positional considerations are clearly irrelevant to the case of values as such, given that these values do not have a physical location apart from their instantiation in valuable things. Differing sorts of "experiential perspective" must therefore be considered if we want to understand how it is that values can appear differently to different subjects.

4.5 Valuative Perspectives: The Source of the Difference

My task, then, if I am to account for the diverse ways in which values can be given, is to spell out some of the conditions according to which such values can be experienced at all. What sorts of subjective qualities are necessary for values to be given to an individual consciousness?[13] Every mode of givenness, of course, has such qualifications; it would be impossible to be given an object in visual perception, for instance, without properly functioning eyes, a visual cortex, etc. (even if that same object could be given in other ways to a blind man, e.g., through touch). The same sort of requirements – though different in specifics – must also apply to valuative consciousness in general, as well as to consciousness of each particular value. These requirements and the subjective conditions that meet them describe the evaluative perspective that conditions the values of valuable things – not altering the values themselves, but modifying the relationships in which those values participate, both to objects and situations in the world of experience, as well as among themselves.

Let us return, first of all, to the case of Bert and Ernie. Clearly, the experience that each man has of *Persistence of Memory* requires all sorts of conditions to be met in order to be possible at all. Both Bert and Ernie must have an appropriately functioning visual system, they must be aware of the social and historical context of the painting to unlock its full meaning, etc. But what are the requirements that are associated with the particularly *valuative* elements of the painting-experience, i.e., the beauty and ugliness that the two observe within the painting? Though I cannot possibly spell out all of these requirements here, it will be useful to look through some of them in order to get a grasp on the nature of valuative consciousness in general.

Although valuative consciousness is a transcendentally necessary component of experience (as I have argued in Chapter 1 of this book, and will continue to demonstrate in the following chapter), values can press themselves upon consciousness with a greater or lesser intensity. Part of what is required to experience values to the fullest extent, then, is the lack of any intervening difficulties that could "turn down the volume" of value-intuition. As an example, one common symptom of clinical depression is anhedonia, an inability to feel pleasure (or an inability to feel passion in general, i.e., apathy) – not sadness, precisely, but a muting of the richness of valuative life as a whole. A depressed person of this sort may well understand that a painting is beautiful to some slight degree, but she would not genuinely *feel* that beauty to its fullest extent. Such depression often has physiological causes. A significant component of an experience like that of Bert or of Ernie (i.e., the *rich* experience of a value, and not merely the experience of a value at a low intensity), therefore, is a body and brain that are open to such an experience (rather than being limited by mental illness or some other such difficulty).[14]

There are also requirements that are unique to particular modes of valuative consciousness or to the consciousness of certain values, just as visual perception has necessary conditions that remain distinct from those of auditory perception. Perhaps the foremost among these more specific requirements, in the case of certain modes of aesthetic consciousness, is the need for contemplative attention to be given to a valuable object in order to ascertain its value (a requirement that is especially salient in the case of beauty).[15] A great deal of what enables Bert to experience the beauty of *Persistence of Memory* is the fact that he has come to a museum specifically to engage in such aesthetic contemplation. Were he simply passing by a storefront on his way to work that had a replica of the painting prominently displayed, he might well ignore the painting completely – particularly if his attention already rested elsewhere, e.g., if he were running late to his job. Certainly, he would *see* the painting, but, without a conscious effort to observe it to the fullest extent, the value it bears might remain largely concealed to him. I am reminded of the famous instance in which violinist Joshua Bell performed a brief concert in a Washington, D.C., subway station. Despite the fact that Bell's concerts typically command great attention and require expensive tickets (a fair indication of the beauty of his performances), many passersby paid little attention to the beautiful music, failing to grasp its valuative character in its fullness – even if Bell's concert held other values for such a person, perhaps even the disvalue of annoyance as the concert interrupted a morning commute. The aesthetic value of beauty and its subsidiary values (e.g., melodiousness or visual harmony) require, at least to some extent and in certain cases, a sort of openness or contemplative preparedness in order to be given to a subject with their full intensity (indeed, it is this requirement that, in large part, distinguishes aesthetic values from other sorts of values).

Certainly, of course, beauty can reach out to us and pull us away from our mundane lives without our explicitly preparing ourselves for aesthetic contemplation. In the case of Joshua Bell in the subway, there were surely those commuters for whom the beautiful music served as a call away from the hustle and bustle of everyday life, who were summoned by their experience towards a full appreciation of the value within it. One can easily imagine a person who, on unexpectedly encountering a painting like *Persistence of Memory*, is immediately struck by its beauty and has a full aesthetic experience out of the blue. Prior preparation and readiness is by no means a strict requirement of experiencing aesthetic value.

And yet, such experiences are all the more notable for the fact that they "break in" to our daily lives, pulling us out of our mundane experiences in a breathtaking way and drawing us into the grasp of beauty. The fact of their existence, therefore, is really a point in favor of the claim that some of our most noteworthy experiences of aesthetic value requires a sort of contemplative consciousness; it is just that, in these instances, the value itself is given so strongly as to draw the experiencing subject away from his accustomed mode of consciousness and into that contemplative mode by its own power. The value and the subject work in tandem with one another; the value, like any element of phenomenological givenness, gives itself, but the subject participates in that giving in important ways. At least with respect to aesthetic values, the subject must either make himself ready to encounter a value like beauty by his willingness to step back in appreciative contemplation, as Bert does when he prepares to go the museum, or find himself already so prepared without his knowledge, as in the case of unexpected aesthetic experiences; in either case, the subject must occupy a certain experiential perspective to open himself up to the connection between beauty and a beautiful thing. Indeed, this connection exists in and through this position on the part of the subject; beauty is a real value, and it is really connected to beautiful things, but this connection must always be understood through the fact of its constitution by the experiencing subject.

Nevertheless, these insights into the requirements of aesthetic consciousness – in particular, consciousness of beauty – have not yet provided an answer to my initial question about the possibility of aesthetic disagreement. Like Bert, Ernie also seems to have come to the museum in a state of mind conducive to aesthetic experiences. And yet, the very same painting that Bert experiences as beautiful is, for Ernie, an object of revulsion. We know from the preceding arguments that this variation must be a result of a subjective difference between the two men. But what are the factors that give Ernie such a different experience to that of his friend, even though their situations seem entirely analogous to one another? To answer this question, we must examine more of the structures by which aesthetic values like beauty and ugliness are apprehended.

When Bert finds *Persistence of Memory* to be beautiful, he is not simply looking at the painting as a blank "X," a variable whose only importance for his aesthetic experience is its horizonal connection to the pure value of beauty. Rather, the genuine content of the object of his experience is an essential component of its valuative character, which, indeed, only takes on its full meaning through its application to these specific instances. As such, the particular artistic qualities that the painting manifests – its surrealism, its color scheme, its portrayed meaning (e.g., the melting clocks symbolizing a dreamlike or muddled sense of time, as in the common interpretation) – are central points of attachment for the pure value of beauty that lies within the painting. Only when these characteristics come together for the observer in what we might describe as a positive manner, a manner that strikes him as aesthetically pleasing, is it possible for beauty itself to be given through the object as a whole.[16] If, on the contrary, the observer's aesthetic constitution is prone to perceive these characteristics negatively, as is Ernie's – if, for instance, he "stands" in such a position as to have surrealism represent a discomfiting disharmony rather than an intriguing novelty – then the painting as a whole will be given with a disvalue instead.

So, what is it about Ernie's aesthetic constitution that prevents him from seeing the same value in *Persistence of Memory* as Bert? (This question could, of course, be asked in reverse; there is nothing particularly privileged about positive values that would make them the default.) There are any number of possibilities here. Perhaps Ernie's cultural upbringing has instilled him with an appreciation for traditional forms of art, and the surrealism of the Dalí painting does not stand in accordance with his own aesthetic judgment. Perhaps the colors used in the painting – the browns of the earth, the drab yellow-white of the clouds – strike his eyes in such a way as to be uncomfortable or harsh, preventing him from seeing any beauty within the painting. Or maybe Ernie's intention in coming to the museum was to see a presentation on the paintings of Degas, and his disappointment at finding that the traveling exhibition on impressionism has already left town has colored his experiences and rendered him incapable of perceiving beauty in any other genre on that day – not to mention any number of other possibilities that could affect his perspective. Whatever is actually the case, it is clear that there must be some factor about Ernie's individual consciousness that conditions what value he will perceive in the painting, just as is the case for Bert.

Again, to emphasize the point, this fact does not mean that values themselves are malleable or purely subjective; the structures by which they condition the consciousness that encounters them remain the same even when the worldly things that serve as the *bearers* of such values fluctuate (and even if the concrete existence of those structures is dependent on their instantiation in such bearers).[17] Nor does it entail that valuable things like *Persistence of Memory* are not genuinely valuable in their own rights. It is true that this interpretation of values could give rise to the erroneous notion that values themselves are simply "added on" to our valuative experiences through the various valuative perspectives of the experiencing subjects – a notion that has been roundly rejected in preceding chapters. To address this objection once again, it could be claimed that values are, through means such as education, acculturation, etc., layered on top of experienced objects in order to produce full-fledged experiences of valuable things, but in such a way that the objects themselves, understood statically and stripped of all these perspectival elements, are envisioned as mere *adiaphora* at the most basic level. In other words, such objects would, in themselves, have no value, but would receive their valuative character only through "value-layers." However, given the arguments for the genuinely and unavoidably valuable character of experience given throughout this project, such an interpretation cannot be valid.

Despite the fact that the value that any given object or situation will hold for a particular subject cannot be predicted ahead of time with any certainty, the genuinely and essentially valuable character of such objects and situations cannot be denied. *What* value a valuable thing might hold in a particular context is open to variation and so cannot be known with apodictic certainty, but the fact *that* it is valuable in one way or another can be.[18] A useful comparison can be made here to Husserl's most famous example of the horizon, i.e., the backside of a visually perceived object. It is always possible for the backside of an object to surprise me once I succeed in bringing it into view; perhaps what I thought was a lone wall standing in the middle of a field turns out to be merely a cardboard prop once I move around it, or perhaps someone has painted the backside of the wall in a way that I did not anticipate. Nonetheless, the fact *that* the wall does indeed have a backside of one sort or another is an essential part of its givenness; its backside is not simply added onto it as a result of my change in perspective. Husserl illustrates this point in the context of an object's color: "If the front side has a pattern, then we will expect the back side to follow this thoroughgoing pattern; if it is a uniform color with a medley of specks, we would also possibly expect specks for the back side, and so forth. But there is still indeterminacy ... What is certain, therefore, is some kind of color in general, or a 'color in general broken up by specks,' and so on, i.e., indeterminate generality" (*Collected Works* IX, 79–80). Similarly, valuable things really are valuable through and through, rather than existing as ur-*adiaphora* that only become valuable through their interactions with perceiving subjects; their appeal to values is an essential part of their givenness, and, indeed, their objectivity (i.e., their position on the object-pole of certain experiences), even if the precise mode of that appeal is malleable with respect to perspectival changes.

What this malleability indicates is simply that the precise details of the connections between valuable things and pure values are made solid only in the context of their apprehension by a consciousness capable of such an act, and therefore that these connections are susceptible to the subjective (perspectival) elements of the experiences whereby they are apprehended. Pure values alone, as the material structures governing value-experiences, are not sufficient to explain why one value might be preferred over another in a particular context: "pure axiological laws give us no criteria to make any decisions here. They cannot help in answering the question of which of two values from different classes ... is better than the other and should be preferred" (Peucker 2008, 317). While Peucker's claim is directed specifically at the laws of a purely formal (rather than material) axiology, what the investigation of values that has been carried out throughout this project has revealed is that it applies equally to the abstract notion of pure values by themselves, devoid of their essential references to the particular experiences in which they are instantiated and the particular perspectives involved in such experiences. As shown, value-experiences as a whole are too heterogeneous to be accounted for on any strictly structural or hierarchical model, which might claim that the relative worth of such experiences could be determined solely from an abstract, impersonal standpoint or known through purely

140 *Values and Subjectivity*

apodictic evidence. That fact holds even if the structures underlying these experiences can nevertheless be analyzed meaningfully in terms of their genuinely apodictic content, even if only from a phenomenological perspective.[19]

Finally, one important question remains about the connection between subjective perspective and the values that are given as horizonal. Namely, if the particular values that are to be experienced in connection with any given object of perception are so malleable with respect to subjective's variations in the experiencing consciousness, can it still be said with any real meaning that certain perspectives or valuative grasps of an object are more accurate than others? Is there, that is to say, an *optimum*, a single best perspective from which the *true value* of a valuable thing can be seen most clearly? This question must be answered in a nuanced way in light of the tremendous variability of the term "optimal." Let me first correct a possible misinterpretation of this term in a phenomenological context. Given the fact that I have already rejected Scheler's notion of an internal hierarchy among values themselves, I certainly cannot claim that there exists some optimal value or set of values that *should* be sought after in our valuative experiences above all others. Beauty is not better than ugliness in any universal sense; as I will discuss later in this chapter, there are even situations in which beauty itself can function as a disvalue. Thus, it cannot justifiably be claimed that Bert's view of *Persistence of Memory* as beautiful is more accurate to the supposed true value of the painting than Ernie's experience of it as ugly. From an abstract perspective, or from any perspective that admits only of apodictic evidence, neither Bert nor Ernie can truly be said to be "in error" about the painting's value, even though they encounter it in quite different (and, perhaps, more or less limited) ways.[20] The painting gives itself just as vividly to either valuative perspective, and the values themselves have no internal hierarchy that could justify such a claim. Such a standpoint on the notion of an optimal valuative perspective – which is not at all the way in which Husserl, for instance, uses the term – cannot reasonably be maintained.

Nevertheless, there is another sense in which the notion of the optimum does remain quite relevant to our experiences of valuable things. That is, we can still meaningfully claim that there exists an optimal perspective from which a valuable thing can be encountered *with respect to each particular value* that the valuable thing in question might bear. Even if none of these values can be preferred over the others in any universal sense, each value does have its own set of subjective conditions that control the vividness with which it can be experienced. Let us consider this idea more concretely. In order for Bert to experience *Persistence of Memory* as beautiful, all sorts of perspectival requirements must be met, as discussed above. Depending on how many of these requirements he meets, and in what way he meets them, his experience of the painting's beauty will be more or less rich. For example, he may be able to grasp the beauty of the painting to some degree if he first encounters it from across a very great distance (say, from the other end of a football field), but that experience will surely be heightened if he then moves closer to the painting to observe it in more detail. It is, therefore, entirely meaningful to speak of an optimal perspective from which the painting can be experienced *as beautiful*, even if that experience itself is not an "optimal perspective" on the painting in any stronger sense.[21] Other experiencing subjects would be able to orient their own experiences of the painting in light of this optimum in order to ensure that their experience of the painting's beauty would be as rich as possible (if, indeed, experiencing that beauty were something they desired). While there are certainly elements of subjective variation operative even in this case (e.g., a nearsighted person might need to get closer to the painting to observe its beauty than would someone with better vision), the notion of an optimal perspective from which the painting can be seen as beautiful is by no means without significance on the horizon-model of values.

Similarly, such an optimal perspective must also exist for Ernie's experience of the painting as *ugly*, an optimum which would make reference to its own subjective requirements. And the same would hold for all other possible valuative perspectives on the painting, including all of the subsidiary values of beauty and ugliness as well; the optimal perspective for understanding *Persistence of Memory* as a breathtaking work of art is naturally different from the optimal perspective for understanding it as a cool decal that one could paint on the side of a van. One could even imagine situations in which other sorts of values entirely could be experienced as part of an encounter with the painting, each of which would have its own optimum.[22] Which of these perspectives one adopts comes down to the attitude in which one approaches the painting; for the museum-goer, the optimum lies in seeing the painting from a certain distance, in a certain reflective attitude, etc., while a more casual fan of surrealism might be directed towards an optimum of an entirely different sort.[23] In this light, it is more accurate to say that there exists a broad set of valuative *optima* for experiencing any given valuable thing, rather than a single optimum. No universal or apodictic account can be given to answer the question of whether one should optimize his experience of *Persistence of Memory* for beauty, for ugliness, or for some other value entirely. Nevertheless, the purely descriptive question of *how* such various optimizations might be carried out can indeed be answered by means of a phenomenological inquiry into the structures governing these different sorts of value-experiences – even if that inquiry would require a more specific and dedicated investigation than can be accomplished in the general theoretical account of values as such that is the focus of this book.

4.6 The Acquisition of Taste: A Genetic Account

Perhaps an even more relevant example of the problem of subjectivity lies in the case of developing taste that is evident in Oscar's growing love for scotch. Here, we see a situation in which the value of an object – a nice glass of scotch – changes over time, not simply between different perceiving subjects, but for one subject who remains, in large part, the same in both circumstances.[24] Let us review the basic valuative situation at the start of Oscar's journey. He finds himself faced with a drink that has a certain taste, certain physiological effects, etc. While he might enjoy some of these effects – I have already posited that Oscar is a drinker – he simply cannot get past the taste of the beverage (admittedly, scotch has a strong flavor). He experiences the drink as a whole as the bearer of what we might call the value of harshness, a subsidiary of the sensual disvalue of disagreeableness. That is to say, when Oscar picks up a glass of scotch and contemplates taking a sip, there are certain structures associated with that disvalue built into his experience. These structures are what cause the glass of scotch to give itself to him in a particularly negative light; they are what makes him slightly rumple his nose at the harsh smell of the beverage, what causes him to hesitate before lifting the glass to his lips, etc. That is, they are entirely responsible for the specific affective character of his experience as a whole. The disvalue of harshness, which exists in and through those structures, is therefore really a part of that experience; the glass of scotch itself is, in this case, really disvaluable in all the ways appropriate to this form of disagreeableness (i.e., it contains those disvalues as a genuine part of its valuative horizon).

And yet, that cannot be the whole of the story if we are to make sense of what happens later in Oscar's journey – namely, his development of a taste for scotch, which is presently so distasteful to him. Over time, the value of scotch shifts for Oscar from the disvalue of harshness to the positive value of deliciousness. As we know from the preceding analysis of Bert and Ernie's day at the museum, what such a change requires is some kind of an alteration in the subjective conditions by which the values in question are apprehended; both harshness and deliciousness are genuine elements of the scotch's valuative horizon, and which of them comes to the fore in a particular instance depends on Oscar's own valuative perspective. Since this example deals with sensual values falling under the categories of the agreeable and the disagreeable, however, those conditions must be different from those that govern the aesthetic values in play in the previous example. It will be useful, then, to bring to light some of the conditions of the possibility of the experience of such sensual values if we are to understand how Oscar comes to appreciate scotch as the bearer of positive values.

It is important to note, at this juncture, the strong connection between these sorts of values and the body itself. Sensual values are, after all, values of *the senses*, i.e., of bodily pains and pleasures of various sorts. A great many of the subjective requirements for experiencing such values lie in the subject's occupation of certain bodily states.[25] Accordingly, part of the alteration that occurs to Oscar is a purely physical one: taste buds, like any part of the body, can change over time. This fact is evident in the method by which Oscar accomplishes this change: he forces himself to drink scotch over a long period of time, despite its harshness. One effect of this persistence is to inure his taste buds to that harshness, which becomes easier to tolerate over time. The fact that his tongue thus grows accustomed to the taste of scotch removes one of the major barriers preventing him from seeing the positive value within it, i.e., it removes a physical block that foreclosed on certain valuative possibilities and thus allows new modes of experience to shine through, in a way analogous to the miraculous healing of a blind man opening up new possibilities of visual experience for him.

And yet, there are other alterations going on in Oscar's experience as well. The truism that "practice makes perfect" holds for valuative consciousness just as it does for many other sorts of experience. Just as someone who studies mathematics for long enough opens himself up to new levels of understanding, or as an athlete might enable herself through consistent practice to have new experiences related to her sport (even when she is not on the court herself; for example, a skilled basketball player is able to notice fine points of technique when watching others play, which may not be obvious to a novice), repeated exposure to scotch allows Oscar to ascertain more subtle flavors than ever before, flavors that eluded him on his first encounters with the beverage. These newly discovered flavors may well be able to deliver to him a more positive value than the overwhelming harshness that was, initially, his only point of contact with the drink. Furthermore, certain more intellectual components of his relationship with scotch might aid Oscar in appreciating its real positive value; for instance, learning certain facts about the ways in which scotch is produced, about various differences in the distillation process, etc., might all contribute to his growing appreciation for the beverage. Again, these examples are merely illustrative – there may well be other points on which Oscar's encounter with scotch could evolve as well, but these few should give the reader some idea of the basic nature of the valuative operation taking place in this example.

However, the changing circumstances that permit Oscar to encounter new values through his experiences of scotch are not all that needs to be discussed with respect to this example. Unlike in the case of Bert and Ernie's differing reactions to *Persistence of Memory*, we have here not simply the manifestation of different values in the same object as a result of differences in the perceiving subject(s). Rather, we have a situation in which the subject makes a *conscious effort* to accomplish such an alteration. Oscar's willingness to do this – the fact that he seems to

144 *Values and Subjectivity*

find some positive value in scotch even when all he can taste is its (disvaluable) harshness – requires some explanation. As will be discussed in further detail in the following chapter, values are inextricably connected to volitional acts; in particular, disvalues are connected to volitional acts that move the subject away from whatever object presents him with the disvalue. We might expect, therefore, that Oscar, smelling or tasting the harshness of scotch for the first time, and thereby being confronted by the disvalue connected to the beverage, would react accordingly. Perhaps he would put down the glass, thrust it away from him across the table, and vow with a look of disgust that he would never touch the stuff again. None of these, however, are what actually happens in our thought experiment (or, at least, they are not the end of the story). Instead of turning him away from scotch, the harshness of the drink seems to draw Oscar closer to it; he devotes himself to the task of acquiring a taste for scotch with a sort of passion that can only correspond to a relatively high value. How is this tension to be explained? Is there any way in which the disvalue of harshness can be reconciled with Oscar being drawn towards scotch nevertheless? What are the conditions under which this counterintuitive result becomes comprehensible?

The answer to this conundrum lies in the fact that valuative experience is, as noted previously, always bound up in the complex web of experiences that make up conscious life. The harshness of the scotch – certainly, at the beginning of the example, a disvalue for Oscar, as seen from the fact that he has to steel himself to acquire the taste for it, the facial expressions that he makes when confronted with the drink, his post hoc comments about his experience, etc. – is not the only value in play in his experience of drinking the beverage. If it were, there would be no question of Oscar's pursuing the matter any further; our tendency to flee those values that we experience as *dis*values is sufficient proof of that fact. Rather, it must be the case that Oscar finds *something* of (positive) value associated with his experiences of scotch in some yet-to-be-determined way, even if that value is by no means that which confronts him initially or most forcefully in his experience of the drink.

Perhaps the most obvious positive value that could be imagined in this situation (though by no means the only one, as I will discuss momentarily) is the aesthetic value of class. Although Oscar's experience of scotch, understood as the bearer of a purely sensual value, might well be characterized solely in terms of its harshness, the drinks that an individual consumes are not always chosen merely for the sake of their pleasant tastes. Even a steady drinker might, as an example, forgo certain alcoholic beverages for some time in order to preserve his health.[26] There are many other benefits that certain drinks might provide as well, e.g., those of "good taste." Scotch (in contrast to many other alcoholic beverages, e.g., tequila or vodka) has traditionally been associated with a more discerning palate. Aficionados of scotch may come together to compare the various subtle flavors of the drink or to debate the benefits of particular brands. It is not difficult to imagine that being an accomplished drinker of this beverage might come with certain social advantages, e.g., acceptance by some crowds that might be wary of those who drink only Tennessee whiskey (as delicious as that beverage might be). It is entirely possible, then, that Oscar could develop his appreciation for scotch as a result of his pursuit of this social identity – an identity that might well, from his perspective, bear a positive value that outweighs the negative value of scotch's initial harshness. Simply because an object or situation bears one negative value does not mean that it cannot have positive values as well (just so long as no two values included at any one time are opposites of one another, e.g., disagreeableness and agreeableness of the same sort).

Nevertheless, this explanation – while it is indubitably part of the picture – does not account for the most likely reason that Oscar might elect to alter his choice of beverage. It is clear from the thought experiment that Oscar does not merely value scotch as a means to an end, but rather winds up appreciating scotch *on its own terms*, at least once the taste for the drink has been sufficiently acquired. It is not as if he simply planned to grin and bear the harshness of the drink forever in order to attain the social status that comes with being a scotch drinker; he genuinely believes that the drink is, in itself, delicious, and that it is merely some fact about his own lack of acclimation to it that prevents him from accessing that value. But how can this be possible, on this model of values? How can Oscar recognize the deliciousness of scotch (that he will experience in the future) at the same time as he faces a far more direct encounter with its harshness? How can two genuinely opposing values be simultaneously present within one experience (rather than in multiple experiences over time or spread out among different subjects, scenarios which have already been explained)? Only if a coherent answer to this question can be given will this model of values be sufficient to account for this difficult scenario.

The only means of answering this pressing conundrum is to point out a vital distinction between the vastly different ways in which Oscar recognizes the opposing values of harshness and deliciousness in the scotch (at the beginning of his journey, i.e., setting aside his experience of that deliciousness after he has acquired the taste for it). That is to say, his experience of the disvalue of harshness is a genuinely valuative experience, a direct exercise of valuative consciousness, while his initial encounter with the deliciousness that he will one day experience more directly is simply an "as if" encounter, a reflection of the value that he will experience in the future, and which he currently knows about through his interactions with other valuing subjects. When it comes to the initial harshness of scotch alone, this value-experience requires little further explanation on the horizon-model. Oscar has an encounter with a certain beverage that is connected to a certain sensual disvalue; the disagreeableness of the drink lies right there on the horizon, calling Oscar on to future acts in the way we have already discussed. Scotch is, in Oscar's early experience, a disagreeable drink in a direct and immediate way.

But this immediacy can in no wise be said to apply to the deliciousness that Oscar sees within the drink at the start of his journey – even if that positive value does call him on to certain acts in a different way. (Oscar may never have been inclined to develop a taste for scotch if he could not, in some way, ascertain this value.) Oscar does not encounter the *genuine* deliciousness of the drink itself at all prior to his acquisition of a taste for scotch. We can see this lack of such an encounter from the ways that he does react to the drink: grimacing, steeling himself for a sip, etc. He must believe that the value is *there* in the drink, but he does not himself encounter it – precisely as a result of his lack of the proper conditions for doing so, as discussed previously.[27] The genuine separation – even a total opposition – between such a positive value and a negative value is thereby preserved; both agreeableness and disagreeableness are *not* encountered in the same way, at the same time, by the same subject in this scenario. The negative value is there immediately in the drink, as a genuinely felt value; the positive value, on the other hand, must have some other mode of givenness.

But how is this model to account for this novel mode of givenness of the deliciousness of scotch, if it cannot be said to lie on the horizon of the scotch in quite the same way as the drink's more immediate disagreeableness? I must be very precise in my answer to this question. The deliciousness of scotch is precisely *not* given to Oscar *in the form of a genuinely felt value*. Rather, it is given to him as a *possibility*, something that he cannot grasp through the ordinary structures of affect that characterize valuative consciousness, but rather must encounter solely as an imaginative enterprise. Consider: how does Oscar come to learn of the drink's positive value in the first place? He becomes aware that scotch is, in fact, a delicious beverage through his associates: by observing them drink scotch with obvious relish, perhaps, or by being told of the drink's myriad virtues directly.[28] Assuming that he trusts his associates, it is quite understandable how he could come to a belief *that* scotch is delicious, even if that value itself is inaccessible to him for the moment. He recognizes that the value is there to be grasped, but also that he cannot grasp it from his current valuative perspective, and therefore concludes – if he wants to become acquainted with said value – that he must make some changes in that perspective, e.g., accustoming his taste buds to the harshness of the drink. In this sense, it can truly be said that Oscar *recognizes* the positive value of scotch even while he *experiences* the opposite value entirely.[29]

Nonetheless, this awareness of the possibility of scotch bearing a positive value is a far cry from the sort of valuative encounter that is the main object of study for a phenomenology of values. Consider an analogy: instead of learning from an associate about the wonders of scotch, Oscar listens to his friend describe certain far-off locales that the latter has seen on his recent vacation (locales that Oscar has never himself visited). Oscar might well find himself constructing a mental picture of these places, considering what they might look like in light of his friend's description, imagining himself walking among such exotic lands, etc. He might very well, therefore, have those locales themselves as the object of his thought – phenomenology certainly makes room for such "as-if" objects of consciousness. And yet, no one would deny that there is a rather monumental difference between Oscar's imaginative experience of these far-off lands and the experience that he would have by going there himself! In much the same way, Oscar can certainly have the deliciousness of scotch as the object of his consciousness, but the givenness of that deliciousness is very different from the genuinely affective (horizonal) givenness of the objects of value-consciousness proper. "As-if" valuation is certainly a possibility for an evaluating subject, but it is categorically *not* the same thing as valuation as such. Granted, these "as-if" values can be the bearers of genuinely felt values in their own right. Oscar clearly sees some positive value in following the advice of his associates by pursuing the reflected deliciousness of scotch that he does experience, as seen from the fact that he does make the effort required to shift his valuative perspective in such a way as to experience that deliciousness more directly. Nonetheless, a rigorous distinction between values that are genuinely felt and those that are encountered only in the "as-if" must always be maintained.

So, the acquisition of taste in the case of Oscar and his scotch can be described as follows. Oscar has a valuative encounter with a glass of scotch. From his valuative perspective, this drink is – on the sensual level – connected primarily to the disvalue of harshness. His experience of taking a sip from the glass is, in this respect, one of disagreeableness. Nonetheless, other (non-sensual) values are operative in this experience as well: the positive value of elegance, for instance. Oscar also recognizes (from the behavior of his associates, from his conversations with them, etc.) that scotch can also bear a positive sensual value, even though this value of deliciousness is not something to which he himself has access (for the moment). With these goals in mind (e.g., the goals of pursuing the class that he sees in being a scotch-drinker as well as the value of a pleasure to be attained later – we often work towards values that are not yet completely in sight), Oscar embarks on the project of altering himself in such a way as to make the experience of scotch's genuine deliciousness available to him. He accomplishes this task by repeated exposure to the beverage, by learning more about it, etc., all of which permit the values that he is pursuing to override the distaste he initially feels for the harshness of the drink. Over time, these factors alter the subjective conditions of his experience of the drink sufficiently that he can now appreciate scotch as a delicious beverage, rather than cringing at its harsh taste. (Indeed, the very qualities that caused this harshness are now perceived by Oscar as genuine positives – e.g., the strong flavor of the beverage might now be interpreted as a pleasing warmth.) All of this alteration has been accomplished without any objective change in the scotch itself; it is the same drink and continues to affect his body in the same ways. What has changed, however, is his own valuative stance; Oscar has made himself into the sort of person who is able to appreciate the positive values of scotch, precisely because he was able to see that value in more limited ways from the very beginnings of his experience.

Of course, returning to our previous considerations in the case of the Bert and Ernie example, it must be noted that we can say relatively little from an abstract perspective about the actual value of Oscar's *transition* from a person with distaste for scotch to an aficionado of the drink. It can naturally be said that this transition has led Oscar to a less *limited* conception of the value of scotch than he had previously attained, at least in certain respects. We might even call Oscar's valuative development here the "education of his palate," a term which seems to imply that the transition should be thought of in terms of improvement, or even as possessing a certain degree of normativity. Nevertheless, as long as we stick to the level of purely apodictic evidence, no such normative claims can be allowed to stand. Just as Oscar's developing palate has unlocked for him the possibility of having certain (positive) valuative encounters with scotch that had previously been unavailable, he has also closed himself off to other such possibilities; it no longer remains possible for him to experience the same distaste for scotch as he once did.[30] While the move from experiencing scotch as a harsh and nigh-undrinkable beverage to grasping it as a delicious and worthwhile drink might ordinarily be understood as an improvement – and while such a claim might even be justifiable on the basis of merely adequate evidence, since many do in fact find this sort of gustatory development to have a positive value – there is nothing to be discovered within the intrinsic structures of these values themselves that could justify this perspective. Only on the basis of some already-adopted valuative perspective, such as the one that Oscar inhabits when he listens to his friends rave about scotch's many virtues, can a judgment be made at all about the overall value of changing one's own perspective.

In any case, this example sheds a great deal of light on the connection between values and subjectivity in general. The case of Oscar's evolving perspective on scotch demonstrates vividly just how much of an impact subjective conditions can have on valuative experience, i.e., on the valuable things that are the only possible way for us to apprehend values themselves. The valuative character of scotch, in this case, is largely dependent on the experiential perspective – broadly interpreted – from which the perceiving subject approaches the drink. For a certain sort of person, unused to the harsh taste of the beverage, scotch can be an object of immense disvalue, its disagreeableness preventing him from attaining any really positive perspective on it on the sensual level. Nonetheless, that disagreeableness, as we have seen, can be bound up with all sorts of other, more positive values – whether non-sensual values that are simultaneously experienced by the subject or other values that are seen only in reflection from a third party. Given the adaptations that these other values might call forth, the disagreeableness of scotch can, over time, fade into its precise opposite.

All of these alterations – as momentous as they might be – are accomplished without any genuine change in the scotch itself, understood as the object of Oscar's experience, or in the values themselves. Agreeableness and disagreeableness mean the same thing whether or not they happen to be attached to a particular object for a particular subject; they condition the consciousnesses that do encounter them in the same ways, they draw those consciousnesses on to the same sorts of acts, etc. But any experience must necessarily consist of both its objective and its subjective components, and a shift in the latter can change the whole experience just as dramatically as a shift in the former. We may not be able to tell from a detached, phenomenological perspective just what valuative relation a particular object might bear towards a specific individual, but we can surely give an account of what these various sorts of valuation mean in general. This task, while perhaps less glamorous than more grandiose theorists might desire, is quite useful nevertheless.

4.7 The Subjective Structures of Valuation: A Descriptive Phenomenology

With this understanding of values and the way that they interact with experiencing subjects through their connection to valuable things in mind, what, if anything, can we say about valuative life as a whole? This question is rather tricky to answer in light of the tremendous variability of valuative experience that has been our focus throughout this chapter. We can know, for instance, how values function in general: that they condition conscious experiences by granting the valuable things to which they are attached their peculiarly affective character, by drawing consciousness towards or pushing it away from those objects and situations, etc. We can know also how each particular value functions in its own unique way: we can understand the difference between values and disvalues, between aesthetic values and moral values, or between particular values within these categories, e.g., between the deliciousness of a beverage and that of a bite of food. That is, we can know the various structures that govern these different values, such as how moral values are associated with emotions like shame in a way that other sorts of values are not.

150 Values and Subjectivity

We cannot, however, know in the same way, or with the same transcendental certainty, which particular objects or situations in the world are going to be the *bearers* of these values for any given subject or in what rank those values will be ordered. That latter fact does not entail that phenomenology must remain totally silent with respect to such questions – a phenomenology of values would be a rather pointless enterprise if we could make no claims in this sphere whatsoever – but it does mean that we must think of such claims in a very different way than those we have made previously. Namely, it is only by moving away from the gold standard of genuinely apodictic evidence and into the realm of adequacy that many of the particular questions we might want to ask about our valuative lives become amenable to investigation.

So, bearing in mind both the preceding account of the relationship between values and valuing subjects as well as the distinction between the apodictic and the adequate, I should be able to say at least something worthwhile about the actual content of particular valuative experiences – even while I acknowledge that whatever claims I make here will be grounded on merely adequate evidence. While it is certainly true that the way in which values are experienced exhibits tremendous variability, both with respect to the different sorts of values that are possible to experience and to the wide variety of experiencing subjects, there are some general claims that I can make about such experiences without straying far from phenomenological rigor. Most notably, value-experiences rarely exhibit a totally chaotic sort of variability; while such experiences do change over time and among different subjects, these changes almost always follow certain regular patterns. In particular, the last section of this chapter will make the following claims: that value-experiences are generally quite stable over time, that they can be traced back to previous events in the subject's lived experience to uncover a process of ongoing development, and that different subjects within a common culture, therefore, frequently hold similar sets of values.[31] Based on these overarching criteria, it should also be possible in the future to make more specific claims about the ways in which the objects we encounter in our everyday lives are experienced as valuable – e.g., the claim that scotch lends itself most easily to experiences of sensual values, whether positive or negative, or that the act of educating one's palate to appreciate its virtues is one that rarely goes unrewarded.

To begin making these claims, I must start from the fact that our valuative experiences do indeed exhibit constant change (even if this fact appears to contradict the first point to be made in this section). As demonstrated throughout this chapter, it is perfectly possible – even commonplace – for the objects and situations that are experienced as valuable by a particular individual to bring forth different values over time as a result of changes in the subjective components of valuation. One day, Oscar experiences scotch as disvaluable, another day as valuable (in opposing ways, no less). Values vary over time, they vary for different individuals at the same time (as seen from the case of Bert and Ernie at the museum), and they are related to valuable objects in a complicated, hard-to-unravel mess (e.g., Aloysius' experience of adultery as simultaneously agreeable and immoral). Indeed, this variability goes so far as to extend to the relative ordering of values themselves, revealed through the ways in which they are experienced. In many cases, for example, an individual might hold that the values of morality are *more important* or *higher* than those of sensual pleasure and pain; Aloysius certainly holds this position when he is on his knees at prayer. And yet, he continues to engage in the act of adultery nevertheless, thereby revealing himself to be more attracted to the pleasure of the act than he is repelled by its immorality.[32] Oscar seems to judge the aesthetic elegance of scotch, combined with its reflected deliciousness, as outweighing the immediate distaste he feels for the harshness of the drink – but it is an easy task to imagine another man who perceives this relationship differently and never sets out to acquire a taste for the beverage.

Indeed, this variability goes so far as to blur the line between positive value and disvalue. While we commonly associate values like beauty and pleasure with the good, identifying them as positive values (and, accordingly, associate ugliness and pain with the bad, thereby making them into disvalues), this relationship does not obtain in all cases. There are indeed situations in which these values undergo shifts with respect to their goodness or badness: for instance, the phenomenon of attraction to the grotesque (a famous example in philosophical history, going back to Plato's use of Leontius' perverse desire to look at a pile of corpses in the *Republic*). In such cases, the ordinarily negative value of ugliness is functioning as a positive value (even if there are other, perhaps opposing values operative as well in the situation, as in the case of Plato's example).[33] All particular values, and even category-values like beauty or agreeableness, are subject to these sorts of shifts, which cannot be predicted ahead of time.[34] Accordingly, it would be ridiculous to assert that values as they are experienced are totally stable or can be classified according to some pre-established hierarchy, or even that we could know with any certainty what sorts of shifts they will undergo.[35] Contra Scheler (see, e.g., pp. 88ff. of his *Formalism*) the act of *preference* – say, for one value over another – can never be carried out totally *a priori*; even if there is an essential stratification of valuative experiences (a "stratification of emotional life," in Scheler's terms), the subjective elements of those experiences ensure that this stratification remains wholly unpredictable.[36] This claim holds true even if pure values do contain *a priori* structures when abstracted from actual experience.

Nevertheless, the shifts in rank and order that values undergo are not themselves completely chaotic. Despite the fact that they seem, on the surface, to come and go as they please, closer observation reveals that they do follow certain established patterns of variation (at least in most cases, but recall that this claim is based only on *adequate* evidence). Very rarely does an individual experience a situation in which the values that she perceives in the world around her undergo a total alteration.[37] If an individual experiences lima beans as an agreeable taste on Tuesday, for instance, she will almost always continue to enjoy the taste on Wednesday. Certainly, room must be made for shifts in these values to occur; it is perfectly possible for that same individual, having abstained from lima beans for years, to find that she no longer enjoys them when she does come to eat them again. We have even seen already how these alterations of taste can be accomplished purposefully, as with Oscar and his scotch. Nonetheless, the fact that there is an extended period of time over which this alteration takes place is indicative of the fact that values do not simply shift wantonly about in our experience of the world; for the most part, they remain the same day after day, even if they do shift over longer periods of time.

Granted, there do exist situations in which the values that an individual encounters in the world seem to be overturned completely, situations in which the individual wakes to find himself confronted by a world that no longer has the affective meaning for him that it once did (but rather a new kind of affective meaning – discounting situations of, e.g., depression, which are often characterized by a slow leaching away of values in general). The most obvious example of such an occurrence is that of religious conversion, as in the case of Saul of Tarsus on the road to Damascus. Prior to his supposed encounter with divinity, Saul saw great disvalue in Christianity, Christ, and so forth; afterwards – after an almost immediate occurrence – he (now more commonly known as the apostle Paul) saw such tremendous value there that he became one of the foremost advocates of the religion.

It cannot be denied that, on occasions like this one, shifts in values can strike without warning, accomplishing almost total renovations of the whole valuative schema of an individual's world. Nonetheless, such extreme instances are all the more notable for their rarity. Conversion experiences stand out to us precisely because they are an unusual occurrence in everyday life. The fact that they do occur from time to time does not disprove the general validity of the observation that shifts in valuative consciousness usually take place over a longer period of time; they are, as it were, the exception that proves the rule. While these exceptions certainly speak to the fact that my claims here are not absolutely certain, I have already admitted as much by classifying this sort of conclusion as based on merely adequate evidence. The basic observation remains useful nonetheless.

Not only do shifts in values, when they occur, usually take place over a longer period of time, these shifts also (for the most part) follow discernable patterns, thereby permitting the phenomenologist who studies them to trace out a path of ongoing valuative development in the experience of any given individual. That is, just as the world of things that are experienced as valuable does not regularly undergo a total renovation for a particular individual, the changes that do occur within it most frequently happen *for specific reasons*. When Oscar's value-intuition of scotch shifts from disvalue to value, it is plain to see that the causes of this alteration lie in his previous apprehension of scotch as an elegant drink, his awareness of the reflected sensual value of the beverage from his associates' praise of it, the actions that he takes on the basis of that awareness, etc. The change by no means proceeds *ex nihilo*. Again, this evidence is only adequate, and not completely certain: there do indeed exist examples of shifts in valuation that are by no means so easily traced back to previous experiences or actions carried out by the valuing subject, shifts that seem to arise from nowhere. The conversion of Saul may well be such an example; his vision on the road to Damascus seems essentially impossible to predict ahead of time, and the massive changes in his valuative life would be difficult to fit into any story of ongoing development – at least, without appeal to a miraculous *deus ex machina*. Nonetheless, the general fact that values do evolve in this comprehensible way in nearly all cases is well established, as before, by the highly unusual character of such occurrences.

The insight that the valuative experiences of an individual tend to evolve through such processes of ongoing development can be usefully related to claims made in other regions of phenomenology. In particular, Husserl's notion of sedimentation within consciousness gives us a handy way of accounting for many of these processes. For Husserl, the meaning of a given phenomenon does not always remain the same over time. Instead, that meaning can be enhanced – can be given new "strata" – when the individual experiencing it has been shaped in the particular ways that are required to unlock those strata. His common example is that of an old Roman milestone. The layman, encountering such a stone in the midst of a walk, might experience it as nothing more than a slab of rock standing (perhaps annoyingly or uncomfortably) in his way. An individual who knew his history, however, and who was therefore aware of the historical significance of the stone, would immediately encounter this object *as* a Roman milestone; this new layer of meaning would be accessible to him in a way that it was not to the layman, precisely because he had been educated in a way that the layman had not. This sedimentation is always, as well, a genetic process; it is always possible for the layman to undergo the process of development by which the experiential content "Roman milestone" would become, for him, an integral part of his experience of this strange standing stone in the middle of his walk.[38] This is a central component of our experience; without it, our encounters with the world around us would be limited to their merely surface-level content, while sedimentation allows our experiences of the world to attain their full richness.

The same sort of process can be said to apply to our valuative experiences. This parallel can easily be seen in the example of Oscar and the acquisition of taste. As a result of his repeated exposure to scotch, the value of deliciousness becomes sedimented in Oscar's experience of the beverage (thereby replacing its previous disvalue of harshness, albeit in ways that maintain the overall tenor of his sensual experience – e.g., the disvalue of harshness is translated into a somewhat corresponding value of warmth). A similar genetic story can thus be told in this case to that of the layman who comes to grasp the Roman milestone as what it truly is. Perhaps an even more obvious example lies in another instance of acculturation: a somewhat unsophisticated individual who comes to appreciate the beauty of opera. When she first encounters the genre, she does not understand the language, the generic conventions at play, the artistic technique at work in the singing, etc. But, as she learns more and more about opera as such, her experiences of operatic performances reveal to her new strata of valuative content. Even if she had initially experienced the opera as beautiful in a rough, crude way, this process of ongoing development opens up for her new dimensions of beauty and greater depths of appreciation. Such a process is nearly always operative in our valuative experiences – again, even if there are exceptions that prove the rule.

Finally, the fact that the valuative experiences of a given individual tend to follow these recognizable patterns also hints at one more useful claim that can – with adequate evidence – be made about valuation in general: that subjects in similar circumstances and with similar subjective characteristics, such as subjects from the same culture or tribe, will, in most cases, experience values in similar ways. Much of what shapes the way in which we experience values is, judging from the previous two points, contingent on the factors that shape the experiencing individual's own valuative perspective: his upbringing, his education, and so on. But many, if not most, of these factors are themselves embedded in the vast nexus that we term culture. Only a culture that studies the ancient history of the west would be capable of instilling in its adherents the experience of a Roman milestone, for instance, and only a culture that held up opera as a worthwhile form of artistic expression would grant its adherents access to the sort of education that would enable them to appreciate the beauty of that genre to the fullest extent (even if its potential value, aesthetic or otherwise, could be appreciated in other ways without such education).

As such, culture – and related factors – have a tremendous role to play in shaping what particular things a given individual will experience as valuable, and in what ways.[39] Individuals within a culture will thus tend to have similar sets of values. This claim is obvious with respect to systems of morality. Few people in modernity would consider the life of a deformed child to be so disvaluable as to warrant infanticide through exposure, but such practices were common (relatively speaking) in many places in the ancient world – to use a particularly egregious example of a shift in valuation.[40] Within a given culture, there tends to be a rather small set of values that are common throughout the population (i.e., the Overton window), a set that shifts only slowly and ponderously.

As with all the other claims made in this section, the culture-dependence of value-experience is prone to exceptions. There will always be instances of individuals who reject or reformulate the typical values of their society, just as there are individuals who undergo dramatic conversion experiences. The deeply motivated serial killer, the fanatical revolutionary, and the founder of a new religion all tend to be examples of such an individual.[41] Indeed, it is very often the case that it is only through such individuals that the valuative framework of a given society can be altered. Consider the founding of a new religion: for instance, Christianity. Prior to the emergence of the religion, the values of the local people are oriented in a particular direction, far removed from the tenets of the new belief-system. And yet, there emerge people – Christ and his disciples, in the case of Christianity – who defy this basic system of values in numerous ways.[42] Although such a difference with the culture at large frequently leads to conflict – for instance, the crucifixion of Christ, the persecution of early Christians, etc. – it can also be the case that the new religion catches on and spreads through the surrounding culture like wildfire. Such a spread does not destroy the values experienced by the converting public; rather, it introduces them to new valuative possibilities that had previously remained closed to them (while also foreclosing on some of those they had previously experienced). So, as with all of these claims, the evidence that members of a common culture will share a closely related set of values is subject to exceptions. And yet, once again, the exceptions merely support the general validity of the claim: Christ and his disciples, as with any great architects of new values, are remembered precisely because they differed from the ordinary run of humanity. Most people follow in the footsteps of their culture, and this fact can tell the careful phenomenologist quite a lot about the ways in which they experience the world of values – even if the conclusions that he draws based on such an assumption must always remain open to further revision.

4.8 Conclusions: Some Things Change, Some Remain the Same

This chapter has focused on giving an account of the historically troublesome fact that values seem simultaneously to be stable, discrete entities capable of being analyzed on their own terms, and yet to exhibit a tremendous level of variation with respect to the way that they appear in the world. This seeming contradiction can be explained by the distinction between values as a whole and pure values; pure values do not themselves change, but their connections to the valuable things that they condition can and do vary widely. Much of this variation is attributable to the changing perspectives of the individuals who perceive values in the world. Bert and Ernie have different personalities and different expectations of an aesthetic experience, and so the encounter that each has with *Persistence of Memory* varies accordingly from one of beauty to one of ugliness. It was even demonstrated, in the case of Oscar and the acquisition of a taste for scotch, how such a variation can be carried out purposefully – and even some of the valuative considerations that might motivate such a shift were discussed (though a full discussion of this point must wait for the next chapter).

Accordingly, while a great deal of transcendental validity can be said about the structures governing valuation in general, the particular values that exist, and so forth, it is impossible to make statements of the same certainty about values as they are experienced through valuable things in the world. That is not to say that no claims about the latter can be made whatsoever – to do so is the ultimate objective of a phenomenology of values – but merely that any such claims must be based on merely adequate, rather than apodictic evidence. They are no less important for that fact, however. The purpose of the transcendental claims made here, apart from their inherent value towards developing our understanding of consciousness in general, is to be able to support philosophical inquiries into the actual givenness of values in lived experience. After having resolved the traditionally vexing question of the supposed subjectivity of values, phenomenologists from here on should be in a good position to carry out these inquiries on the basis of this theoretical exploration of the phenomenology of values in general.

Notes

1 Of course, from a phenomenological perspective, such detachment would not be an appropriate characterization of objects either, which must be thought of specifically as the objects of *intentions*. But this fact is more obvious in the case of horizon-consciousness.
2 The fact that many of his previous admirers – in many cases under the banner of the so-called realist phenomenology of Adolf Reinach – broke away from Husserl after the transcendental turn that followed the *Logical Investigations* (a text that these mutineers wanted to remain the centerpiece of phenomenological inquiry) is emblematic of this debate.
3 The translations of this text in the present project are taken from the 2019 translation by Sebastian Luft and Thane Naberhaus; see Bibliography for details.
4 As Wenjing Cai puts it, what is "self-given in apodictic evidence is not merely the object itself, but rather the impossibility of its non-being" (20)
5 Indeed, this need for apodicticity has been a running thread throughout this project, e.g., my argument in Chapter 1 that Husserl's reduction of valuative

Values and Subjectivity 157

acts to the structures of reason alone relied on the unwarranted (i.e., dubitable) assumption that one single set of structures applied to all regions of consciousness whatsoever. If phenomenology is to be a transcendental *science*, such assumptions must be rejected. As Crowell notes, "only if all assumptions about the nature of mental processes that go beyond how they present themselves in intuitive *Evidenz* were put out of play, could the apodictic grasp of intentional states count as philosophically presuppositionless. The demands on philosophical cognition require that it be based on 'pure' insight, borrowing no interpretive assumptions from other sciences or daily life" (86). See also Hobbs 2020, especially pp. 343ff., for further discussion of Husserl's views on the connection between science and apodicticity.

6 Indeed, even many of those who hold to other models of valuation must grapple with this fact. Hartmann, for instance, despite his claims about the existence of an internal, objective hierarchy of values, acknowledges the difficulty of fitting that hierarchy into a completely developed system (see, for instance, Chapter XXXIV of Volume II of his *Ethics*, appropriately entitled "The Lack of Systematic Structure"). It is obvious to even the most cursory glance at values and value-experiences that they exhibit a vast and troublesome variety, which complicates – though it does not entirely frustrate – any attempt to gain knowledge about them.

7 In the *Ideas*, for instance, Husserl writes that "a distinction should be made between assertoric [i.e. the sort of evidence that admits of being adequate] and apodictic evidence; and the term intellectual seeing should be used, as before, to designate this apodicticity" (§137, 330). A similar distinction obtains in the *Cartesian Meditations*.

8 As S. Kwakman writes, the content given by adequate evidence always possesses an "anticipatory or presumptive aspect" that "means a lack of apodicticity, which affects our belief in the world and in its existence. Its in-itself being never becomes an absolute truth; rather it remains like an open question or like an ideal ... Yet, for that very reason, it keeps impelling consciousness forward to new efforts" (548).

9 This claim agrees with that reached by Theodorou in his exploration of the possibility of carrying out Husserl's phenomenology of values to the fullest: "value is the very *existentio-praxially significance that the value-bearer is felt to have for me as existing and acting person*" (2014a, 80). I agree with this formulation in the main.

10 That is, values are never a direct part of our experience if we set aside phenomenological investigations like the present project. While such inquiries do essentially take abstracted elements of experience as their direct objects – a fact that just goes to show the tremendously insightful character of Husserl's methodology – they do not claim to be concrete examinations of reality as such, but abstractions from the lifeworld that are intended to help us understand in more detail the various structures by which that world is constituted.

11 Husserl makes a similar distinction to that which I draw here between values as such and value-for. In the late ethics lectures, for example, he points out the difference between the value of a sonata and the value that an individual might experience when that sonata is represented, as he puts it, in a concert. He terms the value of the sonata, which is "supertemporal" and remains same in every possible representation, an "ideal value," while the value of the particular, temporally localized concert is a "real value," by contrast (see *Hua* XXXVII, 69f.). By the time of writing the texts composing the *Grenzprobleme*, Husserl prefers the terms "objective value" and "subjective

value" for this distinction. Nonetheless, I will use my own terminology for these concepts, for a variety of reasons. In the first place, Husserl's distinction between "real" and "ideal" values is potentially misleading, since it fails to capture the difference between pure values as conscious structures and value-for as the concrete implementation of those structures that lies at the heart of the distinction. The same applies to the terms "subjective" and "objective" that Husserl later adopts, with the further difficulty that any talk of "subjective values" could lead to the purely subjectivist interpretation that this model of the phenomenology of values opposes entirely. In addition, Husserl's use of these terms is based on his quasi-rationalist and incomplete model of values as a whole, which I have already rejected, as well as bound up with his specifically ethical speculation in the *Grenzprobleme*. While Husserl's insights in this regard are certainly illuminating, I maintain that it is vital to attain a greater level of clarity in our thought about values than would be possible were I to adopt Husserl's methodologically inconsistent and incompletely developed terminology.

12 These subjective elements are essential to any notion of the horizon whatsoever. Cf. Ramirez: "a horizon is the intentional process through which objects or profiles in a given situation appear in such a way that the profile still to come is already anticipated or prefigured in relationship to the object or profile presently in focus, *and this is chiefly due to our habitualities and past similar experiences*" (98, emphasis added).

13 I should point out that, at this juncture, I am discussing only variations among *individual* subjects. The possibility that there might be *collective* subjects who also experience values (and whose peculiarities could therefore affect the ways in which these values are given) is an interesting one, but beyond the scope of the present investigation. In general, I incline towards the view (expressed, for one, by Hartmann – see pp. 106ff. of Volume II of his *Ethics*) that individuals are, at least, the primary or initial subjects of values per se. Nonetheless, given the fact that this question relies on several contentious issues in phenomenology as a whole – the ontological status of a supposedly collective subject, the relationship between this subject and the individual subjects of which it is composed, etc. – I will not deal with it any further in this book. The model of valuative consciousness that I am developing here should remain the same in either case.

14 Conversely, there are also certain physiological states – caused by psychoactive drugs, for example – that could render a subject *more* open to certain types of valuative experience. This requirement for valuative consciousness is more of a continuum than a simple dichotomy.

15 I do not claim that this requirement is necessarily in effect for the optimization of *all* modes of aesthetic appreciation; such questions are a matter for a dedicated phenomenology of aesthetics. Certainly, there are other forms of aesthetic experience that are only heightened by the fact that they seem to strike "out of the blue," as it were. My use of this example is intended merely to elucidate the nature of such valuative requirements in general, and not to give an all-encompassing account of aesthetic consciousness as such.

16 This is not to say that the experiencing subject must be *explicitly aware* of which elements of the painting attract or repel him. Cf. Scheler: "we can possess with *full* evidence the values of the object *without* its being given to us with the same degree of evidence or with the same degree of fullness in its 'meaning' ... We can, for example, possess with full evidence the beauty of a poem or a painting without being able to say to which *factors* this value is attached, e.g., color, design, composition, rhythm, musical characteristics,

speech-values, picture-values, etc." (196). Of course, the possibility of broadening an encounter with such an object later through a more detailed analysis remains open to the experiencing subject, but such an explicit investigation is unnecessary for him to be able to *feel* the object's value.

17 Scheler, although his own conception of values differs quite radically from the horizon-model, makes this point quite clear: "It clearly follows that *value-qualities* do not change with the changes in things. It is not true that the color blue becomes red when a blue sphere becomes red. Neither is it true that values become affected in their order when their bearers change in value ... The value of friendship is not affected if my friend turns out to be a false friend and betrays me" (19).

18 This claim leaves open as well the possibility that more can be said about the particular values attached to valuable things from a standpoint that admits into the discussion evidence that is merely adequate. But this point will be addressed more fully later in this chapter.

19 Indeed, Hartmann supports this claim in his arguments against Scheler's more fully hierarchical model of values, despite his own insistence that values can ultimately be thought of in terms of an essential and objective (though somewhat loose) hierarchy. As he writes, "it is clear to anyone who has gained insight into the valuational realm, that the manifoldness of values is too great to embrace in a linear arrangement the intervals corresponding to their differences of content. The values would need to overflow continually into one another, which by no means corresponds to their actual and often very abrupt articulation, that is, to their difference given in the sense of value" (50). I, of course, take this argument farther than does Hartmann, but his basic point – that the ways in which values are given cannot be accounted for in so simple a manner – is well taken.

20 Of course, it is certainly possible – and even reasonable – for Bert himself to claim that Ernie is perceiving the painting's value incorrectly, not to mention for Ernie to claim the same about his friend, given that they already occupy certain (conflicting) valuative perspectives. We might even be able to make further claims about the "real value" of the painting once we make the move from the level of apodicticity to that of mere adequacy; there certainly seems to be at least some evidence for the painting's beauty in light of its widely positive critical reception. I will discuss similar possibilities further later in this chapter. Nevertheless, it is crucial to note that a claim of this sort is only possible on the basis of adopting some particular valuative perspective or other, whether that occupied by Bert or Ernie or simply one that is justified on the basis of something like the merely adequate evidence of the painting's historical reception. At the level of pure eidetic structures, no such claim is meaningful.

21 This conception of the optimum, in which it refers to the existence of an optimal perspective only in particular contexts, has clear parallels with Husserl's discussion of the notion of the optimum in the field of perceptual experiences. Cf., for example, the end of §4 of his "Analyses Concerning Passive Synthesis," pp. 60ff. in the Steinbock translation.

22 Of course, it is far less difficult to understand how some values could be associated with a painting than others. It is easy to see how *Persistence of Memory* might be encountered as beautiful or ugly, for instance, but if one wanted to imagine how a visual encounter with the painting could be seen as the bearer of certain types of *sensual* values or disvalues, one might be forced to imagine something like a perceiving subject afflicted by an unusual form of synesthesia. At any rate, these considerations must be dealt with at the level

of adequate evidence; the essential structures of valuation itself that can be known apodictically have little to say about questions of this sort.

23 Husserl's example of these attitudes is that of the botanist who is also prone to appreciate the aesthetic beauty of the flowers that he studies. Depending on whether he is presently inhabiting the attitude of the scientist or that of the flower-lover, the beauty of a particular flower will be given to him with greater or lesser intensity (as compared, for instance, to the value it might have as an interesting object of scientific investigation). As Husserl writes

> I may be, as a botanist, delighted by the beauty of a flower, but this delight is not the main action, when I am in the attitude of getting to know it in observation and determining it in classification. Once I am finished with [observing and determining], then, in turn, instead of the theoretical attitude, now the aesthetical joy, which went alongside, may become the main action; and hence I am now in the aesthetic attitude, in that of the heart, instead of in the theoretical attitude, that of the understanding.
> (*Hua* VIII, 101)

24 That is, I am not considering here situations in which there is a major alteration in a subject, to the extent that it is debatable whether or not she remains "the same person" – e.g., conversion experiences and the like. Those situations are certainly deserving of phenomenological investigation, but my present task is to examine a less unusual case to illuminate certain details about the connection between subjectivity and values in general. Many of my conclusions here should remain applicable in those more extreme scenarios, even if they require further investigation in their own right.

25 For instance, it would be quite difficult – to say the least – for an individual to experience the positive sensual value of pleasant coolness that lies in the act of burying one's feet in the sand on a hot day if he had previously undergone a trauma severing the nervous system that conducts such sensations to the brain.

26 Scotch, for example, is often the drink of choice for those with stomach problems. It is perfectly possible that someone might choose to switch from other alcohols to scotch, even if he did not care for the taste at first, for this reason.

27 That is not to say that Oscar does not genuinely experience an encounter with a positive value here. But the positive value that draws him towards his subsequent actions, in this context, does not lie in the scotch itself, but rather in his "as-if" encounter with a future *possibility*. As Scheler makes clear, such a valuative encounter with a not-yet-existent (i.e., not yet *real*, though potentially *imagined*) object is not an unusual occurrence: "For it is not true that value-statements pertain only to existing objects, though they can pertain *also* to them ... Hence one can attribute a factual value to non-factual contents. For example, that a competent man rather than an incompetent man should be the minister has, as a state of affairs, a value, even if the competent man is not in fact the minister" (185).

28 Note that this example also opens up the possibility for phenomenological insights about *inter*subjectivity to be brought into the realm of values. Although I will not dwell on this aspect of value-consciousness in any great detail, the relationship between intersubjectivity and values (e.g., through *fellow-feeling* or *empathy*) has long been a major topic of interest for phenomenologists from the very beginnings of the discipline. See Ferran's "Affective Intentionality" for further discussion of this topic (in particular,

of its treatment by Scheler). This aspect of value-consciousness is certainly deserving of further inquiry, to be carried out in the future on the basis of this fundamental investigation into valuative consciousness as a whole.

29 This distinction is not novel to this project. Hartmann makes a similar point in Volume II of his *Ethics*, noting that "the act of preference is not limited to cases where a number of values is given explicitly. There is also a mere suggestion of the related value in a specific consciousness of a direction upwards or downwards, which from the beginning accompanies the discernment of a special value. Likewise in preference the fact can be present that 'here a higher value exists than the one sensed' – and, indeed, without this higher value itself being in the content of the feeling" (II, 62). We often pursue such dimly-seen values, even if they are not themselves explicitly present to our consciousness.

30 Indeed, this example reveals one of the basic structures of valuative consciousness as such. Although, as we have seen, all values require certain valuative perspectives in order to be encountered in the first place, any such perspective also always has the effect of closing off other valuative possibilities once it is adopted. This constant opening and closing of possible value-experiences cannot ever be avoided in its entirety.

31 Note that only the outlines of these points can be made in this book. The purpose of the present project is to uncover the essential structures of valuation in general in order to lay the groundwork for more detailed investigations into the phenomenology of particular values and value-experiences; my primary focus, therefore, will remain on what is capable of apodictic justification in the realm of values. The present section is intended merely as an example of the sort of work that can be carried out on the basis of this project, and not as an exhaustive investigation in its own right.

32 This point will be developed further and justified more thoroughly in the following chapter.

33 This sort of shift can also function in reverse, or with other sorts of values. I am particularly reminded of a line from *Fight Club*: "I felt like destroying something beautiful." This line reveals a strange desire to get rid of or push away a value (beauty) ordinarily experienced as positive – a reaction clearly associated with disvalues and the bad.

34 Indeed, the only values that are *not* subject to such alterations are the good and the bad themselves. But this is only the case since these capstone values are absolutely the most general values possible, representing only the structural attraction and repulsion that are central to the notion of value itself, while remaining devoid of any content absent their connection to more particular values. The fact that they do not alter in the context of experience is not a sign of any special status they possess, but rather a reminder that they function only at a high level of generality, and require other, more alterable values to unlock their true meaning.

35 The contrary inclination towards valuative hierarchy is a tempting one for any axiologist. Even Husserl himself, although it is his insights that inspired the horizon-model of values that avoids such problems, seems inclined towards such a view at times. For instance, in the *Kaizō* articles, he attempts to make a distinction between values ranked according to preference and according to their "objective altitude." (His example is that of a power-hungry man who prefers the goods of his station to the "objectively higher" good of love for his neighbor; see *Hua* XXVII, 27ff.) Nonetheless, this claim cannot stand up to rigorous scrutiny. There is no way to make sense of the claim that the "height" of a value in this sense, i.e., that of its "worthiness" to be preferred, might be distinct from the value's actually *being* preferred – that is, apart from the

untenable object-model, which might account for such "objective altitude" as a legitimate property of value-objects. On the horizon-model, the existence of values is bound up with their effects on consciousness; their "height," accordingly, is entirely a function of the relationships among the values themselves, the valuable objects to which they are connected, and the individuals who actually experience them (and so is not separable from the acts of *e*valuation that those individuals carry out).

36 I thus reject (in part) what De Monticelli previously asserted as the third "principle" of a phenomenologically acceptable theory of value: that our valuative and emotional lives have "a structure of layers ('stratification'), corresponding (or claiming to correspond) to an objective hierarchy of value-spheres" (2016, 391). That our valuative experience exhibits an essential stratification, with certain values grasped as higher or lower, more or less forceful than others in various contexts, is not to be put into dispute. But the further, rather Schelerian claim that this stratification corresponds to an objectively fixed hierarchy, of whatever sort, fails to account for both the subjective component of value-intuition that this chapter discusses as well as the vast and constantly changing diversity actually experienced throughout our valuative lives (as seen, e.g., in the examples used here). As such, this principle fails to meet the essential phenomenological challenge of returning to the things themselves, as we really experience them. Granted, De Monticelli does introduce the principle with a great deal of nuance and points towards the need for further discussion; for instance, she notes in a somewhat Hartmannian move that "[i]t does not say that there is a complete, objective ordering of values, but of their *types* – of value spheres" (2016, 392). But even this weaker version of the claim still insists that, at least at some level, the valuative components of our experience are in themselves answerable to a fixed and unchanging hierarchy, a hierarchy that is ultimately indifferent to the subjects who experience those values, a point which runs afoul of the critique put forth in this chapter.

37 Thus, even if there is no objective hierarchy among values themselves, De Monticelli's portrayal of the essentially orderly progression of our valuative experiences can still hold true *in practice* or *for the most part*: "Our emotional life is not at all chaotic, nor is it an unstructured flow of 'states'" (2016, 393). She refers to the existence of "motivational chains" as evidence of this point, which I have no intention of disputing when understood in this more limited way.

38 It is important to note that his merely being aware of the fact that such things as Roman milestones exist is by no means sufficient to attain this level of sedimentation. Just after having learned of their existence, he might well realize what the stone is, but it would not be an *immediate* part of his experience; first, he would encounter the stone, and only afterwards remark to himself that it was a Roman milestone. Sedimentation obtains only when the content of a Roman milestone becomes such a habitual part of the individual's experience that it is an immediate feature of his encounter with the stone – a wholly different and more holistic process than a judgment after the fact.

39 Indeed, within the framework of phenomenological axiology, De Monticelli goes so far as to raise the possibility of defining a "civilization" itself "in terms of the value-commitments it fosters and encourages, or as a *tradition of values*," which seems to me to be essentially on the mark, though perhaps only as part of the story (2018, 346).

40 Indeed, the vast gulf between the value-systems of the ancient world and those of modernity serves as an excellent example of this point. Much of Nietzsche's work on the ideas of master and slave morality, for example, can be thought of as an attempt to spell out the conditions in which values have undergone a major shift in the history of the west – at least from a phenomenological perspective, whether or not the historical Nietzsche himself would agree with this characterization.

41 Again, a good example of a philosopher whose work exemplifies such a tendency is Nietzsche – the notion of a transvaluation of all values fits in nicely here.

42 Of course, it is helpful if such figures arise in a time when there are multiple competing value systems or great turmoil among the populace in general, as indeed was the case for the rise of Christianity. But these conditions are irrelevant to the point at hand; the fact is, such contrary individuals do arise in all sorts of circumstances, even if in some more than others.

5 Values and Volition

5.1 Values and the Will: An Overview

By this point in the investigation, this project has developed a plausible idea of what values as such are, the ways in which they are connected to valuable things in the world, and the role that subjectivity plays in valuative experiences. However, one major element of the role that values play in our lives remains unexamined. Namely, how are values connected to the acts of volition that they seem to inspire? Returning to Husserl's tripartite division of experience into the three modes of intellectual consciousness, valuative consciousness, and volitional consciousness, we can immediately see that there are essential points of contact between each of these modes despite their independent and *sui generis* structures. It has been made clear already how valuative experiences are connected to those of intellectual perception; although these two sorts of acts stem from two radically different modes of consciousness, they are nevertheless linked by the fact that values are given horizontally with respect to perceived objects or situations. Similarly, values must be connected in some way with the third and final mode of consciousness, that of volition – but in a very different manner.

It is already apparent that values are defined in part by their propensity to lead the consciousness that encounters them on towards further conscious acts. The claim of this chapter will be that the acts towards which values and value-experiences point can, in the main, be identified as acts of volition. Values call the experiencing subject to *react* to the things with which they are connected in such a way as to draw those things nearer to himself (in the case of positive values) or to push them away (in the case of disvalues). Further, it will be argued that this connection is inherent to the nature of valuative and volitional acts; values *essentially* provoke corresponding acts of volition, while the latter require some value-intuition as their basis. This point will ultimately enable me to prove in more detail my previous claim that all experience is thoroughgoingly valuable in character, that no act of consciousness whatsoever can be carried out without some connection to a value. Intellection, valuation, and volition

DOI: 10.4324/9781003202189-6

are all intimately connected with one another, even if they must be separated from one another as the objects of phenomenological inquiry. Accordingly, it is not my purpose in this chapter to deliver anything like a full-fledged phenomenological ethics or even a full account of the conscious structures underlying acts of volition. My goal here is simply to point out and examine one further essential characteristic of valuative consciousness that, like those discussed previously in this project, plays a tremendous role in shaping our everyday experiences of the world.

Of course, it is imperative to be very clear from the outset of this argument just what is meant by the term "volitional act." This term must be understood in a technical, phenomenological sense, without interference from other common definitions of the phrase. As the third mode of consciousness in Husserl's tripartite division, volition refers to all acts through which the ego thrusts itself forward in the world, actively changing its experiential perspective and drawing itself towards further experiential possibilities. Even though every movement of consciousness involves both a subject- and object-pole, the origin or focal point of those acts differs between volitional acts and other acts of consciousness. In the case of perception, for instance, or of value-intuition, it is the perceived object or value that initiates the act, *giving itself* to consciousness in a certain way. With volitional acts, on the other hand, it is consciousness itself that gives rise to the act; even if a volitional act is ultimately aimed towards objects, it is the ego that takes the leading role. Husserl describes this relationship as a creative one, in which the willing consciousness directs itself towards its objects imperiously, with an assertive "*fiat!*" – an "*es werde!*" or a "let it be done!" As he writes in the early ethics lectures, "consciousness does not say, after a fashion, 'it will be, and thus I will it;' but rather 'because I will it, it shall be.' In other words, the will speaks its creative 'let it be!'" (*Hua* XXVIII, 107).

In this light, volitional acts must not be reduced to acts of "free choice," as the term might often be interpreted. Such a notion of the "free will" is entirely tangential to this mode of consciousness as such, and should be bracketed for the purposes of the present investigation (even if it represents an interesting area of inquiry in its own right). Volitional acts, to put it simply, can be thought of as "act-initiating" acts, where the first "act" is understood in an ordinary sense rather than in its specialized phenomenological meaning. Volition as a category covers all the creative acts by which an individual moves about and accomplishes things in the world, rather than merely becoming aware of or experiencing them.[1]

5.2 Values on the Horizon: The Motivation of Volition

To begin this investigation, let us return to the idea that values lie on the horizons of other conscious acts and attempt to spell out in more detail just what that fact entails. To narrow the investigation, let us focus in particular on our third example: the case of Aloysius and his propensity to commit adultery. Recall the outlines of the example: Aloysius, a devout man who is nevertheless susceptible to the weaknesses of the flesh, is faced with the opportunity to cheat on his wife with another woman. This situation – the hotel room, the woman, his sexual anticipation, etc. – exhibits a great deal of value for Aloysius, both positive and negative. It is obvious from his reaction to the situation (and especially from his subsequent *actions*, which will be the real focus of this chapter) that he experiences the act of adultery as the bearer of positive sensual values. The anticipation and the deed itself are all quite *agreeable* to him, given their connections to an interlocking series of subsidiary values that account for the pleasantness of the act, its specifically sexual character, etc.

And yet, these sensual values are not all that there is to his experience. After completing such an act, Aloysius is, according to the thought experiment, always struck by immense guilt, wringing his hands and praying for forgiveness. These subsequent actions are explicable only if the act of adultery also bears for him the disvalue of immorality (again, subdivided into its constituent components – he might experience adultery as a mortal sin rather than a venial sin, as being more or less grave than other immoral acts, etc., all of which can be thought of as stemming from different subsidiary values within the general realm of immorality). Indeed, to press this point even further, the act of adultery might, for Aloysius, be connected to other sorts of values as well, e.g., to some sort of spiritual disvalue to account for the fact that he might envision his adultery as going against what he sees as the sacred character of the marital bond. Nonetheless, I will focus in the following discussion primarily on the contrasting sensual and moral values connected to this act, in order to keep the example as clear and concise as possible.

The connection between all of these varying values and the single situation of a night of adultery are, of course, quite explicable in terms of the model of valuative consciousness that has been laid out throughout this project. The pure values of agreeableness, of immorality, and all of the subsidiary values involved bring to bear certain experiential structures on Aloysius' encounter with his mistress (e.g., making it both simultaneously pleasurable and agonizing, albeit in different ways). The fact that both positive values and disvalues are in play simultaneously in this experience is no difficulty, since they are not contradictory values; sensually, the experience is totally rewarding for Aloysius (at least in this formulation of the thought experiment; we could also imagine there being certain sensual disvalues mixed into his experience, e.g., if there were a loose bedspring poking him during the act – though even this disvalue would not contradict the general agreeableness of his situation), while morally it is a complete catastrophe.[2] All of the values that are horizontally embedded within his experience of the situation combine to give the act of adultery its unique character for him. It is these values that go beyond a merely physical description of the act, highlighting the truly affective dimensions of his experience as a whole. All of this follows precisely the pattern laid out in previous chapters.

And yet, there remains much of importance about Aloysius' repeated forays into adultery that must be investigated if one is truly to understand the nature of his experience. Namely, this project must account for the fact that Aloysius' experience of adultery is by no means a purely passive one. Sleeping with a woman other than his wife (and subsequently falling to his knees in remorse) is not simply something that happens *to* him, but rather something that he *does*. Aloysius' purposeful activity here – his volitional activity, as opposed to the mere "conscious acts" of perception or value-intuition – is certainly not detached from his valuative experience of the situation.[3] Even from the layman's standpoint, this fact is plain to see. If another person were to ask Aloysius, after the deed had been completed, why he had done it (perhaps in response to his overt shows of remorse for the act), it is easy to imagine Aloysius responding that he simply could not help himself, as the pleasure (i.e., in valuative terms, the sensual agreeableness of the act) was too great. Similarly, if one asked him the reason for his great shows of sorrow for his actions, he might well respond: the act was a sin, i.e., a bearer of the disvalue of immorality. These responses are illuminating, even if Aloysius himself would not phrase them in the explicitly valuative terms that I will use here. It is scarcely to be doubted that there are important connections between the values that we find in the world and our subsequent actions within that world. Nevertheless, the precise character of these connections requires closer investigation, in order that the various structures that govern them might be uncovered.

Let us begin this inquiry by considering the precise way in which, as demonstrated, values are related to the valuable things that they govern – that is, horizontally. For Aloysius, the act of adultery has on its horizons the competing values of agreeableness, immorality, etc. Part of what that fact entails is, of course, the particular affective character of his experience; he encounters adultery in a way very different from someone who had no moral qualms about it, for instance. However, that valuative character is not the only component of Aloysius' experience. He does not merely *observe* an act that bears certain values, but *reacts* to the situation in which he finds himself. That is, he is simultaneously drawn towards the act of adultery – he willingly (even enthusiastically) participates in it – and repelled from it, as evidenced by the moral trepidation with which he approaches the act, his subsequent remorse, etc. This simultaneous attraction and repulsion can be traced back to the nature of the relevant values themselves; positive values, leading ultimately back to the good, are attractors, and disvalues, pointing towards the bad, are points of repulsion. But the necessary counterparts of that attraction and repulsion are the *volitional acts* that they inspire: the act of committing adultery on the one hand and that of regretting it on the other. Values are not impotent with respect to the subjects who perceive them; they give rise to acts of volition that correspond to their particular valuative types (and indeed, as I will argue later in this chapter, they are themselves required in order for those volitional acts to take place).

If values are horizonal, then they are defined by their propensity to give rise to further acts of consciousness. The backside of an object gives rise to the possibility of turning the object around or moving around it to perceive it from that new perspective. In the case of values, the conscious acts towards which they lead always include the acts of volition by means of which the valuing subject either embraces or casts away the things to which the values are connected. Consider the situation in which Aloysius stands in a seedy hotel room, contemplating his intention of committing adultery. He finds himself in circumstances that both attract and repel him, in different ways. On the one hand, he considers the very agreeable sensory pleasure he would get from consummating his desires. This value calls him forward, urging him to cast aside his hesitation and sate his appetites. In response to this call, his knees weaken, he looks onto his mistress with lust, and ultimately he gives into his desires and sleeps with the woman. On the other hand, his apprehension of the moral disvalue of the act has its own effects on his actions. It pushes him away from the deed that he so desperately wants to commit. Perhaps he recoils from the thought of the act, his crisis of conscience manifesting itself physically as he steps back from the bed and clutches his brow in anguish or grits his teeth to bear the guilt that he knows is soon to emerge. Certainly, this disvalue leads to the actions he takes later in the day, as he is driven to visit his local church, to fall to his knees, and to beg his deity for forgiveness. In each case, the act to which the value-horizon of the situation leads is one of volition: Aloysius is brought to certain volitional acts that correspond to each of the varying values that he experiences in that hotel room (and, in novel ways, to the combination thereof).

Values thus have their effects on the world through the volitional acts to which they give rise. In this sense, volitional acts themselves can be thought of as, in part, the activity of values in the world; only through such acts can values make themselves manifest in their real essence, by fulfilling through an appropriate response the attraction and repulsion that are essential to the nature of values as such. Nonetheless, this relationship by no means entails that values dominate or eclipse the individual consciousnesses that carry out these volitional acts. Individual agents are absolutely required for values to make themselves manifest in this way, and – as seen in the previous chapter – subjective conditions on the part of the experiencing ego can have a dramatic effect on the way in which those values are expressed. In Hartmann's terms, the individual consciousness is the "mediator" between value and actuality. "Values," as he notes, "do not, like ontological laws, irresistibly force their way through, subjecting everything actual to themselves ... Only where a being is found which takes hold upon the requirement of the Ought and commits itself thereto, does the ideal law begin to press into the realm of the actual" (III, 21). This assessment is essentially correct, even if Hartmann has a rather different interpretation of what values themselves are: consciousness mediates between a perceived value and the world around itself by moving to actualize positive values (e.g., Aloysius' decision to engage in the agreeable act of adultery) and to destroy or nullify negative ones (e.g., his subsequent attempts to "wash away his sins" through remorse and contrition).[4] The individual acting ego ("man," as Hartmann refers to it) is thus an indispensable component of the relationship between value and reality; without an experiencing consciousness to carry out the volitional acts that they inspire, values are nothing more than an abstract object of study.

Any given value, therefore, can only be fully realized in the connection between an experiencing subject's acts of value-intuition and his subsequent volitional actions. This claim can be generalized as a claim about the essential structures that underlie those modes of consciousness. To each particular value that an individual experiences corresponds a certain reaction (or range of reactions, since our response to values can vary over time and between persons just as much as the valuable things themselves) that is appropriate, at least from that individual's perspective, to the object or situation through which she encounters those values. These actions can be subjected to more particular investigations that are parallel to the phenomenologies of specific values; each value will call forth a different sort of volitional act, even if the precise act that is generated by such a value will also depend on the subjective characteristics of the *re*acting subject. Once again, these more particular investigations represent the long, slow work that lies ahead of phenomenology once these theoretical questions about the connection between values and volition in general have been given a solid answer.

5.3 Values and Volition: An Essential Connection

Nonetheless, certain basic claims about these value-inspired actions can be made despite the very great variability that they exhibit. For instance, the actions that are generated by values that serve as *positive* values within an individual's experience are always intended to bring those values and the experiencing subject closer together. We pursue the positive values that we encounter in the world in the only way that we can: through acts that lessen the distance (in the broadest possible sense of the term) between ourselves and the valuable things through which we encounter them. In contrast, values functioning as disvalues function in quite the opposite way, giving rise to acts that attempt to shove the disvaluable object away or to make it recede in the subject's consciousness.

170 *Values and Volition*

(The particular way in which experiencing subjects pursue these goals is, of course, quite variable.) We aspire to positive values, aiming to make them a greater part of our lives, and just the opposite for disvalues.

Once this basic operation of values on volition has been understood, it is easy to see how any given instance of valuative experience follows this pattern. To run through our previous examples: Bert finds *Persistence of Memory* to be of great (positive) aesthetic value, and so he draws nearer to it, basking in the beauty of the piece. He takes a break from his exploration of the museum to stand in aesthetic contemplation of the work. Perhaps he even purchases a print of the painting to take home with him in an attempt to preserve something of the beauty of his experience – and so on. Ernie, on the other hand, finding the painting to be ugly instead of beautiful, turns his back to the piece, he encourages his friend to accompany him to another exhibit, he rejects the possibility of an experience of aesthetic contemplation in favor of one of (intellectual) critique, etc. In each case, the two men are reacting to the value given to them by the painting; their volitional actions can be traced back to their encounter with beauty, with ugliness, and with their subsidiary values.

The case is just the same for Oscar and his scotch. He finds the act of drinking scotch to be disvaluable in one way, through its disagreeable harshness, and so recoils from the taste at first sip. Just the same, he also finds the drink to be of positive value, through his experience of it as an elegant beverage (and, in a more mediated way, through the fact that he sees the reflected sensual value of scotch in his associates' praise of the drink; he encounters positive value in the *possibility* of such an experience, even if he does not directly encounter the sensual value of the drink itself at this point in time). Accordingly, he acts in such a way as to bring those positive values closer to himself – namely, by removing the impediments that prevent him from ascertaining the genuine deliciousness of scotch. Without such a motivation, Oscar's subsequent actions would remain entirely inexplicable – particularly in light of the sensual *dis*value that he so clearly sees in scotch at the beginning of the example. Once the volitional effects of valuative consciousness are understood, however, every action that an individual might take with respect to a valuable thing suddenly makes sense as a response to some (perhaps quite complex) set of experienced values.

Nonetheless, a purely descriptive account of the way in which many of the particular values that we could consider are connected to acts of volition is not sufficient for our present purposes. I am making a much stronger claim here: that values and valuative acts *as such* are intrinsically and unavoidably connected to corresponding acts of volition. This is a transcendental claim, ostensibly based on apodictic evidence, and so requires further justification than a mere catalogue of instances of such a connection can provide. Rather, this claim must appeal to the essential nature of values if it is to uncover the deep roots of this connection in the structures of consciousness themselves. Recall that values, on the horizon-model, can never truly be said to exist as the objects of consciousness; they do not give themselves to a perceiving consciousness directly. Instead, as discussed previously, values are known only through the effects that they have on valuative consciousness. Indeed, they cannot truly be said to exist at all apart from those effects. Values are structures of consciousness, separate from any individual ego, certainly, but not genuinely separate from egoic activity as such. Values *are* what they *do*, and they have no meaning if considered to be static entities abstracted from their effects on conscious life.

But what is required for the phenomenologist to explicate the effects on conscious life that are so essential to the notion of values in general? It is clear that some of these effects take the form of certain affective qualities that give rise to emotional experiences: the soothing character of an agreeable experience or the psychological discomfort of an immoral one, for example. But surely that is not all that must be said about the matter. It is scarcely possible to imagine a scenario in which an individual completely fails to *re*act in any way to a valuative situation – at least, without some other value overriding that reaction. What would it mean, for example, for an individual to find himself faced with an object of positive value – a pleasing sensation, say – and not desire to bask in or prolong the feelings it inspires in him, acting in such a way as to accomplish that goal? Values are, in essence, attractors and repulsors, but those terms are meaningless without reference to something (i.e., some ego) that is attracted to them or repelled from them; values do not merely exist in the abstract, but rather "are *experientially* efficacious or motivating" (Scheler 247). That is to say, values have an inherent intentionality that cannot be understood without reference to the ways in which they give rise to volitional acts on the part of those who encounter them.[5]

Of course, pure values, as structures of consciousness, can certainly be considered phenomenologically without reference to the particular volitional acts that they inspire. But, as shown, these pure values are mere abstractions when considered in isolation from valuable things and value-experiences. Even if pure values represent "mere" attraction and repulsion in all of their various forms, those terms require instantiation in conscious acts in order to be meaningful at all; *values as such*, values as a whole, must exercise their powers of attraction and repulsion over some consciousness in particular if they are to have any concrete significance.[6] Granted, such instances of attraction and repulsion are not accomplished through any physical movement – beauty does not actually reach out of a painting and draw those who perceive it closer to itself, like a vacuum that pulls in everything around it – but rather must be thought of as movements of consciousness, and specifically movements of *volition*. Although the beauty of *Persistence of Memory* cannot drag Bert closer to the painting by exercising some mystical force, Bert might well feel as if that were the case. Seeing the painting from across the room, he might well feel himself compelled to cross the intervening space to get a closer look. (Ernie, in contrast, might feel compelled to close his eyes, to walk away, and so on, if his revulsion for the painting were strong enough.) Values do and must function in this way; without the intrinsic capability of inspiring such movements, their fundamental structures as attractors and repulsors would make no sense.

Naturally, the power of these values to inspire acts of volition in those who encounter them is not without its limits. There are many situations in which an individual could find himself faced with a positive value and yet refrain from pursuing it – or, for that matter, a negative value from which he does not flee. On the surface, the existence of such instances would seem to disprove the claim that values inherently (and invariably) lead to corresponding volitional acts. However, that counterargument falls apart once it is realized that these failures to pursue or to flee experienced values are always the result of the interference of other, opposing values that ultimately outweigh the values that are seemingly ignored. Many of the complexities of the myriad ways in which we react to values can be resolved by careful attention to the ways in which valuable things and the values that they bear compete with one another to condition the actions of the individuals who encounter them.

The example of Aloysius and his guilt over adultery supports this point quite well.[7] On one level, as noted, the act of adultery bears for Aloysius a highly negative value – indeed, to such a degree that his indulgence in the act causes him to weep, to fall to his knees, to feel the pain of grief, and so on. And yet, he engages in the act regardless of this disvalue. If the immorality of adultery from Aloysius' perspective were all that one could say about the matter, this would indeed be a puzzling fact; who engages in an act that he knows will only bring about an increase in disvalue, that will make the world a worse place for him overall? But other vectors of valuation are in play in this situation, as mentioned earlier. In addition to the disvalue of immorality, the situation as Aloysius sees it is also the bearer of the positive value of sensual agreeableness. From his actions, it is clear that this sensual delight, which lies specifically in the pleasure he receives while committing the act, is a greater value for him than the disvalue of immorality. He does not commit adultery *because* it is immoral; that is a factor that weighs on the negative side of the balance when he makes his decision. It is simply the fact that there are other factors on the positive side of the scale to provide a counterbalance to this disvalue. Indeed, his ultimate reaction to the situation, taken as a whole, is only explicable on the assumption that *both* of these values are conjoined in conditioning his volitional actions; the agreeableness of the deed explains the fact that he does succumb to temptation, while its immorality serves to account for his remorse afterwards. The relative strengths of these two values provide a set of guidelines that render these actions comprehensible, where otherwise they would seem utterly senseless. Certainly, the decision to commit an act of adultery that – as Aloysius knows ahead of time – will lead to great remorse is not a rational one! Once again, the specific structures of valuative consciousness (and now those of volitional consciousness as well) are required to explain this unique form of experience.

5.4 The Value of Living: Values and the Lifeworld

This central point – the claim that values are inextricably connected to the volitional acts that they inspire – is also a major part of the justification of a claim made previously in this book: that values are an essential part of conscious life, and that every experience whatsoever contains valuative elements when considered in its fullness. If the preceding arguments are correct, and volitional acts really are tied to the acts of valuation that inspire them, then the entirety of our volitional lives can be traced back to some (smaller or larger) set of valuative experiences. For each particular volitional act that we might commit – and certainly these volitional acts are themselves absolutely central to our everyday lives – there must be some value or set of values that inspired it.[8] Without such values, there would be no genuine reason for us to do anything at all; any supposed choices that are not informed by values would be meaningless arbitry (i.e., *Willkür*).[9] We do what we do in pursuit of positive values, or as an attempt to distance ourselves from disvalues, and these reactions to our valuative experiences are the sum total of our volitional acts.[10] Accordingly, if we are to react to any object of our experience whatsoever – if such an object is to mean anything at all for our lives – then it must be given with some value or set of values that can serve as the foundation for an appropriate volitional act.[11] Given that we do, in fact, live in a world rife with such meaning, the thoroughgoingly valuable character of our conscious lives cannot credibly be denied.

Let us imagine certain particular situations in order to demonstrate how the preceding claim might be justified. Certainly, the examples used previously in this text lend themselves well to this interpretation of volitional acts. Bert and Ernie's respective reactions to *Persistence of Memory* are clearly informed by the values, positive or negative, that they experience as part of the painting. The same goes for Oscar and his developing relationship with scotch; both the distaste for the drink that he initially displays and his ultimate acquisition of the relevant taste can be traced back to the complex set of values that inform his encounters with the beverage. If we were to inquire into the motivations that could inspire him to indulge regularly in a drink that he finds distasteful, the only possible explanation for such an act would be a valuative one – i.e., he sees some positive value in the act that outweighs its corresponding disvalues. Lastly, the case of Aloysius and his guilty pleasure certainly requires this interpretation. How could we make sense of his constant wavering back and forth between his physical attraction to the act of adultery and his moral abhorrence for it without appealing to the competing values that this act had in his eyes? What would motivate a man like Aloysius to commit such an act, knowing full well the consequences that it will have on his conscience, other than some positive value too strong to be swept aside? Only when the propensity of values to demand action of one sort or another is taken into account can we render intelligible the whole nexus of behaviors in which we engage throughout our daily lives.

Of course, some might make a counterargument to this claim. It could, for instance, be asserted that, while such motivation by values is certainly applicable to many instances of volitional action, including all of those used in our examples, it is not a characteristic of *all* action whatsoever. Correspondingly, the counter-claim could also be made that not all values necessarily lead to volitional action; perhaps there exist some values that could be experienced by an individual without leading him to any particular volitional act. Each of these possibilities must be considered in turn if the main point of this chapter is to be established with apodictic certainty: that there exists an intrinsic and ineliminable connection between acts of valuation and those of the will – as well as between all of those acts and the acts of intellectual consciousness – and that none of these acts can ultimately be imagined without the others (except for phenomenological exploration of their separate structures in abstraction).

Let us begin by confronting the first of these counterarguments: the claim that there could exist some volitional act in no way connected to any act of value-intuition. Perhaps many, even most, of our volitional acts are done in pursuit of or flight from certain values, one might claim, but *some* such acts can be accomplished "for the sake of nothing" or "for their own sakes." To this assertion, the proper rebuttal is to demand an example of such an act, an example that cannot, upon closer investigation, be revealed as the reaction to one sort of value or another. If no such example is forthcoming – if, indeed, any attempt to formulate such an example can ultimately be accounted for as the end result of some instance of value-consciousness – then this is solid evidence that valueless volition is inconceivable, especially in light of the preceding analysis of the connection between the two.

Coming up with possible examples of an act of valueless volition is a more difficult task than it might initially appear. Most acts that an individual might claim to commit for their own sakes have an obvious connection to some value or set of values upon closer inspection. For instance, if someone were to go for a walk, having no particular reason in mind, it would be easy to trace her unrecognized motivations for this activity to the values that the walk, her surroundings, etc., bear for her: perhaps she experiences the cool breeze on her route as agreeable, for example, or finds the scenery along the way to be beautiful. These values, even if she is not actively thinking about them when she decides to take a walk in the first place, certainly play a major role in inspiring that decision.[12] The same could be said for many other similar examples; values do not have to be a patent or thematic component of an individual's choices to be the source of her volitional acts.

Perhaps, though, we could locate instead some act that genuinely has no value, positive or negative, inspiring it – some act that would in no way be understood by an individual to bring him closer to a positive value (or to protect him from a negative value). A possible example of such an act comes to mind: an individual begins, absent-mindedly, to draw aimlessly on the page in front of him during a lecture, church service, or similar event. It seems likely that such an individual would not find much of value in this act of doodling. Certainly, there would be little patent consciousness of value in the act; it is perfectly possible to be surprised by the fact that one has drawn all over a page without one's explicit awareness. But, likewise, there does not seem to be much value in the process at all at first glance, even implicitly. The individual does not engage in the act out of any desire to produce beauty, but simply to pass the time. Similarly, it is unlikely that most such individuals would be distressed in any way if forced to cease the activity; they would not see themselves as giving up anything of value by such a cessation. Perhaps here, the opponent of the present theory might claim, lies an example of an act connected in no way to any felt value.

And yet, on careful examination, value can be found within even this seemingly valueless experience. After all, the individual in question must have *some* motivation behind his choice to draw (rather than, say, to daydream, to stare out the window, to stretch his legs, and so on), *even if that motivation remains concealed from him.*[13] Perhaps the act of doodling is a sensually agreeable sensation for him by keeping his hands and part of his mind occupied, when otherwise they might be uncomfortably stagnant. Perhaps, on the other hand, the act represents for him an *escape* from the disvalue of the lecture or service; it permits him to "tune out" what may be, for him, a disvaluable experience (e.g., a tedious experience, an unpleasant one if the speaker has an annoying voice, etc.). There are numerous possible explanations of such an act, all of which – it is important to note – appeal to some valuative component. Without such a component, we would be reduced to claiming that such acts are *entirely inexplicable*, reducing them to the arbitry rejected above. Such an explanation would be vastly inferior in terms of its explanatory power to the simple claim that some (perhaps hidden) value can be found within any such experience.

Nevertheless, perhaps a more explicit argument for the impossibility of this kind of arbitry is warranted here. Such an argument can indeed be given, on the grounds that motivation (and particularly *valuative* motivation) is an implicit component of the very notion of volitional action itself. In the end, it is only by a comparison of values that such volition can be produced at all. Values, and particularly some value or set of values that is given as superior to all other such sets in a particular context, are necessary to explain why it is that an individual chooses to carry out a specific volitional act. To illustrate this point, let us turn to a famous example in the history of philosophy: that of Buridan's ass. Specifically, let us focus on the version of this problem (not the original) that is described as follows: an ass, suffering from hunger, stands equidistant from two identical piles of hay.[14] It is stipulated in this thought experiment that there is no difference between the two piles, either descriptively (save for their respective places, one on the donkey's right and one on his left) or valuatively; the ass understands each of them to be equally delicious, equally easy to reach, and so forth. The consequence of such a condition, the argument goes, is that the ass will starve to death. He has available to him the sustenance that would both prevent such a fate and satisfy his desire to pursue the values that he perceives in each of the piles of hay, but, there being no *reason* for him to choose one pile over the other, he cannot make up his mind which direction to turn. For our purposes, we may say that the ass lacks an essential condition of volitional action: the presence of one set of values that wins out above all others, and so is capable of inspiring the willful action that would prevent his untimely death.[15]

Of course, this scenario of Buridan's ass is not one that ever does or could occur in reality. It has often been presented as a paradox, crying out for some manner of resolution that would find the error in the formulation of the problem. Many have suggested a solution in the form of a radically free will, a will unconditioned by *any* external factors, which could simply select one or the other pile of hay rather capriciously. This is not, however, a satisfactory resolution; it devolves into the kind of mere arbitry that would leave us wholly unable to explain *why* experiencing subjects make particular choices.[16] Instead, what this example shows in the context of the horizon-model of values is that volitional acts are necessarily based on the predominance of some value or set of values in an individual's experience. If this were not the case, if no value-experiences obtained to found an individual's choices, no decision could be made at all – the ass would starve to death. This would remain the case either if the individual had somehow encountered two perfectly equal sets of values, as with Buridan's ass, *or if* he lacked the value-experiences that would make his volitional act meaningful entirely.

Nonetheless, this example functions perfectly well as a *reductio ad absurdum* for the claim that volitional acts can be separated from the valuative acts that motivate them. No ass – much less a human being – would starve himself to death simply because he could not make his mind up about which way to turn.[17] The impossibility of Buridan's ass lies in the fact that one pile of hay must necessarily be of greater value than the other – even if it is simply because the donkey finds turning his head to the right to be slightly easier than turning to the left, or some other such subjective condition. The fact about volitional consciousness revealed by such an example is that this mode of consciousness is only possible when based on one or another predominant value; without such a grounding, there is no basis on which to accomplish a volitional action at all without resorting to mere arbitry.[18] These considerations thus rule out the first counterargument to the claim that valuation and volition are essentially connected; there is no such thing as a volitional act that is not linked to a value.

The second possible counterargument, however, remains unaddressed. Even if volitional acts are necessarily motivated by valuative ones, the possibility persists that there could exist some value-intuitions that do not themselves inspire acts of volition.[19] Perhaps, that is, the connection between values and volition goes in only one direction. On this model, it would be possible for a value to be given to an individual through value-intuition that, nevertheless, did not impel her towards any particular actions with respect to the valuable thing by means of which she encounters it – a value that left her cold, as it were, with no attraction towards or repulsion from the valuable thing in question, or at least none that results in volitional action.[20]

As an example, let us imagine that a friend of both Bert and Ernie – I shall call him Grover – similarly encounters *Persistence of Memory* in the museum. He glances at the painting briefly, then walks away. When asked later about his experience of the painting, he acknowledges that he found it to be beautiful, but denies that this value had any ramifications on his subsequent actions. "I admit that the painting has value," he might say, "but it had no effect on me." In such a situation, the encounter with a value of some sort seems evident – and yet, the subsequent volitional acts intended to bring that value closer, which positive values are supposed to inspire, are entirely lacking. Perhaps this example reveals a break between value and volition, such that the two are not necessarily always intertwined.

Nevertheless, this counterargument must be rejected as well, for reasons much like those of its predecessor: it fails to account for the strict identity of experientially grasped values with the motivations of our volitional actions. In any situation, even one as apparently mundane as that of Grover and *Persistence of Memory*, we are able to trace out volitional acts that owe their motivation entirely to a set of given values – whether or not the individual who commits such an act acknowledges this link. There are a number of possibilities that might explain why Grover reacts in the way that he does to the painting, and so account for the fact that his response to it is so much more subdued than that of either of his friends. Perhaps, as an obvious solution, Grover is simply prevaricating about the value he experiences in the painting. It is by no means an unknown phenomenon that an individual will claim to enjoy something (i.e., to find value of some sort in it) that he really finds to be trivial or inconsequential. Grover certainly does not want to get a reputation as a philistine, for instance, so he might well claim that he sees the beauty in an acknowledged masterpiece without that beauty being a genuine component of his experience. Indeed, he might well even perceive a sort of reflected value in the painting – i.e., he might understand *the fact that* others experience the painting as beautiful, in the same way that Oscar encounters the deliciousness of scotch through his friends' descriptions – without ever encountering that value through an act of genuine value-intuition. In this case, his claim that he acknowledges *Persistence as Memory* as an object of beauty would not even be a lie, but rather a different way of using valuative language; he understands the beauty of the painting as a *descriptive fact* of intellectual consciousness, and not through the first-level encounter that occurs through specifically valuative consciousness.

Furthermore, it is not even necessary for Grover to lie or equivocate about his experience of value for his reaction to the painting to be genuinely grounded on a value-experience. For one, values can be given with greater and lesser intensity, depending on the experiential perspective of the individual who encounters them. It may be that Grover does indeed find the painting to be beautiful, but only to a very slight degree. In this case, his attraction towards the painting – i.e., that aspect of the painting that should inspire him to attempt to make it a more central part of his experience by approaching it, by lingering in aesthetic contemplation, etc. – could quite easily by overridden by other values he might encounter. Perhaps he experiences the museum as a whole in a way conditioned by the disvalue of tedium, and his desire to hurry through his visit outweighs his lesser inclination to observe *Persistence of Memory* more closely. Perhaps he is hungry, and the sensual disvalue of that plight is sufficient to blunt any motivation he might have to engage in aesthetic contemplation. And there are any number of other possible explanations, all of which can be carried out in purely valuative terms.

It is important at this point to remember that particular values are not tied to *specific* volitional acts, but to *corresponding* volitional acts. The former claim would require that each value be associated on a one-for-one basis with a certain response, such that all individuals who encountered that value would necessarily react in the same way. Given that any value can be experienced in a wide variety of possible ways due to subjective changes in the valuative experience as a whole (as discussed in Chapter 4), this assertion would clearly be ridiculous. Rather, the connection between values and volition is a simple one: positive values attract and disvalues repel, in ways that are conditioned both by the specific structures of the value in question and by the subjective components of the way in which that value is experienced. Values do inspire volitional acts, and they do so in ways that are generally comprehensible in light of the particular values in question, but the acts in which they result can vary widely among different persons and in different situations. Grover's more subdued response as compared with the enthusiastic appreciation of Bert is by no means conclusive evidence that the former does not react to the set of values that he encounters in the painting at all.

On the other hand, it is also possible that Grover himself is mistaken about his value-experience of the painting. It is certainly not an uncommon occurrence for an individual to *believe* that he values certain things in ways that are contradictory to his actual experience. After all, if we can be deceived about what we perceive through visual experience – e.g., mistaking a mannequin in a store window for a lady – there is no reason why we should not be similarly credulous with respect to value-intuition. Perhaps Grover has fooled himself into believing that he experiences *Persistence of Memory* as beautiful – perhaps even for the same reasons as mentioned above, i.e., that he understands that *other people* or *society in general* find this work to be a masterpiece and mistakenly attributes those sentiments to himself as well – while he really experiences the painting as having little aesthetic value, or even being a bit tiresome. In this case, the contrast between his immediate reaction to the painting and his later description of that experience is entirely understandable; he reacts in the moment to the (lack of) value that he perceives in the painting, while he refers later to his mistaken belief about his experience. It is unnecessary to attribute either malice or deceptive intent to Grover in this situation when the self-ignorance that is common to us all presents itself as a perfectly viable explanation.

Indeed, it is often the case that we only discover such deceptive or misleading values through a close examination of the volitional actions that are supposedly committed in response to them. As humans, we are often particularly good at lying to ourselves about what we value (among other things), and particularly about what we value most (or more than something else). For instance, take the case of Aloysius and his adulterous ways that has been discussed throughout this chapter. Aloysius certainly experiences both value and disvalue in the act, as is obvious from his subsequent actions, and he would certainly admit as much if he were to answer honestly. But it is perfectly possible to imagine him, after the fact, perhaps while confessing to a religious figure or a friend, claiming that the guilt he experiences in the act of adultery is so great as to destroy any sensual value that it holds for him. That is, in our valuative terms, he would claim that the value of agreeableness that he experiences within the sexual pleasure of the act is outweighed, from his perspective, by the disvalue of immorality that is also a component of the deed (perhaps he would blame his own weakness of will or some external coercion for his actions).

Nonetheless, Aloysius' actions give the lie to his words. In the moment in which he found himself confronted by two competing values, Aloysius was clearly more attracted than repelled. In that moment, the sensual values were of greater importance to him than those of morality – as much as he might protest that ordering of values on a more level-headed occasion. And while it is surely possible for values to change over time, such that one might speculate that the moral values could *become* of greater value to him once the act has been completed and he has time to repent, part of the thought experiment is the postulation that adultery is a regular activity for Aloysius. He will return to the act again and again, despite all his protestations of morality. He can prevaricate with others about the valuative ranking of his world, and he can even lie to himself about his own experiences, but his actions always speak more loudly than his words.[21] The connection between values and volition is therefore one of the most important tools that a phenomenologist has for studying values as they are experienced; although the ways in which the two are connected are complex and multifaceted, the latter always provides at least some means of access to the former as they are instantiated within an individual's experience.[22]

The reason that such valuative judgments are possible, that we can conclude from an individual's actions what sorts of values she sees in the world, is that the inspiration of action is utterly essential to the nature of value itself. (This claim is a transcendental one, since it is a condition of the possibility of any act of valuation that it be directed towards some corresponding set of volitional actions, though it is important to point out that our conclusions about any particular individual's values from her actions will always be based on merely adequate evidence or worse. Once again, the phenomenology of values, while utterly solid when reduced to its transcendental claims, only permits of varying degrees of certainty once it is applied to individual cases.) That is to say, values simply are not values *unless*, when experienced by an individual, they necessarily influence her behavior with respect to the objects that they condition.[23] While value-consciousness itself is certainly an independent region of phenomenological study, possessed of its own unique and *sui generis* structures as discussed in Chapter 1 of this book, it can never be separated from the other modes of consciousness *in practice*.

Values exist as the foci of phenomenological observation, but what that observation always reveals is that they are defined by their existence on the horizons of an individual's experiences, calling him forth to corresponding acts of volition. This is why we can say truly that values *are what they do*; positive values are nothing more than attractors (including, of course, reference to the particular modes of their attraction so that we can distinguish, e.g., moral values from aesthetic ones) and disvalues are nothing more than points of repulsion. But the notions of attraction and repulsion as such make no sense without necessary reference to something that is attracted or repelled (something in general, speaking theoretically, though in practice that term will have to be filled in with content by some *particular* thing). In the case of values, this "something" is always an experiencing subject, since it is only these who encounter values through experience. To imagine a value without an individual to experience it, to strive towards it in an attempt to bring himself closer to that which it conditions or, conversely, to attempt to remove himself from its presence, is to imagine an empty "X" that is precisely the purely formal, utterly contentless nothing that those phenomenologists who have considered the question have rightly rejected. Indeed, the world of values as a whole is only meaningful on the supposition that it inspires individuals to willful action.[24] Values, if they are to mean anything at all, require an essential connection to volition.

5.5 The Three Modes of Consciousness: A Summation

At this point in the investigation, it should be clear how values and valuative acts fit in with the other modes of consciousness, with the intellect and with the will, at least in general terms. As argued in previous chapters, values are horizonal with respect to perceptual acts, i.e., acts that fall under the general category of the intellect. All such acts give their objects with some value or set of values attached to them, not directly as properties, but lurking on the horizon. What this horizonality entails, at first, is that the valuable things given in such perceptions (ranging from individual objects, whether real or ideal, to entire situations, or even the world as a whole) are given with a particular affective quality, shaped by the values that govern them. Beautiful objects are given as objects towards which aesthetic contemplation is appropriate, for instance, and immoral acts are accompanied by a bold "thou shalt not!" – though any further analysis of these qualities will have to wait for the phenomenological investigations of particular values and category-values that can be built on this theoretical model. The world of our perceptual experience is shaped through and through by acts of valuation that run in tandem with acts of perception; though these acts are distinct in terms of the structures according to which they shape experience, they are constantly found working together.

Of course, it is not enough to say that values are horizonal with respect to perceptual acts without specifying the sorts of acts to which they lead the experiencing subject, given that a key element of the horizon in general is its propensity to tie various acts of consciousness together, to give rise to ever new possibilities of experience (just as the planet's horizon gives rise to the possibility of traveling towards it, exploring new vistas and discovering new horizons). As demonstrated in this chapter, the ultimate aim of values is to inspire in those who encounter them the volitional acts that will bring that individual closer to the value, in the case of positive values, or drive him away from it, in the case of disvalues.

Indeed, this connection to volition is the primary way in which we can come to know values more coherently than through a pure encounter with valuable things; although these more direct encounters give us the actual content of values quite dramatically, they can also obscure the subtler gradations of such values. We know values primarily not through any direct grasp of pure values – such an understanding would be impossible, given their horizonal character – but through the effects they have in our everyday lives, including the volitional acts that they inspire. This fact entails that an awareness of the essential interconnections among all three modes of consciousness – the horizonal attachment of values to perceptual acts, and the position of volitional acts as part of the content of that horizon – is central to understanding the role that valuative consciousness plays in our lives.[25]

These essential interconnections are ultimately the only way that we can make sense of countless aspects of our everyday experience, as discussed throughout this book. Certainly, the thought of valuative consciousness without (dispassionate, intellectual) perception is meaningless *in practice*. Values can never be encountered in the absence of valuable things – pure values themselves are merely structures of experience, and not its (direct) objects – and how could such valuable things be encountered other than through the perceptual acts of sight, hearing, etc., that give them to consciousness? No element of valuative experience is to be thought of as "mystical" or "floating in the aether"; values are always embedded in the concrete world of our experience.[26] But no more can these values be omitted from experience if it is to remain in any way explicable. The link between values and volition means that all of the willful actions that we accomplish in our day-to-day lives are meaningful only on the basis of the values that inform them.[27] It is certainly not the mere act of dispassionate perception that inspires Bert to approach *Persistence of Memory* to get a better experience of it, nor the merely descriptive thought of a glass of scotch as, e.g., bearing a certain taste and texture, having a certain appearance, etc., that causes Oscar to grin and bear the discomfort of drinking it in order to produce in himself the changes that are required to appreciate it. Rather, it is only on the basis of the *values* that these men perceive in those objects that their subsequent actions make sense. It is the value with which the painting or the beverage is connected, and not merely the act of perception that gives those objects to consciousness as physical things, that gives rise to the possibility of the volitional acts that the two men carry out; there would be no question of Bert appreciating the painting if it were given to him as aesthetically mediocre (and valuable in no other way), nor of Oscar training himself to enjoy scotch if it were a merely indifferent experience for him. Values permeate our experiences, and it is only by recognizing this fact that we can make sense of the world in which those experiences take place on a philosophical level.

5.6 Values and Morality: Towards a Phenomenology of Ethics

This account of the connection between values and volition is by no means the end of possible phenomenological investigation into the matter at hand. Even at first glance, it is immediately apparent that the same breadth of investigation that lies open with respect to particular values – e.g., a phenomenology of aesthetics, of morality, of sensuality, of spirituality, and of all their subsidiary values – remains relevant in the context of volitional action. The acts that are appropriate with respect to aesthetic values are quite different from those that might obtain in response to moral values, and so on. Each of these regions remains a possible target of phenomenological exploration, and it is here that the truly practical conclusions of phenomenology will reach their apex. The present project, which focuses on the phenomenology of values in general, is a necessary component of those more specific inquiries, but it is not at all a resting point for this task. The aim of such an inquiry must always be to help us live in and understand the lifeworld, as Husserl might put it, and not to capture transcendental truths solely for the sake of philosophical exactitude (as noble as that goal might be in its own right).

Perhaps one of the greatest possibilities that lies ahead of the phenomenology of values as put forth in this book is that of delivering a full-fledged phenomenological account of moral philosophy, an account that must grapple with some of the most vexing problems of philosophy as a whole. It has long been a matter of grave concern *what an individual should do* in a given situation. Given the essential interconnection between values and volitional acts that has been laid out in this chapter, it is clear that any such moral philosophy will have to be built on top of a phenomenological account of values. What we *should* do is inextricably related to the valuable things (situations and acts, primarily) that are given to us in a particularly moral way. As such, a phenomenological exploration of morality will have to be carried out in the context of investigating what it means to pursue the morally valuable. And, indeed, the most famous attempts to carry out such a task follow precisely this pattern. For Scheler, to behave in a morally correct manner is – in an oversimplified formulation – to pursue those values which are the highest, in line with his insistence on an essential hierarchy of values. Hartmann follows much the same path, although he goes, in many ways, into greater detail about the modes in which values may be morally given – for example, distinguishing the "ideal ought-to-be" of a value from the "ought-to-do" with which it might be given to a particular individual. In all of these cases, what lies at the heart of ethical speculation is the pursuit of moral values in general (though the precise outlines of these points of view are not the proper focus for this chapter).

To see the beginnings of how a phenomenological account of moral philosophy might be carried out on *this* model of values, however, it is necessary to return to the tentative forays into this field carried out by Husserl himself (and, from there, back to Brentano's "new categorical imperative," which Husserl took up in his own work). For Brentano and Husserl, the whole content of moral philosophy – as complicated and multifarious as that discipline may be – can be summed up by the following dictum: when confronted by a choice among a number of possible actions, an individual should always choose "the best among what is attainable," i.e., he should pursue the best among all possible ends (or, more properly, those which it is practical to attain in the given context). In the abstract, of course, this is an entirely pointless statement; calling on the individual to choose "the best" action seems only to restate the basic problem of this discipline, the problem of deciding *what is best*. Nevertheless, in light of this phenomenological conception of values, the actual content of this dictum comes to light more clearly. "The best" is explicitly a valuative term. It refers to that which lies closest to the good, i.e., that which is of the greatest positive value (though perhaps, in this context, the scope of the term should be limited to that of *moral* values – a question that cannot be answered until the phenomenology of morality is carried out in its own right). To choose the best among the possible means to pursue that value which is given to the individual as "higher," as closer to the good, than all others in a given situation.[28] As such, any such claim requires something very like the account of genuinely felt values as the root of action that has been developed here; as Sonja Rinofner-Kreidl puts it in discussing Husserl's ethics as a whole: "Every person who is concerned with the practical sphere at issue has to act according to this imperative *under the condition that* she acknowledges the relevant material values" (199). While a claim of this sort would require a great deal of further explication, the basic way forward for such an account is now clear.

This conception of a phenomenological account of morality thus serves to prepare the way for a rigorous investigation of that dimension of human life, which has long proved to be a particularly troublesome area of philosophical inquiry. It neatly avoids certain problems with the ethics given by (especially) Scheler and (to a lesser extent) Hartmann – namely, the requirement for such an account to rest on an externally established hierarchy of values, which is quite a difficult point to prove, as countless moral philosophers throughout the ages have discovered. At the same time, it accounts for many of the insights delivered by these philosophers in this sphere: the reliance on varying degrees of "height" with respect to the values that we pursue, the idea that values (even moral values) can be in tension with one another, etc.

This formulation also takes into account the pattern for moral philosophy that was laid out by Husserl himself. Husserl, throughout his lifetime, constantly emphasized the need for moral philosophy to be just as rigorous a discipline as any other (a high standard indeed, coming from the great phenomenologist). He held that moral claims and duties could only be understood in their proper context once they came to be seen from a purely rational point of view (once again, in the sense of the generalized, pre-theoretical rationality that he also believed to underlie value-consciousness). That is, for Husserl, it is simply impossible for a human being to live a moral life unless and until he pursues the highest values in a completely consistent and rational manner.[29] While this quasi-rationalism cannot be maintained as fully as it was by Husserl himself on the model of values put forth in this project – though finding a replacement for this claim is a task that must be left to the phenomenology of morality itself – the basic aim of such a sentiment remains valid. Namely, an important element of any phenomenological account of moral philosophy is the need to be very clear about what values, in a given situation and for a given individual, are the highest or closest to the good, or, indeed, count as "possible" at all. Granted, as Hart notes, "we do not know in advance in the particular situation what the best is. We only know that if there are things of value a best will surface" (1990, 210–211).[30] The myriad moral questions that confront us throughout our daily lives can never, except in the broadest of terms, be answered with anything more than adequate evidence. As seen throughout this book, values can often be confusing and unclear, requiring great perspicacity to come to light; the same applies to the moral duties that are based on such values. Nonetheless, the rigor of phenomenology must be applied no less in the latter enterprise than in the former.

Of course, the phenomenology of morality is by no means a trivial task even once the phenomenology of values has been carried out. At the very least, such an account would require a detailed examination of the special structures of moral values as such, and likely of other modes of values as well. (How, for example, could we give an account of the moral substance behind Aloysius' adulterous acts if we did not have a good understanding of the sensual values that inspire them?) A phenomenological account of moral philosophy is a detailed undertaking in its own right and deserves the phenomenologist's full attention – as seen in previous attempts, such as the texts of Husserl, Scheler, and Hartmann on which this project has relied. Much work naturally remains to be done; as I have reminded the reader again and again, much of the ultimate payoff of phenomenology lies in the difficult, grinding, quotidian work of a descriptive phenomenology based on adequate evidence, and not necessarily in the theoretical work that makes such an endeavor possible in the first place. Nonetheless, the phenomenology of values remains an irreplaceable grounding for any phenomenological speculation about moral philosophy whatsoever. Now that this project has carried out a detailed analysis of values as such, the way forward towards these closely related investigations should be an easier path to take than before. At least, this is now true: this account has provided a solid idea of what is meant by the

186 *Values and Volition*

term "good," at least in its most general sense. It should now be possible to delve further into that idea, fleshing it out in various ways, applying it in the realm of morality in the form of the moral good, and so on. That, at least, is no mean accomplishment.

5.7 Conclusions: The Indispensability of Value-Consciousness

The content of this chapter stands in an unusual position with respect to this project as a whole. Much of the work accomplished herein is a necessary component of the phenomenology of values as such that this project set out to investigate. Values, as shown, are inextricably connected by their very nature to the volitional acts that they inspire. Pure values must be understood only as points of attraction and repulsion, and such a notion is meaningless without reference to that which is attracted and repelled – namely, experiencing subjects, pushed towards and pulled away from, through volitional action, the valuable things that they experience. In this sense, this chapter is an integral part of the story about values as they appear in the world that this project has set out to tell. And yet, this chapter also points towards other, quite different investigations that must be carried out in the future. Volitional action is manifestly *not* subject to the same laws as those of valuative consciousness; as a distinct mode of consciousness, it stands on its own terms. This chapter has by no means intended to carry out a detailed investigation of this mode of consciousness, which indeed would require a separate project of at least the magnitude of this whole book. Yet again, the discussion contained here is not meant as a pale substitute for any specific inquiry into another region of consciousness, into its subregions, and so on, but rather as an attempt to illuminate the ways in which these regions of consciousness are inextricably interconnected with one another.[31]

The primary point of this chapter is once again to emphasize the fact that values cannot be understood fully apart from their instantiation in the real lives of those who experience them. Values are what they are only through the individuals who react to them, who pursue them and flee from them. Just as values have no internal hierarchy in themselves, they have no real existence outside of the ways in which they structure individual experiences. They are not limited to such particular circumstances – they are conscious structures, and not mere properties – but neither can they be said to exist in total abstraction from them. On the path towards developing an accurate phenomenological understanding of values, therefore, this is yet another region of consciousness that must be examined in some detail. The preceding examination has illuminated its outlines, showing us how values can inspire volition in general and how values can be known beyond the possibility of deception only through such a connection, but the practical details of volitional consciousness itself remain to be investigated. It is enough for now, however, to rest content in the knowledge that another vital region of value-consciousness has been explored – even if, like values themselves, that region always points beyond itself to further possibilities of investigation.

Notes

1 Ullrich Melle's description of these acts in his "Husserl's Phenomenology of Willing" is particularly cogent. In brief: "In the ordinary sense, willing is directed towards something in the future that is to be actualized through a creative act. Willing can only be directed towards something in the future that is, ontologically speaking, real. It is necessarily founded in the consciousness of what is practically possible, in the consciousness of the 'I can'" (1997, 178). The category of volitional acts is comprised of all acts that are directed towards bringing about certain states of affairs in the world, rather than merely grasping that world as it is (or ought to be).

2 Of course, one could also imagine a situation in which the moral disvalue of adultery contributes, in some way, to Aloysius' sensual enjoyment of the act; the forbidden fruit may sometimes taste all the sweeter. But this is not a problem for this model of values, since we are not dealing here with a positive and a negative value of the same sort; the two can exist alongside one another and even influence each other without contradiction, since they are not strict opposites. Examining such interconnections among values is certainly a worthwhile topic for future, more specialized investigations in particular regions of value-consciousness.

3 Nor, for that matter, is it unconnected to his perceptual experience of the situation, to bring in the third mode of consciousness. After all, it would be rather difficult for Aloysius to engage in adultery at all if he could neither see, hear, nor feel his partner through some perceptual experience!

4 Indeed, most of the third volume of Hartmann's *Ethics* is devoted to exploring the consequences of this necessary mediation. Although the specifics of his thought here are not entirely relevant to the present project as a result of his adherence to the object-model of values, the work as a whole remains insightful.

5 De Monticelli identifies these two elements – the valuative and the volitional – as "two 'moments'" that are "apparent in most emotional phenomena: (a) *Being affected by* or receptivity, 'passivity,' being 'struck' or 'impressed' by something: in short, the *receptive component* of an emotional episode, a kind of perception. (b) *Being inclined to*, 'moving' to or from, drives/desires (*Strebungen*) or in short the *conative component*, the urge to action" (2016, 389). Apart from the somewhat imprecise description of value-intuition as "a kind of perception," this portrayal of these two essential components in any such experiential complex seems to me to be basically on the mark – although I maintain that they can only be understood in full when grasped as the contributions of two entirely distinct and *sui generis*, though intrinsically related, modes of consciousness.

6 Hartmann agrees with this claim: "As ideal essences, values are self-existent and need no authorization from a subject. But in the real world this self-existence does not suffice. Here for the actualization of the Ought-to-Be, issuing from values, there is need of authorization. A real subject must affirm them in contrast to what already 'is'" (I, 262).

7 As, indeed, does the case of Oscar. But I will focus for the moment on Aloysius' more poignant example.

188 *Values and Volition*

8 Cf. Husserl's claim about humanity as a whole in the *Kaizō* articles: "It furthermore belongs to the essence of human life that it constantly takes place in the form of striving; and thereby it always ultimately takes on the form of *positive* striving and is therefore directed to an achievement of *positive values*" (*Hua* XXVII, 25). I would also mention here that this striving can aim just as much at a rejection of negative values, though Husserl would not agree with this formulation (see Chapter 3 of this book).

9 The term *Willkür* is notoriously difficult to translate into English. I am indebted to Hoke Robinson for the felicitous (though admittedly somewhat archaic) term "arbitry" to serve in this role.

10 Thus, it might almost be said, mirroring the early Husserl, that acts of volition are themselves *founded* on the acts of valuation that motivate them (alongside the intellectual acts of perception that allow us to navigate the world as we exert our will). I am, however, hesitant to adopt this formulation; it seems to me that acts of volition are themselves as closely intertwined with the other types of consciousness, in a multitude of ways, as intellectual and valuative acts are with one another. I am inclined to believe that they too are reciprocally necessary, with all three modes of consciousness being ultimately *equiprimordial*. Nonetheless, such a specific claim would be a matter for a detailed phenomenology of volition, and will thus not be discussed any further here.

11 In this claim, I agree with Crowell's portrayal of Husserl's theory of volition: "Unlike perception, however, affective grasp of value has intrinsic motivational force. For Husserl, both aspects of feeling are necessary for practical intentionality [i.e., in this context, for volitional consciousness]. Without the motivating force it would be impossible to explain what distinguishes such intentionality from mere belief" (266). Crowell himself supports Heidegger's theory of volition as an advance over that of Husserl on the grounds that Heidegger's view better accounts for the centrality of what we might call instinctive or automatic actions to our everyday lives (q.v. Chapter 12 of his *Normativity and Phenomenology*), but I maintain that Husserl's late work – in particular, the *Grenzprobleme* – addresses these issues in a quite satisfactory manner. In any case, this debate is mostly immaterial to the project at hand.

12 This argument has a well-established philosophical pedigree. Variations on this claim go back at least to Aristotle's assertions in the *Nicomachean Ethics* that all actions aim at some good; even actions like relaxation that seem to be done "for their own sake" ultimately have such a purpose. (See Drummond's "Husserl's Phenomenological Axiology and Aristotelian Virtue Ethics" for an interesting discussion of the potential compatibility between phenomenology and Aristotelianism with respect to the teleology of values.) Explicating this notion of "the good" in these particularly valuative terms is a useful innovation, to be sure, but it is important to point out the historical roots of these claims in general, if only to understand how philosophy as a whole has long been more or less on the right track in investigating such matters.

13 Cf. Husserl on the difference between "rational" and "irrational" motivation (*Hua* XXXVII, 107ff). Although I do not endorse all of his claims here – in particular, I would hesitate to employ the term "rational" motivation in the context of values, as discussed in Chapter 1 of this book – the distinction that he draws between the two forms of motivation is, in general, both valid and necessary.

14 Alternatively, in some variations, the ass is equally hungry and thirsty, and so stands equidistant between a pile of hay and a pool of water. The exact formulation matters little.

15 This particular thought experiment is not, of course, the first formulation of the problem in the history of philosophy (though it may well be the best known). The conundrum, in general terms, goes back to the ancient Greeks at least. I am particularly fond of the formulation of the problem put forth in al-Ghazali's *Incoherence of the Philosophers*: "For we will suppose that there are two equal dates in front of someone gazing longingly at them, unable, however, to take both together. He will inevitably take one of them through an attribute whose function is to render a thing specific, [differentiating it] from its like" (23). Nonetheless, I have chosen to use the Buridan formulation as my primary example simply due to its enduring popularity.

16 Furthermore, I find the arguments against this kind of mere arbitry that have been delivered by many philosophers throughout the history of the discipline, from Hume to Hegel and beyond, entirely persuasive. These arguments are not, however, the proper focus of this project.

17 That is, setting aside cases of catastrophic mental illness such as extreme anxiety. But these unusual cases must be analyzed in other terms, e.g., as subjective conditions that interfere with the individual's ability to translate motivation into action, and not as evidence of a break between value and volition in general. The fact that they are the unfortunate exception, rather than the rule, is sufficient proof of this point.

18 Husserl's various models of volition action tend to agree with this claim (despite the fact that he revised these models continuously throughout his career). He writes in the late ethics lectures, for example, that "I can desire nothing and will nothing without being determined to it by something, namely determined by a previous act of valuation, and furthermore it is the same whether or not the striving is also motivated by another striving. My willing has either one ground of determination or manifold grounds of determination in certain acts of evaluation, in which lies that on the basis of which I desire or will exactly that and with exactly that meaning" (*Hua* XXXVII, 81–82). Values, he continues, are the *goal* of volition. Husserl's own employment of the phenomenological method thus leads, in this respect at least, to the same conclusion that I have drawn here: it is essential to acts of volition (whatever other qualities might be appropriate to this mode of consciousness) that they are motivated by their connection to some act or acts of valuation.

19 This is a separate argument from the claim that there could exist certain *values* that do not inspire particular acts of volition. Hartmann puts forth such a claim in his *Ethics*: "In the actional sphere of the real subject, the end [i.e., of volitional action] corresponds to what the value, behind it, is in the ideal self-existent sphere. Not every value with its material becomes the content of an end set up. For not every value is the aim of a positive Ought, and certainly not of an Ought-to-Do directed to a subject" (I, 262). There are a number of ways to interpret such a claim. On the one hand, what Hartmann says here could simply be interpreted as a reference to the fact that pure values differ, phenomenologically speaking, from value-experiences as a whole. If the claim means only that there are certain values – i.e., certain material structures of experience – that have not yet been encountered by any particular consciousness (but which could be encountered by some consciousness at a later point), then it does not contradict the horizon-model of values at all. Pure values are, as noted, abstractions when isolated from the valuative acts of which they form a major component, so they can certainly be separated from the volitional acts that they inspire for the purposes of phenomenological investigation, without thereby implying that *valuative*

consciousness as such can be separated from volition. However, Hartmann's claim could also be interpreted to mean that these "values that are not the content of an end" exist as *more* than possible structures of future conscious acts, that they exist as objects in their own right – in which case, the claim would run afoul of the criticisms of this position discussed in Chapter 2 of this book. In either case, a claim of this sort is not a threat to the viewpoint that valuative consciousness as a whole is essentially connected to volitional consciousness.

20 Although explicating the possible causes of such a reaction is not my present focus, I will note that there may be certain psychological conditions (sociopathy, for example) that could result in a person failing to be moved by the same values as others – though whether or not such a person genuinely experiences the values in question must be answered by my discussion in the following paragraphs. There are, of course, other possible explanations for this sort of behavior as well.

21 This is, of course, a classic example of Sartrean bad faith. Nonetheless, any connections between this phenomenology of values and the insights given by Sartre must be left for another project entirely.

22 Here is another useful example to support this point. Imagine that you have a friend who constantly talks about his desire to go skydiving. To listen to him, you would think that this activity held the greatest positive value within his experience: it is thrilling, laudatory, etc. One day, you happen to win two tickets to go skydiving from a contest on the radio. Of course, you invite your friend along. Once he is presented with the opportunity to make his dream a reality, however, he immediately begins to backpedal, telling you how he is sick, how he is busy that day, and so on. The tickets are not for any particular date, so you continue to ask him to accompany you, each time being met with an increasingly ridiculous excuse. Soon enough, it becomes clear that he does not value skydiving quite as much as he claims! Once again, actions put the lie to words in the sphere of values, all thanks to the essential connection between values and volition.

23 Accordingly, to return to the example of sociopathy raised previously, we must say not that the sociopath experiences certain values (e.g., those related to empathy) but remains unmoved by them, but rather that she never genuinely experiences those values at all – even if she might understand, perhaps after having spoken with others who possess a greater measure of empathy, that finding value in the well-being of others is possible in general, and thereby enter into an "as-if" encounter with such values.

24 As Hartmann puts it:

> He who stolidly passes by men and their fates, he whom the staggering does not stagger nor the inspiring inspire, for him life is in vain, he has no part in it. The world must be meaningless and life senseless to one who has no capacity to perceive life's relationships, the inexhaustible significance of persons and situations, of correlations and events.
>
> (I, 35)

25 Similarly, just as acts of perceptual consciousness permit the experiencing subject to engage in acts of valuative consciousness, which, in turn, lead him towards acts of volitional consciousness, so too do those volitional acts give rise to new acts of perceptual consciousness, completing the cycle. For instance, Bert, upon seeing *Persistence of Memory* and appreciating its beauty,

walks (through a corresponding act of volition) further into the exhibition hall to get closer to the painting, thereby opening up new sights for him to see, with valuative horizons of their own, and so forth.

26 That is, values are always part of what Husserl calls the *Umwelt*, the "environment," the world understood as a holistic and thoroughly interconnected nexus of meaning, rather than as an abstract collection of objects. Crowell's depiction of this "surrounding world" in his *Normativity and Phenomenology in Husserl and Heidegger*, although it is directed towards a vastly different line of questioning, makes this connection plain; he writes that the *Umwelt* "differs from naturalistically apprehended nature in that it is a world of beautiful, pleasant, and useful things; a world in which I am in communicative communion with others; a world of generations, traditions, and institutions ... these meanings are inseparable from our practical engagement in the world" (161).

27 Indeed, human existence as a whole can be thought of as the lived pursuit of values in the world. As Husserl writes in the *Kaizō* articles, "the subject lives in the struggle for a 'value-filled' life, which is secured against subsequent devaluations, decreases of value, lack of values, disappointments, which increases in its level of value, [the struggle] for a life that could vouchsafe a continually harmonious and secure overall satisfaction" (*Hua* XXVII, 25). Husserl's writings in *Kaizō* as a whole are devoted to the concrete details of what it might mean to pursue such a life (particularly in the context of the aftermath of the Great War), and are thus – perhaps – a fruitful point of departure for future inquiries into the subject.

28 This categorical imperative naturally goes beyond particular situations as well; it culminates in the claim that the individual should pursue that value which is given as the "highest" among all others, taking into account all of the vast horizons of possibility that are open to him. As Hart puts it, Husserl's claim is that fulfilling this dictum requires us to "seek out what we truly want in life and determine what is best among the widest field or horizon of our life. The best which encompasses the widest circles of life is *no longer able to be absorbed* by any other good and therefore is not a relative best. Here there is no longer possible a further horizon that would contain a practical good that would be better" (1997, 209). This portrayal certainly requires further exploration in light of our novel perspective on values – Hart's discussion here is based only on Husserl's earlier thought on the subject, a point of view that can no longer be maintained – but it provides tantalizing glimpses into the connection between values and ethics nonetheless.

29 This formulation is expressed primarily in Husserl's late ethics lectures, though with important insights also contained in the *Grenzprobleme*. Nonetheless, anything more specific about the content of this speculation lies outside the scope of the present project.

30 Of course, Hart maintains that even this latter certainty remains ambiguous – for instance, he argues that "[s]everal of the things might be equally good, there might be no best" (1990, 211). The model of values that has been developed throughout this project, however, is perfectly capable of clearing away at least some of that supposed ambiguity, even if much work remains to be done in that respect.

31 That is, many questions about volitional consciousness – including its connection to value-consciousness as seen from the other side, as it were – remain to be answered by a dedicated phenomenology of willing. Husserl wrote on this subject extensively (though ambiguously, and without any clear solutions

in the end; see Henning Peucker's "Hat Husserl eine konsistente Theorie des Willens?" for an excellent summary of Husserl's evolving thought on the subject), as did many other phenomenologists and philosophers of related schools. Nonetheless, particular considerations like the task of distinguishing willing from wishing, desiring, etc., cannot be answered by the current project alone; the laws governing the will are, as pointed out in Chapter 1 of this book, quite distinct from those of value-intuition, and no less deserving of an extended treatment in their own right.

Conclusion

Overview of the Book

This project has been both challenging and – ultimately – rewarding. From its very beginnings, it was obvious that it would require a great deal of rigorous effort, and that even a very detailed investigation could only illuminate the theoretical outlines of our valuative lives. Nonetheless, this book does fulfill a critically important role in the phenomenology of values. First and foremost, it hopes to have demonstrated conclusively, at least from the standpoint of transcendental phenomenology, the real nature of values as such, which has been quite a troublesome question throughout the history of axiology. It discusses the general role that these values play in conscious experience, it answers some of the most puzzling issues surrounding the givenness of values (e.g., the problem of subjectivity), and it illuminates many of the structures that link valuative consciousness to the rest of our experiential lives. Although much work remains to be done, especially in the context of carrying out phenomenological investigations into the givenness of *specific* values in particular situations, this explication of the essential structures of valuative consciousness as such is a major step forward in the realm of phenomenological axiology. Certainly, such a project is absolutely necessary for any further investigations in the field, or into any of the sub-disciplines of philosophy that depend upon it (e.g., into ethics or aesthetics).

Nonetheless, it is also important to remember that this book builds on much previous phenomenological work in the field of value theory, the insights of which cannot be overlooked. This project could not have been carried out without the help of philosophers like Husserl, Scheler, and Hartmann, who put this investigation on the right track by their careful and rigorous investigations into valuative life, as well as the assistance of later commentators who clarified and criticized many of the central points raised by their predecessors. Even if the ways in which these previous works interpreted values are ultimately insufficient for one reason or another – a claim that the early chapters of this book discussed at length – my debt to such thinkers is immense. Whether it be the tripartite

DOI: 10.4324/9781003202189-7

194 *Conclusion*

division of consciousness discussed by Husserl (and by Brentano), which has been the organizing principle behind this project as a whole, Scheler's division of values into their various categories, or Hartmann's lucid analysis of the good itself – not to mention the many other insights discussed throughout this text – this project builds on the wisdom of others. To paraphrase yet another great thinker, if I have seen farther than these men by carrying out the horizon-model of values to its inevitable conclusions, this has only been possible because I was standing on their colossal shoulders the entire time.

Beginning in its second chapter, this book has delivered what I believe to be a firm account of the basic nature of values in general. To reiterate: values as such are always bound up with our daily lives, i.e., with the things – situations and objects in the world – that we experience as beautiful, as immoral, as agreeable, and so on. They cannot be abstracted from this nexus of experience save for the purpose of phenomenological exploration of their unique and *sui generis* structures. To explain their ontological status, we have no need to posit a Schelerian realm of independently existing value-objects or to attribute to values, as does Hartmann, an "ideal" existence parallel to that of mathematical entities. Instead, relying on Husserl, we can see that values are always experienced on the horizons of the valuable things through which they are encountered. What this means is that values shape our experiences of the world (often in rather dramatic ways) but can never themselves be known except through the effects that they have on those experiences – they can never be encountered directly.

While this elusiveness might seem, on the surface, to make values rather difficult to understand, nothing could be further from the truth. Values are just as they appear to be in our everyday experience. Beauty *is* the way in which a beautiful painting stands out from all other objects, calling us to appreciate its aesthetic qualities; immorality consists in the repulsion that we feel for a reprehensible act. Once this fact is understood, once it is realized that axiology does not require a painstaking analysis of some mysterious and ultimately elusive object, but rather a rigorous investigation of certain genuinely felt aspects of our experience, many of the problems traditionally associated with the discipline simply melt away. It is this insight – certainly nascent in the work of Husserl, but remaining quite opaque and insufficiently explored in his own writings – that is perhaps the most important idea discussed in this book, since it is the cornerstone of this entire investigation of values (and, if my arguments here hold true, of a phenomenology of values in general).

Once the horizon-model has been accepted, it is a relatively simple task to explicate the way in which a phenomenology of values should be carried out in general. Since values lie on the horizons of other experiences, it is plain to see that the distinction between pure values and valuable things that is the focus of the third chapter of this text must be upheld in order to attain an understanding of the relationships between values and the world as a whole. Pure values are the focus of phenomenological analysis, but never of direct intuition; they give themselves only through other experiences, through the valuable things that are our primary means of access to affective life. This distinction is critical, since it allows us to explain the difference between values as static *structures* of experience and the dynamic, unpredictable nexus of values as they are actually experienced in the world around us. Pure values remain the same: they affect consciousness in similar ways over time, with positive values drawing subjects towards them and disvalues pushing subjects away, even while the valuative experiences through which these pure values are given vary wildly.

This discussion of pure values also revealed the fact that values do indeed possess their own hierarchy – not one of height or importance, as Scheler would have it, but one of classification. Values run the gamut from the most specific – the melodiousness of a particular bell-like tone, perhaps, or the scratchiness of an uncomfortable shirt – to the most general – the good and the bad themselves, which exist only as the ultimate points of attraction or repulsion towards which other values point, and not in any truly independent way. In between, there exists a series of cascading categories of values, most notably the four divisions of aesthetic values, moral values, sensual values, and spiritual values that I have adapted from Scheler. All of these pure values have their own unique effects, their special ways of conditioning the valuable things with which they are associated. Valuable things and valuative experiences themselves can, in turn, be classified according to these schema – even if that task becomes enormously more complicated once we bring in the hustle and bustle of everyday life.

One of the greatest of these complications lies in what I have chosen to call the problem of subjectivity, i.e., the difficulty of accounting for the fact that values and value-experiences seem to vary among different subjects without simply reducing all values to merely subjective choices, a problem that we see exhibited in cases like that of Bert, Ernie, and *Persistence of Memory*. Fortunately, the horizon-model of values has provided a way of explaining this puzzling fact. Pure values do not vary, but the things that are given as valuable certainly can due to the experiential perspective of the individual subject. Just as a visually perceived painting can appear in very different ways as a result of the varying locations from which it can be seen, valuable things can participate in the structures of radically different values when "observed" from a different valuative perspective. One man might see a painting as beautiful while another experiences it as ugly, all without effecting any changes in the values of beauty and ugliness themselves or in the painting. While this fact certainly reduces the scope of what we can say with apodictic certainty about values – transcendental claims as such can only be made about pure values and the structures that they bring to bear on valuable things, not about the specificities of any particular valuative experience – that is simply an inevitable characteristic of the complicated world in which we live, a point that phenomenology has acknowledged many times over. Once we move to the level of adequacy in our investigations of particular regions of value-experience, it should be possible to draw further distinctions and to make more robust claims about values as they are actually experienced (although spelling out any such claims in detail remains a task for another occasion). At any rate, the problem of subjectivity is no problem whatsoever for the horizon-model of values – at least, assuming that the aforementioned distinction between pure values and valuable things is rigorously maintained.

Finally, this book has also explored some of the further-reaching elements of valuative consciousness, most particularly those which connect values to the other modes of conscious life. As noted, values are known by the effects that they have on the consciousness that perceives them. Perhaps the most notable of these effects is the attraction or repulsion that values inspire in those who encounter them, attributes that make sense only in the context of the volitional acts that those subjects subsequently carry out. Values are not experienced merely as static entities lurking within other experiences, but as the very engine of conscious life itself. Whenever we act purposefully, pursuing our various ends and bringing about new experiences for ourselves, we do so on the basis of the values that we encounter within those ends and experiences.

Of course, this text has not been able to explore volitional consciousness itself in any fine detail; carrying out a full-fledged phenomenology of volition is not the purpose of this project. Nonetheless, outlining the essential connections between value-consciousness and the will is a necessary component of understanding values at all, and so this task required at least some investigation. Values operate in the world by means of their relationships to those who encounter them, by bringing about volitional acts on the part of the latter, and to deny this fact would be to deny the real character of such values just as much as any attempt to throw them in with objects of intellectual perception. Although it is the work of a more detailed phenomenology of volition to carry this investigation further, the basic nature of this connection can be seen solely from a study of valuative experience itself. As they are realized in practice, values always reach beyond themselves.

Closing Comments

Overall, the basic nature of values is to be embedded in the concrete lives of the individuals who experience them. While this investigation has primarily consisted in a theoretical look at pure values themselves and the various structures whereby they have their effects on our lives, it should never be forgotten that the real payoff of such an inquiry lies in the practical conclusions that can be drawn from it through further phenomenological analysis. All the transcendental claims in the world are of little use without the ability to apply them in concrete situations. Nonetheless, those transcendental claims – claims like those made throughout this project, about the horizonality of values, their relation to subjectivity or volition, etc. – are a *conditio sine qua non* of any pragmatic results that might proceed from a phenomenological perspective. Phenomenological rigor must be maintained; the philosopher cannot speak with any certainty about the structures embedded in various particular values without knowing in advance what values are in general. It is the latter task that, if I have been successful, has been accomplished in this book. It has been well worth the effort, and it is to be hoped that this project will lead to future investigations into the givenness of values in a more specific way. Like values themselves, phenomenology always leads its adherents onwards towards greater and greater possibilities.

Values are an indispensable component of our daily lives – and, indeed, are by definition the only way in which we have access to anything of worth. Although they have traditionally presented philosophy with a rather difficult set of problems, many of these can be resolved with a rigorous application of phenomenological methods. Although these methods are by no means trivial to carry out – after all, even the task of illuminating the bare outlines of values has taken the space of this entire book – they allow us to carry our inquiry into values farther than any others. Granted, it is not my intended task to defend phenomenology as a whole at this time; such a defense has already been carried out quite satisfactorily by Husserl himself, among others. Nonetheless, it is to be hoped that, having seen the explanatory power of this phenomenology of values, the reader will be persuaded that this perspective is best suited to answer some of the most conventionally difficult problems in axiology as a whole, and therefore that the phenomenological model of values should be considered as the best way to approach such troublesome questions. The fulfillment of that hope, of course, lies in the hands of the reader. As for myself, I have done my part, and I trust that this rigorous investigation of values will be an important source of insight for any future inquiry into the subject.

Bibliography

Adorno, Theodor. 2013. *Against Epistemology: A Metacritique*. Trans. Willis Domingo. Cambridge, MA: Polity Press.
Al-Ghazali. 1997. *The Incoherence of the Philosophers*. Trans. Michael Marmura. Provo, UT: Brigham University Press.
Baumgartner, Wilhelm. 2002. Franz Brentano: The Foundation of Value Theory and Ethics. In *Phenomenological Approaches to Moral Philosophy: A Handbook*, ed. John Drummond and Lester Embree, 119–138. Contributions to Phenomenology, Vol. 47. Dordrecht: Kluwer Academic Publishers.
Brentano, Franz. 1889. *Vom Ursprung Sittlicher Erkenntnis*. Leipzig: Duncker & Humblot.
Brough, John. 1997. Image and Artistic Value. In *Phenomenology of Values and Valuing*, ed. James Hart and Lester Embree, 29–48. Dordrecht: Kluwer Academic Publishers.
Cai, Wenjing. 2013. From Adequacy to Apodicticity. Development of the Notion of Reflection in Husserl's Phenomenology. *Husserl Studies* 29: 13–27.
Crowell, Steven. 2013. *Normativity and Phenomenology in Husserl and Heidegger*. Cambridge: Cambridge University Press.
De Monticelli, Roberta. 2016. Sensibility and Values: Toward a Phenomenological Theory of the Emotional Life. In *Analytic and Continental Philosophy: Methods and Perspectives. Proceedings of the 37th International Wittgenstein Symposium*, ed. Sonja Rinofner-Kreidl and Harald Wiltsche, 381–399. Boston: De Gruyter.
De Monticelli, Roberta. 2018. On Pluralism, Value Disagreement and Conflict: A Phenomenological Argument for Axiological Universalism. *Journal of the British Society for Phenomenology* 49.4: 342–355.
Donohoe, Janet. 2004. *Husserl on Ethics and Intersubjectivity: From Static to Genetic Phenomenology*. Amherst, NY: Humanity Books.
Dreyfus, Hubert. 1990. *Being-in-the-World: A Commentary on Heidegger's Being and Time, Division I*. Cambridge, MA: The MIT Press.
Drummond, John. 1995. Husserl's Phenomenological Axiology and Aristotelian Virtue Ethics. In *New Perspectives on Aristotelianism and Its Critics*, ed. Miira Tuominen, Sara Heinämaa, and Virpi Mäkinen, 179–195. Leiden: Brill.
Emad, Parvis. 1977. Heidegger's Value-Criticism and Its Bearing on the Phenomenology of Values. *Research in Phenomenology* 7: 190–802.
Ferran, Íngrid. 2016. Affective Intentionality: Early Phenomenological Contributions to a New Phenomenological Sociology. In *Phenomenology of*

Sociality: Discovering the "We", ed. Thomas Szanto and Dermot Moran, 219–233. New York: Routledge.
Ferrarello, Susi. 2014. Brentano's and Husserl's Axiology. In *Phenomenology of Intersubjectivity and Values in Edmund Husserl*, ed. Susi Ferrarello, 95–112. Newcastle upon Tyne: Cambridge Scholars Publishing.
Ferrarello, Susi. 2015. *Husserl's Ethics and Practical Intentionality*. London: Bloomsbury Academic.
Fröhlich, Günter. 2011. *Form und Wert*. Würzburg: Königshausen & Neumann GmbH.
Geniusas, Saulius. 2012. *The Origins of the Horizon in Husserl's Phenomenology*. Contributions to Phenomenology, Vol. 67. Dordrecht: Springer.
Gubser, Michael. 2014. *The Far Reaches: Phenomenology, Ethics, and Social Renewal in Central Europe*. Stanford, CA: Stanford University Press.
Hackett, J. Edward. 2018. *Persons and Values in Pragmatic Phenomenology: Explorations in Moral Metaphysics*. Wilmington, DE: Vernon Press.
Hart, James. 1990. Axiology as the Form of Purity of Heart: A Reading of Husserliana XXVIII. *Philosophy Today* 34.3: 206–221.
Hart, James. 1997. The *Summum Bonum* and Value-Wholes: Aspects of a Husserlian Axiology and Theology. In *Phenomenology of Values and Valuing*, ed. James Hart and Lester Embree, 29–48. Dordrecht: Kluwer Academic Publishers.
Hartmann, Nicolai. 1932. *Ethics*. Trans Stanton Colt. New York: The Macmillan Company.
Heidegger, Martin. 1998. Letter on "Humanism". Trans. Frank Capuzzi. In *Pathmarks*, ed. William McNeil, 239–276. Cambridge: Cambridge University Press.
Hobbs, D.J. 2019. Who Is the Subject of Phenomenology? Husserl and Fink on the Transcendental Ego. *The Journal of the British Society for Phenomenology* 50.2: 154–169.
Hobbs, D.J. 2020. Philosophical Scientists and Scientific Philosophers: Kant and Husserl on the Philosophical Foundations of the Natural Sciences. In *Husserl, Kant and Transcendental Phenomenology*, ed. Iulian Apostolescu and Claudia Serban, 333–357. Boston: De Gruyter.
Höffe, Otfried. 1994. *Immanuel Kant*. Trans. Marshall Farrier. Albany, NY: State University of New York Press.
Husserl, Edmund. 1956. *Erste Philosophie (1923/4). Erste Teil: Kritische Ideengeschichte*. Husserliana, Vol. VII. Ed. Rudolf Boehm. The Hague: Martinus Nijhoff.
Husserl, Edmund. 1959. *Erste Philosophie (1923/4). Zweiter Teil: Theorie der phänomenologische Reduktion*. Husserliana, Vol. VIII. The Hague: Martinus Nijhoff.
Husserl, Edmund. 1970. *Logical Investigations*, Vol. II. Trans. J.N. Findlay. Ed. Dermot Moran. London and New York: Routledge.
Husserl, Edmund. 1980. *Phäntasie, Bildbewusstsein, Erinnerung. Zur Phänomenologie der anschaulichen Vergegenwartigungen. Texte aus dem Nachlass (1889–1925)*. Husserliana, Vol. XXIII. Ed. Eduard Marbach. The Hague: Martinus Nijhoff.
Husserl, Edmund. 1988a. *Aufsätze und Vorträge (1922–1937)*. Husserliana, Vol. XXVII. Ed. Thomas Nenon and Hans Rainer Sepp. Dordrecht: Kluwer Academic Publishers.

Bibliography

Husserl, Edmund. 1988b. *Vorlesungen über Ethik und Wertlehre: 1908–1914*. Husserliana, Vol. XXVIII. Ed. Ullrich Melle. Dordrecht: Kluwer Academic Publishers.

Husserl, Edmund. 1999. *Cartesian Meditations: An Introduction to Phenomenology*. Trans. Dorion Cairns. Dordrecht: Kluwer Academic Publishers.

Husserl, Edmund. 2001. *Analyses Concerning Passive and Active Synthesis: Lectures on Transcendental Logic*. Collected Works, Vol. IX. Trans. Anthony Steinbock. Dordrecht: Kluwer Academic Publishers.

Husserl, Edmund. 2004. *Einleitung in die Ethik: Vorlesungen Sommersemester 1920 und 1924*. Husserliana, Vol. XXXVII. Ed. Henning Peucker. Dordrecht: Kluwer Academic Publishers.

Husserl, Edmund. 2014. *Grenzprobleme der Phänomenologie*. Husserliana, Vol. XLII. Ed. Rochus Sowa and Thomas Vongehr. Dordrecht: Springer.

Husserl, Edmund. 2019. *First Philosophy: Lectures 1923/24 and Related Texts from the Manuscripts (1920–1925)*. Trans. Sebastian Luft and Thane M. Naberhaus. Dordrecht: Springer.

Jordan, Robert. 2002. Nicolai Hartmann: Proper Ethics Is Atheistic. In *Phenomenological Approaches to Moral Philosophy: A Handbook*, ed. John Drummond and Lester Embree, 175–196. Contributions to Phenomenology, Vol. 47. Dordrecht: Kluwer Academic Publishers.

Kant, Immanuel. 2003. *Critique of Pure Reason*. Trans. Norman Kemp Smith. New York: Palgrave Macmillan.

Kelly, Eugene. 2011. *Material Ethics of Value: Max Scheler and Nicolai Hartmann*. Phaenomenologica, Vol. 203. Dordrecht: Springer.

Kwakman, S. 1974. The Beginnings of Philosophy: On the Apodictic Way to the Object of Transcendental Experience in the Philosophy of Edmund Husserl. *Tijdschrift voor Filosofie* 36.3: 521–564.

Lauer, Quentin. 1961. The Phenomenological Ethics of Max Scheler. *International Philosophical Quarterly* 1.2: 273–300.

Levinas, Emmanuel. 1986. Phenomenology and the Non-Theoretical. In *Facts and Values*, ed. M.C. Doeser and J.N. Kraay, 109–119. Martinus Nijhoff Philosophy Library. Dordrecht: Martinus Nijhoff.

Lotze, Rudolf Hermann. 2015. The World of Ideas. In *The Neo-Kantian Reader*, ed. Sebastian Luft, 85–92. New York: Routledge.

Melle, Ullrich. 1988. Zu Brentanos und Husserls Ethikansatz: Die Analogie zwischen den Vernunftarten. *Brentano-Studien* 1: 109–120.

Melle, Ullrich. 1991. The Development of Husserl's Ethics. *Études Phénoménologiques* 7: 115–135.

Melle, Ullrich. 1997. Husserl's Phenomenology of Willing. In *Phenomenology of Values and Valuing*, ed. James Hart and Lester Embree, 29–48. Dordrecht: Kluwer Academic Publishers.

Melle, Ullrich. 2002. Edmund Husserl: From Reason to Love. In *Phenomenological Approaches to Moral Philosophy: A Handbook*, ed. John Drummond and Lester Embree, 229–248. Contributions to Phenomenology, Vol. 47. Dordrecht: Kluwer Academic Publishers.

Melle, Ullrich. 2012. Husserls deskriptive Erforschung der Gefühlserlebnisse. In *Life, Subjectivity & Art: Essays in Honor of Rudolf Bernet*, ed. Roland Breeur and Ullrich Melle, 51–99. Phaenomenologica, Vol. 201. Dordrecht: Springer.

Merz, Philippe. 2015. *Werterfahrung und Wahrheit: Phenomenologische Ethikbegründung nach Husserl*. Paderborn: Wilhelm Fink.
Mohr, Eric. 2015. Phenomenological Intuition and the Problem of Philosophy as Method and Science: Scheler and Husserl. *Symposium* 16.2: 218–234.
Nenon, Tom. 1991. Willing and Acting in Husserl's Lectures on Ethics and Value Theory. *Man and World* 24.3: 301–309.
Peucker, Henning. 2008. From Logic to the Person: An Introduction to Edmund Husserl's Ethics. *The Review of Metaphysics* 62.2: 307–325.
Ramirez, Ignacio. 2015. Intentionality of Moods and Horizon Consciousness in Husserl's Phenomenology. In *Feeling and Value, Willing and Action*, ed. Marta Ubiali and Maren Wehrle, 93–103. Phaenomenologica, Vol. 216. Cham: Springer.
Raynova, Yvanka. 2017. *Sein, Sinn und Werte: Phänomenologische und Hermeneutische Perspektiven des Europäischen Denkens*. Frankfurt am Main: Peter Lang.
Rinofner-Kreidl, Sonja. 2010. Husserl's Categorical Imperative and His Related Critique of Kant. In *Epistemology, Archaeology, Ethics: Current Investigations of Husserl's Corpus*, 188–210. London and New York: Continuum.
Roth, Alois. 1960. *Edmund Husserls ethische Untersuchungen: Dargestellt Anhand Seiner Vorlesungmanuskripte*. The Hague: Martinus Nijhoff.
Sanford, Jonathan. 2003. Affective Insight: Scheler on Feelings and Values. *Proceedings of the ACPA* 76: 165–181.
Scheler, Max. 1973. *Formalism in Ethics and Non-Formal Ethics of Values*. Trans. Manfred Frings and Roger Funk. Evanston, IL: Northwestern University Press.
Schubbach, Arno. 2016. *Die Genese des Symbolischen. Zu den Anfängen von Ernst Cassirers Kulturphilosophie*. Cassirer-Forschungen, Vol. 16. Hamburg: Felix Meiner.
Staiti, Andrea. 2018. Husserls Liebesethik im Kontext des südwestdeutschen Neukantianismus. *Phänomenologische Forschungen* 2018.1: 151–167.
Szanto, Thomas and Dermot Moran, eds. 2015. *Phenomenology of Sociality: Discovering the "We"*. Routledge Research in Phenomenology, Vol. 3. London: Routledge.
Theodorou, Panos. 2014a. The Aporia of Husserl's Phenomenology of Values and Another Beginning. In *Phenomenology of Intersubjectivity and Values in Edmund Husserl*, ed. Susi Ferrarello, 65–82. Newcastle upon Tyne: Cambridge Scholars Publishing.
Theodorou, Panos. 2014b. Pain, Pleasure, and the Intentionality of Emotions as Experiences of Values: A New Phenomenological Perspective. *Phenomenology and the Cognitive Sciences* 13: 625–641.
Toombs, S. Kay, ed. 2001. *Handbook of Phenomenology and Medicine*. Dordrecht: Kluwer Academic Publishers.
Ubiali, Marta and Maren Wehrle, eds. 2015. *Feeling and Value, Willing and Action*. Phaenomenologica, Vol. 216. Cham: Springer.
Zhang, Wei. 2011. Rational a Priori or Emotional a Priori? Husserl and Scheler's Criticisms of Kant Regarding the Foundation of Ethics. *Cultura* 8.2: 143–158.

Index

Page numbers followed by n indicate notes.

adiaphora 58, 82–87, 138
Aloysius 60, 86–87, 106, 151, 166–168, 172–174, 179–180

Bell, Joshua 136
Bert and Ernie 59–61, 63, 67–71, 75–78, 82–83, 86, 95–97, 101–102, 104–105, 117–118, 126, 135–138, 140–141, 151, 171–173, 182
Brentano, Franz 6–7, 184
Buridan's ass 176–177

categorical imperative, new 6–7, 9–10, 12, 184–186
culture 154–155

Dalí, Salvador 22, 34–35, 59, 63, 67–71, 75–78, 86, 95–97, 104–105, 117–118, 126, 135–138, 140–141, 171–172, 177–179, 182

ethics 67, 110, 183–186
evidence, adequate 129–131, 150
evidence, apodictic 128–129, 149, 170

Grover 177–179

Hartmann, Nicolai 13–14, 44, 46–48, 61, 64–71, 80, 85, 168–169, 183
Heidegger, Martin 15, 90n16–91n16

hierarchy of values 66–67
horizon 56–57, 71–81
horizon-model of values 56–57, 71–81, 171, 181–182, 194
Husserl, Edmund 4–5, 7–11, 30–43, 48–50, 71–76, 78–80, 128–131, 139, 153–154, 165, 184–186

ideas, transcendental 97–99
intersubjectivity 41–42

Lotze, Rudolf Hermann 6

object-model of values 61–71, 80, 194
objects, ideal 13, 65–66, 194
Oscar 59, 86, 105, 126–127, 142–149, 151, 170, 173, 182

reason 36–43, 48–50
reason, pre-theoretical 39–41, 43, 48–50
Rickert, Heinrich 14, 65

Saul of Tarsus 153
Sawyer, Tom 45
Scheler, Max 11–12, 44–48, 61–64, 66–71, 80, 109, 111–112, 183
Stein, Edith 12–13
sui generis structures 30, 36–50, 66–67

temporal extension, law of 39–40

valuable things 68–69, 94, 100–103, 171–172
values, pure 68, 71, 94–100, 171–172
Vernunftarten 8, 30–36, 39

visual consciousness 2–3, 72–74, 97–98

Willkür (arbitry) 173, 175–177
Windelband, Wilhelm 14

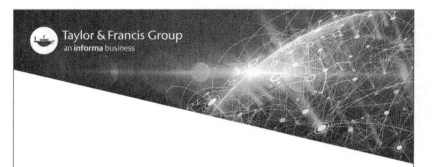